The A-Z of House Plants

CRESCENT BOOKS

New York

in association with Phoebus

Editor	Susan Joiner
Assistant Editor	Pamela Hunter
Design	Mary Cooper
	Roger Hammond

We are indebted to Hugh Young for
his translation and to Mary Everett
for her expert advice.

Made and printed in Great Britain by
Purnell and Sons Ltd, Paulton (Avon)

G. E. Hyde

ABOUT THIS BOOK

No one has 'green fingers' – it's just a matter of knowing how to handle plants the right way.

This complete A–Z guide to more than 100 popular house plants, compiled by an international team of experts, will tell you all you need to know to make your plants thrive.

It contains a wealth of information on the basics of cultivation for each plant – its soil, light, heat, and water requirements, when to cut back, and how to propagate.

In addition there is a section on plant care that answers the questions indoor gardeners ask most frequently:

Where is the best place to grow ferns?

How can I make my hippeastrum flower?

When should I cut back the begonias?

What should I do with my plants when I go on holiday?

Why does that rubber tree look so bare?

And – more important – it gives you enough 'dos and don'ts' so that you never need to ask, 'What did I do wrong?'

Lavishly illustrated throughout with beautiful full-colour photographs of every plant and its variations, as well as clear step-by-step pictures of plant care, *The A–Z of House Plants* is an indispensable, authoritative addition to any gardener's bookshelf.

Passiflora caerulea

CONTENTS

CARE OF HOUSE PLANTS   5

Nature Indoors   6
Warmth   6
Light   7
Water   8
Fresh Air   9
Soil   9
Where to Put Plants   10
Plants for the Shelf   10
Plants at the Window   11
Plants on the Move   11
Plants in a Terrarium or Bottle
  Garden   12
A Modern Conservatory   13
Flowerpots   14
Repotting   15
Feeding Plants   16
Pruning   17
Propagation   18
Pests and Diseases   20
Hydroponics – Plants without
  Soil   22
Holiday Care   23

A·Z OF HOUSE PLANTS   24

indoor plants arranged under
their botanical names

PLACES FOR PLANTS   154

GLOSSARY OF TERMS   158

DICTIONARY OF POPULAR NAMES   160

CARE OF HOUSE PLANTS

NATURE INDOORS

When the Indian rubber tree sheds its leaves, when the African violets wilt, when the Easter cactus refuses to flower, inexperienced indoor gardeners often give up and declare, 'I haven't got green fingers.'

This myth of 'green fingers' goes back a long time, but it is still only a myth. No one has 'green fingers' —it's just a matter of handling the plants in the right or wrong way.

We must always bear in mind that every plant is a fragment of nature—that in the hall, in the living room, on the windowsill, even in the greenhouse with all its technical equipment, plants are being kept alive in surroundings that are foreign to them. They will flourish only if the indoor gardener can manage to reproduce the actual conditions in which they lived in the open air.

So anyone who supposes he can come back from a holiday in the Canary Islands smuggling a dragon tree past customs officials and into his home and get it to grow on the sunny balcony right away has simply overlooked the fact that the dragon tree has not had time to adapt itself to another climate. Unless the climatic conditions of the Canary Islands can be reproduced fairly exactly in the conservatory, it will die.

It is possible to imitate nature indoors only when you are quite clear how many different factors have to be combined and adapted. Plants—either flowering or simple foliage plants—depend on many different environmental conditions, each one of which must be satisfied. There is, first, the warmth of their natural habitat, then the amount and intensity of light that reaches them there, the moisture of the air and of the ground and the general constitution of the soil. If any one of these demands is not met, the plants will react; they wilt and shed their leaves, run to seed or die completely.

WARMTH

If you are to give an indoor plant the right amount of warmth, you have to know where it comes from. Plants from the tropical rain forests naturally need more warmth than plants that are at home in the Alpine highlands. Indoor gardeners have agreed on three different categories of plants.

Cold-house plants in our houses must, in winter, have a temperature of not more than 12°C (54°F) and not less than 3°C (37°F). You can put them outdoors altogether in the summer, either on a balcony or terrace or, if you like, actually planted in the open.

Temperate-house plants are the plants typically found in living rooms. They can stand the temperatures of rooms with no heating as well as those in well-heated rooms. The normal temperature range for them in winter is 12-20°C (54-68°F). In summer quite a few of these plants can be put out in the open, but some of them must only go in light and airy places.

Hot-house plants are the ones you see in the conservatories at botanical gardens. In the house you must take special care to keep them warm. In the winter they need temperatures of over 18°C (64°F); in summer they want humidity and temperatures of 20-25°C (68-77°F).

These three categories are not inflexible. After all, we must not forget that even in their natural habitat plants sometimes have to cope with exceptionally warm winters or cool summers. There is really no point in constantly hovering over them with a thermometer. The three categories—cold-house plants, temperate-house plants and hot-house plants—are useful as guides that can always be varied for limited periods. There is no harm in keeping cold-house plants and temperate-house plants together. They will do very well. But if you ask a hot-house plant to pass the winter in temperatures of 5°C (41°F), it will freeze.

Plants' need for warmth is not constant. That is because in their natural surroundings all plants pass through periods of rest and periods of growth. Since they need water and warmth to make them grow, they take their rest periods in the cool, dry season.

The countless house plants that originally lived in the tropical regions of Africa, Asia and South America illustrate the adaptability of nature. In the tropical heat they grow to really enormous size—*Dracaena draco,* the dragon tree, reaches a height of nearly 20 m (65 ft) in its native habitat—while in our houses they are satisfied with a normal room size. This more limited growth is a direct result of the lack of warmth. If you transfer these plants to the hothouse of a botanical garden they will reach heights that would make them unsuitable as house plants.

You should, however, be warned against trying to acclimatize tropical plants yourself, even if you are allowed to bring them into the country. To begin with, such experiments call for expert knowledge and the equipment of a nursery. Secondly, the plants do not really like reducing their growth; if they are not warm enough they simply die. Thirdly, you must remember that as a rule younger plants need more warmth than older. Actually this is an advantage. Older palm trees, for example, can be left out on the balcony in summer, whereas for the younger plants it is not advisable.

LIGHT

Light, like warmth, is vital for plants. Without light plants cannot live. They need sunlight to manufacture their food from the carbon dioxide in the atmosphere and from water. But essential as sunlight is to plants, it can also be deadly. Too much light —direct sunshine, or the sun shining straight on to a window so that it works like a magnifying glass—will burn the plants.

As with warmth, plants are divided into three groups according to their light requirements: plants that need sunny, half-shady and shady positions. Unfortunately the human eye is not an adequate measure of light or dark, sunny or shady. Many an indoor gardener wonders why his favourite fuchsia, although it is standing on the windowsill, presumably in full light, suddenly sheds its flowers and leaves. The reason may be that a great pot with a sansevieria (mother-in-law's tongue) is standing next to it and taking so much light from the fuchsia that it finds its position permanently shady, and protests.

The need for light varies greatly, not only between different families and species of house plants but also at different times of the year. In their periods of growth and flowering, plants need a great deal of light. The smaller amount of light that most plants need in their rest period fits with the short days of winter. But the rest period of cultivated plants does not necessarily correspond with the seasons. During the winter, Northern Hemisphere gardeners must reserve a favoured place by the window for plants that come from the Southern Hemisphere.

Instructions for the care of plants often specify a light position. Do not make the mistake of confusing light and sunny. Plants that need bright light but cannot tolerate direct sunlight must be properly protected. You can use curtains for that, drawing them at the time of day when the sun is shining directly on the window. Venetian blinds are especially useful as they can be adjusted to control the amount of light coming in as required. It is not advisable to keep moving the plants about simply to keep them out of the direct sunlight.

In considering how much light house plants need, we can look back again at the conditions in which the plant grows in nature. Even a pure

shade plant like saintpaulia (African violet), which comes from the rain forest of East Africa, can never in its natural habitat find a position that is free from the sun all the year round. So you can put your African violet permanently in a north window, where it will still be reached by the first rays of the morning sun. The same is true of cyclamens and rhododendrons (azaleas). On the other hand you need not worry that the most sun-hungry cacti and echeverias will suddenly cease to flourish because they are no longer in full sunlight. These are adaptable plants.

As a general rule, flowering plants need more light than foliage plants, and plants with brightly coloured leaves more than dark green-leaved plants.

The best source of light for house plants is the sun. Sometimes you cannot rely on it, however, and then artificial light will work quite well. Not ordinary electric light bulbs, though; the least you will need are fluorescent tubes giving a warm-toned light. But once again, as always with house plants, too much is harmful. The plants cannot really stand it if you leave the light on all the time. You are actually stimulating their growth night and day, which is what gardeners do in the forcing

Prevent climbing plants from overshadowing light-loving varieties.

house to make flowers blossom before the natural season.

Whether the plants are standing in sunlight or artificial light, it is not good to move them too often. Experienced indoor gardeners, especially when working with particularly delicate plants—the rhododendron, or even rhipsalidopsis (Easter cactus) or zygocactus (Christmas cactus) —use what are called light marks. They make marks on the flowerpots and on the window ledge or wherever the plants are standing, and then if they have to move them they can always put them back in exactly the same place.

To get enough light, plants, both outdoors and indoors, will always grow towards the source of light. The phenomenon is called phototropism. If their position is changed, or even if the pots are turned around, the plants will no longer get the accustomed amount of light. In some cases they react very markedly; for example, Christmas and Easter cacti shed their buds. As a rule, foliage plants are less sensitive than flowering plants. But even they should really be allotted a place of their own in the house and not moved.

WATER

It has been only a hundred years or so since scientists abandoned the notion that plants 'ate' soil. They then discovered that plants consume nothing but liquid food—apart, that is, from such curiosities as carnivorous plants. This is because plant foods are dissolved in water. So you do not have to water your plants because they are so thirsty. It is true that plants do suffer if they are not watered enough. But what they suffer from primarily is not thirst, but hunger.

Water also maintains the plant's 'circulation'. A steady stream of water is sucked up by the roots, rises through the plant's vascular system and evaporates through the leaves. In the reverse direction, the product of assimilation (that is, of the conversion of carbon dioxide into starch with the aid of sunlight) is carried out of the plant into the storage cells. If the supply of water is interrupted the plant breaks down in the truest sense of the word. First it does not extract enough food from the earth, secondly the supply system does not work any more, and finally the circulation itself breaks down: the plant withers.

The water that plants need can be supplied in various ways. Watering lets them suck up water through the roots. Spraying raises the humidity of the surrounding air and so reduces evaporation. So in high

No wonder that the watering can is smiling! It is only in the last hundred years that scientists have realized plants absorb food from water.

humidity plants need less water because they have to lose less, though actually they can absorb only very little of the water sprayed on them.

Occasionally the earth around a plant dries out so much that it no longer gets properly moist again with ordinary watering. Soil that has dried into dust does not absorb water well, and the water simply runs through it so that the roots can absorb only a very small amount. If this happens you should put the flowerpot or tub into a bucket of water until the soil is completely damp.

Everyone in a hard-water area knows that from time to time the kitchen kettle or saucepans have to be 'scaled'. The 'scale' consists of lime, which is dissolved in drinking water and is precipitated when the water is boiled. So if you water your plants with water out of the mains, in the course of time they acquire a substantial, unwanted deposit of lime. The lime settles into the soil and there follows a slow process of leaching, chemically known as alkalization, which acts as a poison to many plants.

Lime shows its presence by 'lime flowers' on the russet brown of the flowerpot. Flowerpots that leave whitish or brownish rings on glass-topped tables or china plates also indicate an excess of lime in the water used for watering.

To be able to water plants properly you should understand a little about chemistry. Scientists have developed a scale of pH values to measure acidity and alkalinity (lime content). At one end, at pH 0, is hydrochloric acid, and at the other, at pH 14, a normal solution of caustic soda. Pure water has a pH value of 7. Water with a pH value of less than 7 is chemically acid; if the pH value is greater than 7, it is alkaline.

If you make a regular practice of using water that has a pH value of

more than 7, then soil that started by being slightly acid will slowly but surely be given a greater concentration of lime and will gradually begin to be chemically too alkaline. Eventually the plants find themselves standing in the wrong sort of soil and begin to droop. They have been poisoned, quite slowly, by the water they were watered with.

What can you do about it? The safest method is always to work with distilled or previously boiled water, which is chemically completely neutral and does not change the composition of the watered soil. This, however, is quite a nuisance, and it is usually enough to repot your plants when necessary in fresh soil. It is not necessary to throw the old pots away. Soak them in vinegar overnight and the lime will be dissolved.

In unpolluted areas the best thing for watering is rain water, unless it is collected from the roof by way of gutters and drainpipes, because then it will be teeming with bacteria and dirt. Rain water has a pH value of exactly 7, so that it is soft, and it also comes at a temperature that the plants like.

You can also damage your house plants (and garden plants, for that matter) by watering them with cold water. The plants suffer a severe cold shock and temporarily stop absorbing as much water as they need. You can often see the plants begin to wilt when this happens. As a general rule always use water just at or below room temperature.

Insufficient water will cause the plant's circulatory supply system to break down.

Cold water can send plants into such a state of shock that they will not take in the water they need.

FRESH AIR

Plants, like most living things, cannot live without air. Plants of course need a different gas in the air; while it is the oxygen that is vital to men and animals, plants need carbon dioxide. The plants absorb it almost exclusively through tiny pores in their leaves. We are therefore not far wrong if we describe the leaves as the lungs of the plant.

And just as men can be poisoned by foul air, so can plants. Both need fresh air. If the carbon dioxide in the air is almost exhausted, then plants react just as men do when they have to live in a room that is short of oxygen—they begin to droop.

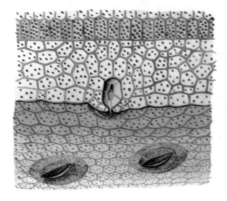

This magnified section of a leaf shows the stomata, or tiny openings in the epidermis or outer layer, through which the leaf breathes in carbon dioxide and exhales oxygen.

The supply of fresh air to house plants does however have its problems. Plants can easily 'catch cold' and if placed in a draught will before long begin to drop their leaves. Next to draughts, what house plants like least is dry air from the heating, which forces the plants to exude moisture continuously. Unless they are watered all the time, they dry up. But even a continual supply of new water does not really help. It overloads the plants' circulation. However often you water them, the plants will eventually begin to wilt. Instead use humidifiers or put a bowl of water on the radiator to keep the air sufficiently moist. It also helps to spray plants regularly with a fine mist, using a hand pressure sprayer.

SOIL

Coming up with the perfect soil for house plants is something of an art. Only this much is certain: ordinary garden earth is no good at all for indoor plants. It will contain weed seeds, pests and maybe diseases, though it can be sterilized. And unless you get professional help you will not know if it has the necessary nutrients and trace elements.

This need for special soil is also logical when you consider the origin of most of our house plants. Only a tiny proportion come from northern latitudes; the others almost all come from the forests of the tropical and subtropical regions. The soil in those forests consists largely of rotted leaves and only to a small extent of mineral materials like sand and clay, so it is easy to understand why we most commonly use a soil consisting of three parts leaf mould, two parts old cow dung and one part sand.

Nowadays it has become more and more difficult for the ordinary townsman to get cow dung, so industry has taken up the problem and produced composts consisting mainly of peat, animal manure and the necessary trace elements. What is true about pH values of water applies equally to soils. The pH value of soils consequently should lie between 4.5 and 7.5. Unfortunately there is still no control over the composts marketed by the trade, and it is only too easy to get composts that are far too acid or too alkaline.

Most house plants that originated in the tropical rain forests need humus-rich soils with an acid reaction of 4.5 to 5.5 pH. You need not be too meticulous: variations of 1 or 2 in pH values are normal and plants can tolerate them. But it is important not to put acid-loving plants like coleus in alkaline soil, or the lime-loving campanula (bellflower) in acid soil.

In case of doubt, you can avoid mistakes by seeking information from a professional about the right soils for your flowers or foliage plants. There is, however, one mistake that you should never make, though it is quite common. Never store compost in an open container or where it can get damp. Nothing is so susceptible to animal and plant parasites as unused, slightly rotting soil, and any fertilizers it contains become inactive after a while.

No less important than the composition of the soil and its chemical reaction is its warmth. Pot plants, especially if they are standing on window ledges, often suffer from 'cold feet'. Sometimes this is because the window lets in a draught. In addition they suffer from 'evaporation chill' through evaporation of water from the soil.

It may be that you are keeping a hot-house plant in a soil temperature which would be more suitable for a cold-house plant. That can cause serious damage to the root system. In the worst cases the plants die. As a general rule, soil should never be at less than room temperature.

House plants from tropical countries are simply not at home in common garden soil.

Even if you pot the immigrants in special compost they will not thrive if temperatures are low.

WHERE TO PUT PLANTS

Light and air, water and warmth and the right kind of soil are the factors that have to be satisfied if plants are to grow and flower properly. Too much or too little light, widely fluctuating air or soil temperature, too little or too much water, even a type of soil that does not meet the plant's requirements—any of these can seriously impair the plant's growth.

Since you can influence and adjust all these factors, you can in theory—and also, very nearly, in practice—construct the ideal site for house plants. Of course, if you live in an apartment you may find you have certain imposed limitations. But, if you keep the structural conditions of your apartment or house in mind, you can always choose for your indoor garden those plants that will do best in the conditions available.

It should be obvious, but must be stressed because so many shocking examples make it necessary: plants are not furniture, not pictures, not simply ornaments. Plants are living creatures and must be treated as such. So if you want to keep plants in your apartment or your house, the first thing to decide is where they are to stand even before you make up your mind what sort of plants you want to stand there.

PLANTS FOR THE SHELF

If you want to keep plants on a bookshelf, on a stool in a corner of the room or in a niche in the wall, you must remember that only the most robust will flourish there. The fluctuations in temperature are generally too great, and not enough sunlight will reach the plants. You will do best to stick to foliage plants.

For heated rooms, a good choice will be from tillandsia, *Dracaena draco* (dragon tree), and aspidistra.

For rooms that are not continuously heated, or for the hall, there are chlorophytum (spider plant), sansevieria (mother-in-law's tongue or snake plant), fatsia (fig leaf palm or castor oil plant), and asparagus fern.

In cool rooms you can keep the typical cold-house plants such as phoenix (date palm), monstera (Swiss cheese plant), and araucaria (Norfolk Island pine).

All these plants are suitable for what indoor gardeners call shelf positions. This means that the plant shares the general climate of the room, which you can do nothing to improve. At best it is possible to improve the lighting conditions by fitting lights over the shelves where the plants stand. If the source of heat in the room is near the shelf, you must take that into account in your choice of plants. As a rule humidity will be lower in a room where the temperature is higher. As far as possible, avoid hanging plants in such positions; the rising warm air is bad for them.

The Swiss cheese plant or shingle plant (monstera), a robust climbing shrub, does well in the shady corners of cool, airy rooms. Mature specimens, as on the left, will easily reach 4 m (13 ft) high, but younger plants will thrive in a flowerpot.

PLANTS AT THE WINDOW

Conditions for plants kept on the window ledge are very similar to those on shelves. In most centrally heated houses the radiator is fitted under the window so even in winter the house plants kept there have a good, warm spot. But they are exposed to very dry air and above all to draughts. If you want to keep plants on the window ledge, you really must fit the window with draught-proof strips.

Plants standing by a window get a great deal of light, which suits many of them but does make some special precautions necessary. Venetian blinds are a good way to keep out the fierce sunlight of a south window, and as a rule the circulating air keeps the room cool and prevents spots on the leaves and curled-up foliage. If this does occur in plants on the window ledge it will generally be those standing in the corners that are affected. It is often due to curtains hanging down at the sides of the window and preventing the air from circulating in the corners, so damaging the plants.

PLANTS ON THE MOVE

One answer to the question of the plants' position—one that is actually contrary to nature—is the use of flower benches or flower tables. Contrary to nature, because plants are static and anchored to their positions, whereas the plant benches or tables are specifically intended to be pushed from one part of the room to another.

A plant bench does make the work of caring for plants easier: you simply put the plants in a loose row on top of the bench, which should be at least 20-25 cm (10 in) wide.

A plant table, on the other hand, is better from the plants' point of view, because of the foundation put in the tray on which the plants stand. A damp foundation will prevent the evaporation of water through the pots and the consequent cooling off of the root system. It is a good idea to cover the bottom of the tray with a layer of medium coarse pebbles—

about 1 cm ($\frac{1}{2}$ in) deep—and then spread wet peat over it. The tray itself must be watertight and not susceptible to damage by humus acids and fertilizers. Glazed upper surfaces are not only resistant but are easy to look after.

If you were thinking of making a flower table yourself with a tray made of tinplate, remember that the tray will need a protective coating which must be renewed twice a year. Not only does this cause extra work but some plants can be harmed if you take them out too often.

11

PLANTS IN A TERRARIUM OR BOTTLE GARDEN

Giving your plants the care they need sounds a good deal easier than it is. You may intend to do your best by them, but what if your home is suitable for humans yet difficult for plants? Your family may be used to central heating, draughts, cigarette smoke and drastic changes in temperature, and no plant will thrive in these conditions. The answer may be plant cases, properly called terraria, and bottle gardens.

It all started with a Victorian, Doctor Ward. He discovered, quite by accident, that some very delicate ferns which had previously died when he tried to grow them in the open air thrived in a completely closed glass container where they were protected from dust, fumes and dry air. What is more, he was able to leave the container for years without attention. The ferns had been able to create a perfect microclimate in the container. His discovery led to a tremendous interest in this kind of gardening, and elaborate plant cases took pride of place in many homes.

Modern terraria are not so elaborate as the Victorian originals, but you can heat them and provide artificial lighting. You can grow almost any plants in them depending on size.

For those with little time, foliage plants are probably the best as they need less attention than flowering ones. Obviously do not include any plants that are going to grow rapidly and spoil the whole effect. The main thing to remember is that all the plants in a case or bottle must be compatible. Do not mix moisture lovers with cacti, for example. If you want to put the case on a sunny windowsill, be sure that all the plants will be happy in such a situation. If the only place for it is a dark corner, fill it with shade-loving woodland ferns. And if the case is placed so that the plants receive only artificial light, change them at intervals. They could not survive long without sun.

You can have fun with these cases, too, by creating a miniature landscape with soil to resemble hills, or studding them with rocks. Make a desert with sandy soil and cacti. Or just fill a terrarium with exotic foliage plants and light it from behind for tropical drama.

Bottle gardens work on the same principle as plant cases, and most plants, safe from outside hazards, will thrive—except, of course, for those which need a dry atmosphere. Inside a bottle garden the humidity is always fairly high. Clear glass is best, although it is possible to get healthy growth in tinted glass.

Planting a case is easy because you have plenty of room to manoeuvre. Bottle gardens need more dexterity, as you will discover. Both types of container must be scrupulously clean before you start, and good drainage is essential for success. Washed shingle or pea gravel is a suitable foundation, and over this you must have a layer of horticultural charcoal, which filters out impurities and keeps the soil 'sweet'. The charcoal is especially important to the more enclosed conditions of a bottle. The growing medium goes on top of the charcoal. This can be a soil-based compost or one of the soilless mixtures.

Take your time arranging plants in a terrarium so that each is shown to advantage. Make sure each individual plant looks well next to its neighbour. You can either plant them all on the same level, or by building up the compost, have them at different heights. Finally, firm the compost lightly round the roots and

water. Be careful with the watering —you want neither to flood the case nor to splash compost up against the glass you have cleaned. A case full of moisture-loving plants needs a lid, just a little bigger than the case for easy handling. Plants that like drier air should be uncovered.

Filling a bottle needs more patience and the plants you use should be small enough to pass through the neck undamaged. Drainage material, charcoal and moist compost can be poured in through a funnel of stiff paper or a long cardboard tube, then spread out evenly with a teaspoon lashed or wired onto a long stick. It is very important not to dirty the sides of the bottle while you are doing this as it can be so difficult to get the glass spotless again. You can see where the dexterity comes in. Next drop in the little plants and when they are in position make small holes for their roots in the compost. Manoeuvre the plants into the holes (use two sticks if it helps) and work some compost over the roots. Firm it lightly. The roots will soon take hold.

Finally, watering. It is all too easy to wash the compost away from the plants or make muddy splashes against the glass sides, so tilt the bottle slightly and let the water run gently down the sides—it will soon soak through to the middle of the bottle. Do not pour in too much at first for it takes a long time for the moisture to evaporate from a bottle.

To cover or not to cover the bottle is arguable. Certainly it is a good idea to keep it closed while the plants are settling in. Use the bottle's own cork if it has one, or cover with something like plastic wrap if not. But if the glass is running with condensation then the top must come off until the compost has dried a little. Aim to have the top half or so of the bottle covered inside with light condensation and use this as a guide to watering, too. It may take a little time before you can judge how much water is needed to keep a healthy balance of moisture, but it will come with experience. The main thing is that eventually you will be able to leave the bottle alone for months.

Even the healthiest terrarium or bottle garden will need grooming now and then. Caring for a terrarium is easy, but you will need a long bamboo cane with a razor blade stuck into the end to remove dying leaves or to prune away too vigorous growth from a bottle garden. Remove the debris with two sticks, using them like tongs or chopsticks.

A MODERN CONSERVATORY

Years ago most large houses had a conservatory. These were deliciously romantic places with cool tiled floors, wicker chaise-longues, or lacy wrought-iron tables and chairs tucked away under giant palms or among green ferns. Bougainvillaeas climbed up to the vaulted glass roof, the air was filled with the sweet scent of jasmine, there were tubs of tender camellias, immaculate in flower and leaf, perhaps an exotic bird tethered to a pillar, and to lull the senses even more, the gentle splash of a fountain. Just the setting for gentle courtship.

It was all very grand and rather delightful. But the really exciting thing about these conservatories was that they were marvellous places for growing plants. They had space, all the light a plant could need, a certain amount of humidity, and enough heat to encourage growth.

Life is not so lavish now. Few of us have room for such spacious structures, or could afford to heat and maintain them. Courtship would be a teeth-chattering affair and most of the plants would turn up their toes in the cold winter months. The next best thing is a home extension.

Usually these are built on to the sunny side of a house to provide extra living space for the family, but with a little planning you can turn them into a jungle of happy, healthy plants. Buy the largest extension you can afford and have room for. You can buy components in many sizes and materials to suit your site and house. Then, when you have made sure the family have enough room to sit and move around without knocking things over, start furnishing the remaining space with plants. If you have chosen an extension with a glass or clear plastic roof, so much the better. You will have more light, though you will lose more heat. You can, of course, buy models with double roofs or double glazing to overcome this problem, but be sure that there are enough windows to ensure good ventilation.

Unless you are sure you can provide lots of heat, which you probably would not want anyway in a living area, choose only those plants which will tolerate cold, provided that they are protected from frost at night. A small heater will prevent night frosts, and during the day the extension will be quite warm if the sun is shining,

even in winter. Some of the warmth from the house wall will be trapped inside the extension too.

If you grow tender plants in pots outside during the warm weather, bring them into the extension during the winter. Then have a look at the plants already in the house. Many of them, however much you pamper them, can never look their best in living rooms. That monstera, for instance, will become quite exuberant in a light and airy extension. If you give it something like a moss-wrapped branch to cling to, you will get some idea of what it should really look like.

For scent, grow stephanotis on trellis or wires. Have hanging baskets full of the heavenly *Campanula isophylla*, the plants our grandmothers were so fond of, or ivy-leaved geraniums, ferns, and, of course, as many varieties of fuchsias as you have room for.

Nor is there any reason why you cannot have a small pool and fountain. The pool need only be a large plant container, fitted with a small submersible pump. Decorate it with plants like cyperus and let a few fish slip among the stems. If you cannot have a fountain, choose plants that are at home around still water, like zantedeschia (arum lily). Many of the plants we call marginals—that is, those which grow on the boggy edges of ponds—will grow in a shallow, water-filled container with perhaps a layer of colourful pebbles lining the bottom. They will be magnified by the water.

Unlike a greenhouse, where some plants can be grown in an earth border, you will want to keep extension plants in pots, and some will eventually need quite large ones. This will keep the more vigorous kinds under control and means that you can change them or move out any that are not doing too well, or simply resting.

In a room which is really intended for living you will probably have to prune back growth that threatens to interfere with the family's activities. Climbers particularly will need trimming, to prevent them from covering the windows and blocking out all light.

If you really have no room for an extension but feel you must have a good home for your plants, alternatives include small hexagonal greenhouses that stand on a balcony or patio, or even in a sunny room, or greenhouses which you fit with a few screws and plugs over a window on the outside of the house.

FLOWERPOTS

Once the clay flowerpot was virtually the only kind ever used, but more recently a number of other kinds of plant containers have been introduced. Clay pots have given way to plastic, papier mâché, metal, even concrete, as gardeners learn more about the behaviour of plants. People used to think that flowerpots had to be porous, permeable by both air and water; they used to lay a clay shard over the drainage hole to make sure that the water could get out. Now we know that what matters is not the porosity of the pot walls but the soil with which it is filled.

If you do use clay pots, new ones must be thoroughly washed and plunged in water. This washes away all traces of the firing, and the pot soaks up water until it is saturated. If you were to put a plant into a new clay pot without soaking it, the porous material of the pot would suck water out of the soil and so out of the plant, and the plant would wither. It is amazing what a lot of water a clay pot can swallow.

Plant composts used to be finely sieved, so that they were very compact and admitted very little air. Modern composts are much looser and admit more air and water, so that the porosity of the container is unimportant. Fertilizers also move through these light, spongy mixtures more easily and are readily available to the roots.

The root system of a plant is even more important than what grows above ground. If stalks, leaves or flower buds are damaged, they just stop growing, but damaged roots affect the entire well-being of the plant.

Roots have three functions. First, they anchor the plant firmly to the ground; secondly, they absorb the water and food that the plant needs; and thirdly plants—to some extent, —store food in their roots. The roots of plants may take a variety of forms, according to the conditions in the plant's natural habitat. We divide them into tap roots and plate roots.

Tap roots extend deep into the ground, with a strong main stem. Plate roots spread out equally in all directions, at no great depth. You must choose the shape of flowerpot that is suited to the roots of your plant.

Clay pots are graded according to size and, like plastic pots, come in different shapes. Conventional plant containers taper towards the bottom. The only object of that is to make it easier to get the plant out when you are repotting, for the root system of a plant would fill a wide-bellied pot just as well since the fine rootlets of the plant make for the wall of the pot. Most commonly the top diameter is equal to the height. You can also get pots of special shapes for special purposes—flatter pots for plants with plate roots, for example. The additional outer pots often used nowadays (correctly called cache pots) are purely decorative and have no effect on the plants.

Which is better for the plants, clay or plastic, is the subject of much vain discussion. The good old clay pot has served its purpose for hundreds of years and has done the plants no apparent harm. On the other hand, plastic pots are lighter, easier to clean and less likely to break, though cheaper qualities become brittle and crack quite quickly.

The only important difference is that a plastic pot is not porous and water cannot evaporate through the sides, so water less frequently.

There is one more thing about pots that causes controversy among indoor gardeners: the drainage hole. While it is not essential, a drainage hole at least does no harm. Even experienced gardeners overwater sometimes, and a drainage hole will let the excess escape so that it does not collect in the bottom and rot the plant's roots. And, of course, if you see roots growing out of the drainage hole, this is a sure sign that your plant needs a new pot.

REPOTTING

If something like two-thirds of the amount of soil—which also, of course, means the amount of food—in a pot has been displaced by roots, the time has come to give your plant a new and larger pot.

The job needs a bit of preparation. To start with, if you use new clay pots you must begin by washing and soaking them 24 hours in advance. If you are reusing old pots, scour off any lime deposits and clean them thoroughly to reduce the risk of infection to your new plants. Any old soil left in them may harbour pests.

As a general rule, never repot in the rest period of a plant or when it is in flower—except for plants that flower continuously, like the pelargonium (geranium). During the rest period the plant's roots will not grow into the soil, which will go sour. When a plant is in flower repotting interferes so seriously with its growth that the flowers will be destroyed. Even if the plant tells you unmistakably that its pot is too small by raising its root ball, you should never disregard this rule—never in flowering and never in the rest period. A few weeks will not make that much difference. The only exception is if you drop the pot and damage it.

To repot, take the plant carefully out of the old pot simply by turning it upside down and either giving the bottom one sharp tap or bringing the rim down sharply on a table. With very delicate plants, break the old pot to be sure of avoiding damage to the roots or shoots.

The old soil at the top of the root ball, where the plant breaks the surface, is generally just thrown away. To clean the bottom part of the ball, just shake gently. Cut out diseased roots or any parts affected by pests, and snip off dead roots. If you have delayed repotting too long, so that the root ball is thickly matted, you can carefully cut out a part of the roots from below. That will be especially necessary with young plants, which always tend to form too many roots.

The root ball should be put into the new pot right away and packed in with new soil. Only beginners leave root balls lying about while they look for a knife or the soil they need. Then replace the upper layer of soil on the root ball, pressing the new soil down lightly. Finally, water the plant, but do not drown it.

Dislodge hardy plants by upending the pot and bringing its rim down sharply on a hard surface.

Extract the plant and discard old surface soil, taking care to keep the root ball intact.

Sink the plant with root ball in a larger pot and fill it with new soil until the soil level reaches the same height on the plant as before.

Firm the plant in gently, pressing the soil down with both hands. Keep the repotted plant out of direct sun for a few days and water well.

You can tell by looking at the root ball whether a plant is healthy or diseased. Healthy plants have light brown roots, and the tips are almost white. Diseased roots are dark brown to black or quite rotten. They must be cut out and so must roots that are broken or have been damaged in repotting. If you leave the damaged part on the root ball it will soon begin to rot and cause the plant to become diseased.

Avoid using a pot more than two sizes bigger than the old one. If you use too large a pot, unless the plant is very vigorous, it will not send roots into all the new soil, or it will spend all its strength at first in forming new roots at the expense of top growth.

But for very large plants it is not always possible to find a bigger pot, so all you can do with them is reduce the root ball. Do not make the mistake of just cutting underneath and all round the root ball. That would be fatal—you would be killing all the most vital roots. Instead cut out a small section from the middle and then press the reduced root ball together again.

Make sure when you repot that the plant reaches the same height above the rim in the new pot as it did in the old. Since larger pots are normally also taller, you should put the old, possibly cut-down, root ball on a correspondingly higher layer of soil in the new pot.

As a final measure, keep repotted plants out of direct sunlight as much as possible for the next two weeks. Repotting will have interfered with the absorption of water through the fine roots, and if the plants stand too much in the sun you cannot be certain that the water will be replaced. If a plant is not too big—you cannot do this of course with a large indoor shrub—you can increase the humidity of the air around the plant by putting a plastic bag over it. That will ease the shock of repotting. Or you can spray it with a fine mist of tepid water twice a day for a week or two.

FEEDING PLANTS

Plants require more than the proper position. Not only must they be given enough light and air, warmth and water and the right soil; they must also have all the food they need, regularly and at the right times. Watering and feeding are inseparable in plant care, unless you want to stand in front of plants that grow more and more unattractive, complaining, '. . . but I've always given them plenty of water!' Good watering by itself is not enough.

Besides light, water and the carbon dioxide they draw from the atmosphere, plants live on nitrogen, phosphorus and potassium. These are the three principal foodstuffs that fertilizers can supply, plus small amounts of other necessary elements, primarily boron, iron, calcium, magnesium and manganese. These substances occur naturally in soil, if not always in adequate amounts.

The foodstuffs in a small flowerpot are consumed quite quickly and must be replaced. And since the plants can only absorb food in water, fertilizers must be given in a liquid form. Modern inorganic fertilizers are made up in such a way that they do not dissolve all at once—if they did the plants would get a severe shock from overfertilization. The foods are absorbed gradually as the plants are watered.

It is vital for plant development to give nitrogen and potassium at the

Lack of nitrogen inhibits growth.

right time and in the right quantities. Nitrogen promotes growth and is important in the formation of chlorophyll, the substance that makes the leaves green. A plant that gets too little nitrogen stops growing; its leaves turn yellow and the flowers are small and of poor quality. Too much nitrogen, on the other hand, means that the leaves turn an unnaturally pale green and grow large and sappy. Flowers that get too much nitrogenous fertilizer also become particularly susceptible to diseases and lose their resistance to parasitic fungi.

Too much potassium has much the same effect on plants as too little nitrogen. Too little potassium causes discoloration of the leaves: what was originally green will show yellow and red at the edges. But plants that get enough potassium grow very strong and have brilliantly coloured flowers and fruits.

The main importance of phosphorus, the third of the principal foodstuffs, is in the growth of roots and the formation of buds and flowers. A plant that gets too little phosphorus becomes stunted, and its leaves become discoloured.

There are excellent balanced fertilizers on the market for house plants, containing essential trace elements as well as the three main foodstuffs. If you buy prepared soil from the nursery you can take it for granted that it will contain adequate amounts of the basic necessities, but you will have to start fertilizing eventually, depending on the type of soil you use.

In addition to fertilizers, it is a good idea to give plants some organic manures if you can get them.

You should always combine the operations of manuring and watering, for again it is only through water that the plant receives a sufficiently diluted supply of food. If you manure without watering you may inadvertently damage the roots when they absorb the food.

There are five rules for manuring.
● Feed in the evening, preferably on an overcast day.
● If you manure by day, you must give the plants extra protection from the sunlight so that they do not lose too much water.
● After manuring, plants must be well watered and sprayed.
● Never manure plants if the soil has dried up; the plant must first be well watered so that the fine roots become capable of absorption again.

● Do not get any on the leaves! If you do, spray it off at once with clear, tepid water.

Nothing is more important in plant cultivation than understanding the 'life rhythm' of the plants. That applies to every aspect of cultivation. Plants orient themselves in their growth to the rhythm of light and darkness. Some start to form flower buds when the days are growing shorter and so are called short-day plants. Others flower when the days grow longer. These are called long-day plants. Between the two extremes are the plants that can flower and grow regardless of the length of day or time of year.

Only during the growth period do plants need a lot of watering and feeding. For the remainder of the year, when growth and flowering are over, the plants rest. To feed them then is not only superfluous but actually dangerous; it can cause damage to the roots.

After the growth and flowering period, which differs from family to family, from species to species, even from one plant to another, you must stop feeding. But do not stop watering. Although plants need less water in their rest period, hardly any of them can tolerate completely dry soil. Only quite robust plants like the sansevieria (mother-in-law's tongue) and other succulents can survive a dry root system, but it is not good gardening to let them get that dry. It is impossible to give precise instructions; this is where you have to learn by trial and error.

Feeding resting plants is harmful.

PRUNING

Pruning does more than make plants look nice and neat. Faded flowers and withered leaves are a permanent source of danger. Points of infection can quickly form on them which in a short time will endanger the whole plant. Remove fallen flowers and leaves before watering. If there are faded flowers hanging on to stems in which the sap is still flowing, you must take off the dead head and the stem with it. The withered flowers of the cyclamen are pulled off; withered blooms of the saintpaulia (African violet) or begonia, for instance, are broken off; with primulas the stalk must be cut off. What remains of the stems will dry and can easily be plucked off shortly afterwards.

Withered foliage and faded or spotted leaves must always be removed with the stalk. If a leaf is difficult to remove, then it must still be in contact with the sap circulation and the plant has not yet extracted all the reserves of food out of it. If you have to make an effort to tear off the leaf you may damage the plant tissue. That is dangerous, not so much because it harms the plant as because parasitic pests can infect it.

Often it is hard to remove leaves that clasp the stem or stalk as soon as they wither. This problem arises with the monstera and dieffenbachia. You have to cut off the leaves or their stems along the stalk with a sharp knife. What remains of the leaves is not picked off until later, when it has dried up completely.

Pruning also controls growth and can make the difference between a weak spindly plant and one that is bushy and flourishing. When shoots are removed from a young plant, it immediately tries to develop new shoots, often two or more, just below the cut. *Ficus elastica* (the rubber tree), for example, must be pruned as soon as it reaches a height of about 45 cm (18 in) above the rim of the pot. Prune at the end of the rest period, before the plant starts to put out new shoots. The pruning point (and this is true also of cutting back) should be no more than 1 cm ($\frac{1}{2}$ in) above the base of a leaf or side shoot. Botanists call this a node. If the stump left above the shoot is too long there is a danger that it will become infected and so a source of disease to the plant.

Pruning to alter the appearance of a plant is especially necessary with hanging or bushy plants. But you

must prune with care. Hard pruning can so check the growth, especially of flowering plants like fuchsia, peperomia, and pelargonium, that it damages their blossoming.

Cutting back older plants restores their youthful shape and encourages them to form new, more productive shoots. On the rubber tree, for instance, you can cut back as far as the woody parts. The plant will look desperately bare for a time, but it will recover and form new shoots.

If a bushy plant grows too quickly and begins to crowd the plants around it, then you must cut it back, simply to make room. Do this before and during the growth period

Breaking dead blooms from the begonia, seen here with other house plants, will ensure fine, healthy growth.

(younger specimens will generally stand more cutting back) and aim for a balanced shape.

One more job in caring for indoor plants is the occasional cleaning of leaves. Wipe off dust and remove any chalky residue from watering using a cloth dampened with lukewarm, previously boiled water. You do not have to use detergents or soap, milk, olive oil, or beeswax. They clog the pores in the leaves and the plants cannot breathe.

PROPAGATION

It is always a thrill to raise new plants from ones you already have. You may not always have much luck with tropical plants like orchids and cacti, but even trying is fun.

Unlike those grown outdoors, house plants are hardly ever grown from their own seed, because they seldom set ripe seeds from the flowers. Also, hybrids and some varieties will not come 'true' from seed, that is the seedlings will not be like the parent. And some species simply take too long to propagate by seed.

Usually you will have to rely on vegetative propagation for the second growth of house plants. The most important of all forms of vegetative propagation is propagation by **cuttings,** which are parts of a plant separated from the main plant. They may be cuttings of side shoots and the tips of leading shoots, or stem cuttings, for which the stem of the plant is cut into a number of finger-length pieces. Then there are leaf

Propagating cuttings in bottles or jars of water will allow you to see how the roots progress. Transfer the cuttings to pots when they are 10-15 cm (4-6 in) long.

bud cuttings (a leaf plus a bud) and finally leaf cuttings, which are particularly easy to work with.

Shoot cuttings generally need a very warm soil to make them root. The shoots are cut from the old plant and put into sandy soil immediately after separation. Always work with a sharp knife. If you do, the stem below the cut will not be damaged, but if you use secateurs the stem gets crushed before the cutting is separated.

At the base of the cutting the cells form a growth of harder tissue called a callus. If you insert the newly separated cutting into slightly damp, sandy compost before the callus begins to dry, new roots are formed from the callus which will support the life of the cutting, or from which new young plants develop. When the callus dries on the parent plant, corky cells form and the wound heals over.

Basically, the procedure with stem, leaf bud and leaf cuttings is the same as for shoot cuttings. Propagation by stem or leaf bud cuttings is very rare, but leaf cuttings are frequently used. Choose fully grown leaves and cut them off with their stems. Leaf and stem are inserted in the compost and new plants form at the base of the leaf blade. Propagation by leaf cut-

ting is particularly simple with the pelargonium (geranium), saintpaulia (African violet) and related plants, and most succulents.

You must take cuttings only from healthy plants or shoots. The best time is when the plant is beginning to awake from its rest period and sending out new shoots. Do not take cuttings if the plant is already in flower; the formation of roots then is very slow and hesitant. Flower buds at the tip of shoots taken as cuttings should be carefully removed, for they will develop even on cuttings and deprive the young plant of the strength to form roots. Whether or not to prune shrubby cuttings that have plenty of leaves depends on the species, but remember that even a cutting needs leaves to breathe. On the other hand transpiration from a big leaf area may be so great that the tiny new roots cannot supply enough water.

You can, of course, root cuttings under glass. In a glass frame—or even a plastic bag—you get high humidity, so that the plants do not lose so much water by transpiration. But do not try to create humidity by overwatering the soil or the cutting will rot.

A cutting must always be kept in a warm, light position well sheltered

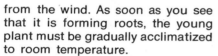

From left to right: slice the shoot almost through, plug the cut with moss to prevent healing, cover with moss and seal in a polythene strip, secure with string or adhesive tape. Roots will soon form in the bag.

Stem, shoot and leaf cuttings can all be used in vegetative propagation. Do not take a cutting from a plant in full flower and remove even the tiniest bud or it will develop at the roots' expense.

Shrubby ferns are easily propagated. Upend the pot, tap the base to dislodge the plant, then work the root ball loose until you can see where the roots will easily divide. Cut through here. Repot.

from the wind. As soon as you see that it is forming roots, the young plant must be gradually acclimatized to room temperature.

Certain house plants—like tradescantia, pilea (aluminium plant), African violet, or geranium—root incredibly quickly and easily. But woody plants—like *Ficus elastica* (rubber tree)—give a good deal more trouble. If you are not successful at first, put the cuttings on to a warm foundation so that the temperature in the rooting medium stays at about 25°C (77°F). The other way is to stand the cuttings in bottles filled with water. In full sunlight, when you occasionally have to spray the outside parts of the cuttings with water, the submerged parts will begin to form roots. When these are 10-15 cm (4-6 in) long, gently take the cuttings out of their bath and pot them carefully.

A method of vegetative propagation that has proved very effective especially in the cultivation of the rubber tree is called **air layering**. Here you can do two jobs at once. When the rubber tree has grown so tall that it must be pruned anyway, you cut the shoot nearly half way through, preferably just below a leaf node. To stop the plant closing the wound at once, put a small piece of wood or a little moss into the cut, then cover it with a thick layer of damp moss, and wrap some polythene around this, securing it with string or adhesive.

Within three months, roots will have formed at the point where you cut the stem, under the moss covering. Then cut the head off just below the roots, remove the covering, and

set the new plant in loose soil. If this seems too complicated, you can, of course, simply cut the top off the rubber tree and root it in warm sand or water.

Layering is also one of the best methods of propagating creepers. Lay a shoot along the ground and fasten it down carefully with wire at intervals of 8-10 cm (3-4 in), covering these points with soil. If the soil is kept moist the plant will form roots at the points where it is buried. Sever them from the parent and pot up.

The simplest of all forms of vegetative propagation is **division**. Shrubby plants like ferns, which have grown so luxuriant that they threaten to burst their pots, can be cut apart

vertically with a sharp knife. There are still so many roots on each part that it will grow in a new pot with no trouble. It is not always necessary to divide the plants with a knife; sometimes it is enough to tease the roots apart and then carefully divide them. But tuberous plants like begonias must be divided with a sharp knife and each piece must contain at least one eye. This form of propagation is also particularly suitable for zantedeschias (arum lilies) with their fleshy rootstock.

Cuttings need special care. Create a sheltered environment with a tank where they will have ample warmth, light, humidity and air.

PESTS AND DISEASES

There is no doubt that house plants are more delicate than anything that grows outdoors—more susceptible to errors in cultivation and pests and disease. This is not only because nearly all our house plants come from regions with very warm climates and have difficulty with the climatic conditions far from their native habitat. They also have to live in places that are designed primarily for men, and men make different demands on their environment.

Plants which sicken as a result of cultivation errors are a sad sight. Drooping leaves, shrivelled flowers, weak growth or rotting or damaged foliage can result, damage that is difficult to remedy.

One of the commonest mistakes is standing the plant in the wrong position, with too much or too little light, too much or too little warmth, too much or too little water. And not enough care is taken to provide for plants' urgent need of humidity in the atmosphere, especially in winter when indoor heating makes the air extremely dry.

If you do not look after your house plants properly, it may not only cause damage to them directly but may also make them more susceptible to pests of all kinds, animal parasites, bacteria, fungi or viruses.

Sometimes it is hard to tell where all the aphids and red spiders, mildew and cutworm, mites, even snails, come from. You may have carefully sealed the terrarium, meticulously disinfected all the soil and inspected all the tools you use. But the pests arrive just the same. Even professional gardeners shrug their shoulders resignedly when you ask them where the pests come from. 'Out of the air!' they will often tell you. It sounds unlikely, but it can be true enough. The air actually contains countless bacteria, viruses and fungus spores, most of which are harmless, but which can suddenly discover suitable food on a plant that has been damaged by inadequate care and attention, descend on it all at once and do serious harm.

Many diseases—particularly white fly—are introduced through other plant material, or they may be present on your plants already and, in the right conditions, thrive. And you should not be too surprised to find even earthworms or eelworms, espe-cially on plants that have been out-doors in summer, as the eggs of these creatures can for short periods withstand temperatures up to boiling point. Even steam has sometimes proved inadequate for disinfecting garden soil.

Remember when you use pesticides that you are not only exterminating the harmful parasites but you may also be harming human beings and pets (especially fish, birds and cats) in the house. Never use them in closed rooms. If you cannot work on the balcony or in the garden, at least you should have a window open, and keep children away. Check labels for warnings, follow all instructions and wear gloves. Always use the prescribed amount —too much can be harmful.

If in doubt seek professional advice before beginning any treatment. Garden shops or centres are glad to help, too, provided you do not walk in with a pot plant covered with disease germs which could infect all the healthy plants there.

Even without professional advice, you must always take a plant that shows symptoms of disease away from the others. Plants with bacterial or virus infections must be destroyed at once. Never use them for composting; the source of infection can remain active for years.

Here is a list of some common plant diseases and their sources, possible ways of tackling them, and the appearance of the disease symptoms.

Plants affected by **bacteria** begin to wilt. They stop growing, and growths appear on the plant tissue—on the roots, the stems, the leaves or the flowers. The plant develops soft patches, generally yellowish or grey. Drooping leaves and yellowing foliage are also signs of bacteriosis, as are galls on roots or stems. The begonia, pelargonium (geranium) and various cacti are often affected this way.

Bactericides are only effective against bacterial infection as a prevention. To avoid infection, keep the plant in an airy and dry position. Diseased plants must be destroyed, and no seeds or cuttings from them may be used, since they are almost certain to be affected.

Fungus diseases have much the same effect on plants as bacterial infection. They are caused by little thread-like parasites on the plant. They enter through wounds in the plant, but they can also enter through the natural pores in the tis-sue. After a short time they become visible on the plant in mouldy patches. Fungi can affect both the roots of a plant and the parts that grow above the ground. As with bacteria, prevention is the only way to deal with fungi. Spray with fungicides and destroy infected plants immediately.

Among the commonest fungus infections are powdery mildew and downy mildew. Even experts cannot easily distinguish between the two—in both, the plants are covered with a silvery, floury powder. With powdery mildew the leaves shrivel; with downy mildew they fall. Powdery mildew is caused by too dark a position and too much nitrogen in the fertilizer. Downy mildew may be brought on by too much moisture in the air and in the soil.

Plants with bulbs, corms or rhizomes are prone to fusarium foot rot. Dark, almost black spots appear, mostly at the neck of the roots, which later become moist and rotten. The plants wilt and cannot be saved.

Botrytis, often confused with mildew, arises from excessive humidity, generally only on dead parts of the plant. Healthy plants are seldom attacked by it. It causes brown spots on leaves and flowers. If the plant is only mildly infected you can remove the spotted leaves and spray with preparations of copper. That will save most plants. You may get this disease in the cyclamen, pelargonium (geranium), and saintpaulia (African violet).

You will quite often find spots on the leaves of house plants, but you need not always suspect the worst. Often they are burns caused by strong sunshine or spots of water. But they can also be due to fungus infections that even experts find hard to diagnose. Rust causes spots of an almost orange colour on the underside of the leaves, from which patches of mildew later develop. Red spots on the underside, and also on bulbs and on flower stalks, are a sign of red burn. But if the leaves have rust-red spots, later turning black, on their upper sides, then the plant has septoria. In all three cases you can use preparations of copper and sulphur, and take the plants out of the room or window. With injuries only to the stalk or stem you can occasionally hope for recovery.

Virus diseases, carried mostly by animal pests, are especially dangerous for all plants. They are indicated by serious interference with the growth and extreme colour changes.

There is no hope of saving plants once they are diseased but, to avoid more serious harm, take the affected plants out and burn them at once.

Among virus diseases are leaf roll, which makes the leaves roll up like paper bags, leaf curl and mosaic disease, in which light and dark patches of discoloration appear on the leaves. Another virus disease may cause chlorosis.

The only thing you can do about virus diseases is to control the animal pests that carry them, either with insecticides or by removing the pests by hand—in practice not generally very effective.

There are many **animal pests** that can trouble an indoor gardener. Among the most common are scale insects, woolly aphids, root lice and, especially, white fly, a scourge to house plant growers and very difficult to control. These all feed by sucking sap from plants, not only depriving them of essential nourishment but also causing the leaves to curl up and eventually drop. They also spread every kind of virus disease, and fungus infections settle in their secretions and damage the plants still further.

Infection is a sign that the plant is not standing in the right conditions. Generally it is too warm, and the air too dry. You can prevent infection by increasing the humidity and by thorough watering.

If the plants are already infested, wash them with a mild solution of soft soap, or simply use a spray. Some insecticides work entirely on contact, so that they have to be directed on the pests. Others are systemic—that is, they are absorbed by the plant which itself then becomes toxic to the pest. These are more effective and longer lasting than contact poisons, and you do not have to cover the whole plant. With

any product, read the manufacturer's instructions to make sure it is safe.

Other common pests found on plants are the dangerous mites, who also suck the green parts of the plants. Wherever they occur light spots will appear on the leaves, which soon fade to a pale green, shrivel and fall. This kind of damage is caused most of all by the red spider, a tiny mite which is not always as red as its name suggests. The little creatures can sometimes be white, yellow, green or orange-brown. You can spot them when you see infected leaves covered with a fine, glittering web. Red spiders are a sign that the plant is standing in too dry air. Spray the plants with water and then with an insecticide.

In contrast to the red spider, both root mites and soft-skin mites are signs of too high humidity. You can control them by spraying and by giving the plants plenty of air. The soft-skin mite in particular is responsible for many ugly changes in plants—twisted, corky patches on

the leaves and stems, leaves turning brown on the underside, shrivelled buds and spotted flowers.

More a nuisance than a menace are ants and woodlice. Both feed on all parts of the plant. Woodlice eat only at night, and their presence is a sign that the plant is not being kept clean. The best way to deal with ants is to block the way from their nest, usually outdoors. With woodlice, hunt them out of their hiding places —under fallen leaves or in any unused flowerpots that are lying around—and make sure there are no places where they can lurk. Only when these measures fail should you consider using various poisons.

The pelargonium (begonia), cyclamens, and ferns are infested by a particularly harmful insect, the vine weevil. It is as dangerous as a larva as it is as a mature beetle. The larvae, white with a brown head and growing to nearly 1 cm ($\frac{1}{2}$ in) long, feed from late summer until winter on roots, corms and bulbs. If a cyclamen suddenly falls sick, you should turn it out of the pot at once and look to see whether the corms are being eaten by one of these larvae. If the damage is not too great you can generally rescue the plant by cutting out the part that has been eaten and dusting with charcoal. The mature beetle, nearly 1 cm ($\frac{1}{2}$ in) long with a broad snout, avoids daylight and hides under flowerpots. Leaves eaten from the edges are a warning signal that the vine weevil is about. Control this pest by reducing its hiding places and using insecticides.

Finally, beware of the minute, transparent eelworm. They live in plants, sucking the sap from the cells and causing growths and distortions. You find them in the leaves as well as in the roots. Chemical control is difficult; it is safest to destroy infested plants.

Greenfly or aphis.

The black ant (_Lasius niger_).

Black leaf spot.

HYDROPONICS - PLANTS WITHOUT SOIL

When botanists discovered that plants did not live on soil but got their food solely by absorbing inorganic substances dissolved in water, they had the theoretical basis of hydroponics. The botanists asked, quite logically, why plants should have to stand in soil at all. From there, as a complement to geoponics (soil cultivation), grew the concept of hydroponics (water cultivation), a revolutionary idea first brought to public attention in the United States in 1929 in a work by Professor W. F. Gericke.

As with so many scientific discoveries, the full significance of this one became evident only as a result of wartime conditions. During World War II the Americans found difficulty in supplying their troops in the barren Pacific islands with fresh vegetables, and then they remembered Gericke's discoveries. They began to grow vegetables in huge troughs full of a nutrient solution, arranging the plants on wire netting above the troughs so that their roots grew down into the fluid they fed on. The vegetables grew marvellously well without soil, and what is more they were absolutely free from infection by the fungi and bacteria found in the soil of the islands. Hydroponics had passed its first practical test.

But of course plants need soil not only as a source of food but also as a support to hold them upright. The Americans' lettuces had all the support they needed on the wire netting over the hydroponic troughs, but a house plant would just not be able to stand up once it had grown tall. Unless its roots are anchored in the soil, it simply falls over. So now a number of artificial cultivation bases have been developed, or natural substances have been pressed into service as bases for hydroponics.

A cultivation base must provide more than support for the plants; it must contain air so that the roots can breathe. (This is also true for ordinary house plant soil, and it is a good idea to break up the soil in pots occasionally.)

It really does not matter whether the cultivation base or aggregate is quartz or gravel or coal slack, basalt chips or crushed granite, pumice or cinders, broken bricks or the popular

vermiculite. What does matter with all these aggregates is that they should be inert, that is they should not react chemically with the nutrient solution, because only then can the substances in the solution be extracted to meet the plants' needs. Secondly, the aggregate must be absorbent, so that it can absorb the nutrient fluid quickly and yield it up slowly. Finally, whatever this artificial soil is made of, it must be something

Loose absorbent aggregate supports the plants while the roots feed on the nutrient solution.

that has no sharp corners that can hurt the delicate root system.

In geoponics a plant needs a container full of soil. In hydroponics it needs two containers. The lower container holds the nutrient solution, while the plant supported in the aggregate stands above it in the inset container. This upper container has holes in the bottom of it so that the roots can grow down into the nutrient solution. Roots cannot tolerate bright light, so use only containers with a protective tint for the fluid. This not only shields the roots from the rays of the sun but also prevents the sunlight from encouraging algae formations in the solution. Be sure also to use containers of the right shape. Bulb plants are best kept in cylindrical containers, because they form long roots. For all other plants, round solution containers and tapering inset containers have proved best.

The nutrient fluid must contain the right ingredients in the right concentration and the right proportions. You need not worry too much about the ingredients and the proportions, for the various fluids on the market contain all the necessary ingredients for the nourishment of the plants. All you need to know is what pH value your plant requires.

The concentration of the fluid is more of a problem. Since the dissolved inorganic substances do not evaporate with the solvent, the concentration of the fluid gradually grows stronger, and the roots can get seriously burnt. And finally you must always keep the level of the nutrient fluid constant. If there is too little the roots will not reach their food; if there is too much, the roots will not be able to breathe and will start to rot. The hydroponic containers commercially available have either a little window In the fluid container through which you can observe the level, or a little tube that shows you how much nutrient fluid there is in the container.

If you have plants grown in soil that you want to transfer to hydroponics, you must realize that this involves a certain risk. Transplant plants only at their most active, just after the rest period. First rinse the root ball thoroughly in lukewarm water, then put the plant for ten to twelve hours in a pot of boiled water cooled to room temperature. Remove only those roots that are diseased or damaged. As you fill the inset pot with aggregate, hold the plant loosely until the aggregate is supporting it. Never press the artificial cultivation base down as you would ordinary house plant soil or you will crush the roots.

As with ordinary repotting, be careful that when the plant has been placed in its 'hydro-pot' the aggregate comes no higher than the old soil mark on the stem. It is best to use a height mark and a light mark.

To give the plant time to get used to its new conditions, go on feeding it with liquid fertilizer for ten to fourteen days and keep it in water with the right pH value. During this period of acclimatization make sure that the plant has a light, warm position, but protect it from direct sunlight. Remember that its whole circulation has been reorganized and supplies to it have been interrupted.

HOLIDAY CARE

Every year it's the same problem: what to do with your plants when you go away on holiday. If you have a lot of plants you can hardly hire a removal van to take them to relatives or friends. And even then you can never be sure they know enough about plants to look after yours properly.

So here are a few tips to help your plants last out the holidays, so long as you are not going to be away for six or eight weeks. Remember, though, that these are emergency measures—things might still go wrong. A plant-loving neighbour is always better.

Before leaving for your holiday, stand the plants in a bath and give them a long drink; then put them in transparent plastic bags loosely tied at the top. In this sealed enclosure the moisture will last for a long time, and if you put some liquid manure in the water the plants will not suffer from hunger. Although you cannot treat indoor shrubs quite the same, it will be enough to put the pot and the base of the stem in a large plastic bag and tie it up around the stem.

More robust house plants can be put into a bath on the balcony in a position sheltered from wind and sun. Put a layer of clay crocks or aggregate 5-8 cm (2-3 in) deep on the bottom of the bath and saturate them with water and nutrient. Clay flowerpots put into this material will absorb water and nutrient fluid through their porous walls, and both clay and plastic pots can take up nutrients through the drainage holes.

Another well-tried method is to put the pot over a bowl so that the bottom of the pot stands immediately above the nutrient fluid. Push a wad of absorbent material through the drainage hole to act as a wick, through which water and nutrient are sucked up. A similar method uses one or two woollen strands laid on the soil and then led into a container of water; if you put the water container at least as high as the flowerpot the water will be slowly and steadily transferred to the soil in the pot. This is no substitute for real watering, but at any rate it will keep the plants from drying out completely, which could be fatal.

Plants that have to be looked after during the winter holidays require extra precautions. A simple but adequate protection for all cold-house and temperate-house plants against draughts from the windows is to wrap pots and plants together in several sheets of newspaper so that only the tops of the plants show.

Plants often suffer more from the dry air of central heating than from the cold, so it is important to turn off the heating unless you can somehow arrange to keep up sufficient humidity. Dry cold is not so dangerous for

Feed plants by sinking absorbent pots in a liquid feed or by 'piping' water along woollen strands.

plants as dry warmth.

Hot-house plants must of course be kept in their special cases with a high air temperature.

A-Z OF HOUSE PLANTS

24

Abutilon hybrid

ABUTILON

Indian Mallow

Small tropical flowering shrub with colourful hybrids, a few suitable for house plants.

Position light, warmish, airy room, otherwise outside.
Height up to 1 m (3 ft).
Flowering summer.
Propagation by cuttings or seeds.

The wild species which grow in Mediterranean countries and in South America are not so colourful as the hybrids developed by crossbreeding. They can be made to grow more than 1 m (3 ft) high and have hanging and climbing species.

Species
Beside the hybrids, two true species should be mentioned. *Abutilon*

striatum is a climber with orange, dark-veined, bell-like flowers growing singly in the leaf axils. The variety 'Thompsonii' has yellow-mottled leaves.

Abutilon megapotamicum is a hanging plant with narrow wedge-shaped leaves. Its beautiful flowers grow singly almost all year round.

Cultivation
Abutilons are fresh-air fiends. They do well by an open window, but are sensitive to draughts. Put them outdoors in summer, but with the first cool days bring them back into the house. There they like a light, cool place with a minimum temperature of 12°C (54°F). Water the plants freely while in flower and feed them once a fortnight. When flowering is over, keep them dry and do not feed them. Repot in spring and later clip back the foliage to encourage bushy growth.

Propagation
Leaf tips of about 5-10 cm (2-4 in) can be taken as cuttings. They need warmth and moisture to root in spring. Plant them 2 cm (1 in) deep in a pot of sandy soil with a glass cover to protect the topsoil from drying. The young plants will begin to grow when they have put out roots. Water them freely and pot on when necessary. They develop best in a room temperature of 18°C (64°F), or out in the warm sunshine. Keep them from draughts, or aphids will easily attack them.

Acalypha hispida

ACALYPHA

Copper Leaf, Red-Hot Cat's Tail

Indoor shrub with ornamental leaves and in one species attractive flowers.

Position essentially sunny and warm, with high humidity, in loamy soil.
Height up to 3 m (10 ft).
Flowering winter through autumn according to species.
Propagation by cuttings.

Acalyphas belong to the spurge family of which about 400 species are known in tropical and subtropical countries in all parts of the world.

Species
Only one of the commonly seen species, *Acalypha hispida*, has attractive flowers. It has bright red tassels of blossom up to 50 cm (20 in) long from which the nickname 'red-hot cat's tail' is derived.

We value *Acalypha wilkesiana* only for its marvellously coloured foliage. The flowers are so small and dull that they are almost invisible against the dazzling leaves. Most commonly we see the many hybrids of this South Seas species. Among the most attractive are the varieties 'Marginata' (olive green leaves edged with pink), 'Musaica' (greenish brown, dark red and orange-speckled leaves), and 'Obovata' (dark green iridescent leaves bordered with orange).

Cultivation
For the leaves to retain their lovely colours the plants must stand in a light place, but not in full sunlight. *Acalypha hispida* does well in half-shade. The air must not be too dry, the temperature not below 16°C (61°F).

The loamy soil must be kept good

and moist. Feed twice a month from spring through summer. Older plants bush out if you cut them back from time to time. Remove dead flowers regularly.

Propagation

Insert cuttings in sandy soil under glass. With *Acalypha hispida* plant shrubby cuttings from summer to winter and do not prune them during the growth period. *Acalypha wilkesiana* hybrids can be propagated all year round. To encourage growth, cut off the tips of cuttings from time to time.

Below: *Acalypha wilkesiana*
Middle: *Achimenes*
Bottom: *Adiantum*

ACHIMENES

Perennial flowering house plant.

Position warm and light in ordinary garden soil, but not in direct sun.
Height 20-50 cm (8-20 in).
Flowering summer and autumn.
Propagation by tubers.

Most species of achimenes are relatively modest, but numerous splendidly flowering hybrids have been developed by crossbreeding. The rather flat flowers grow in the axils of the transverse growing leaves. The petals, of various colours, unfold at the top of a narrow tube.

Species

Achimenes grandiflora grows to 50 cm (20 in). The big, elongated leaves are slightly hairy and reddish underneath. The red flowers are violet inside the tubes.

Achimenes longiflora grows to no more than 20 cm (8 in) and has small, pointed leaves, with big, bluish red flowers with yellow centres.

Cultivation

Achimenes do best in a light but not too sunny position with steady temperatures of about 18°C (64°F). Water well until near the end of flowering. When flowering is over and the leaves wilt, cut the stem off just above the ground, but leave the yellowish rhizomes, with their scaly surface, in the pots.

Propagation

Cut off 5 cm (2 in) lengths of rhizome in spring or summer and insert eight to ten pieces in a medium-sized pot of sandy soil. Cover the shoots with soil at most 2 cm (1 in) deep and at first do not water them much. Later give them more—and only softened —water, and after a month feed them once a fortnight.

ADIANTUM

Maidenhair Fern

Evergreen house plant.

Position shady positions and slightly acid humus-rich soil.
Height 30 to 60 cm (12-24 in).
Propagation by division.

The maidenhair fern is a citizen of the world. You can find hardy species near the polar circle, while others are at home in the tropical rain forests of South America. This wide distribution has naturally brought about considerable variation in the appearance of the different species, but all have shiny generally dark brown leaf stems.

Species

Adiantum macrophyllum is a delicate species with large leafy fronds which are red to start with but later turn green.

Adiantum raddianum, a species of many varieties, forms magnificent bushes. Long pinnate leaves with many leaflets, mostly light green to yellowish green, grow on long stems. Famous varieties are 'Brillantelse' with leaves that start red-brown, 'Fragrantissimum' with long, narrow, dark green leaves, and 'Gracillimum' with little ornamental leaflets.

Cultivation

Indoors, adiantums need watering with lime-free water early spring to autumn and also plenty of food. The plants like a warm position with high humidity. They lose their foliage in dry soil, and in insufficiently moist air the tips of the leaves dry up.

Propagation

Older plants are propagated most easily by division. Propagation by spores is possible but difficult.

AECHMEA

Urn Plant

Popular perennial house plant with exotic inflorescence.

Position warm, light place with no direct sun and a constant temperature.
Height up to 18 cm (7 in).
Flowering spring through autumn.
Propagation by suckers.

As a house plant, aechmeas need what they were used to on branches of trees in the Brazilian forests—constant warmth, light and humidity.

It is undoubtedly one of our most beautiful house plants. Extraordinary, pink bracts grow in a thick cluster on a long stem with, between them, short-lived little yellow, red or violet flowers. Even though flowering time is quite short, the attractive bracts last for months.

Species
Its pretty flowers make the *Aechmea chantinii* particularly impressive. Fiery red with yellow-mottled points, they grow close together on branching stems. Beneath the spikes hang long, narrow spathes, like a ruff round the neck of the flowers. The leaves of the cup-shaped rosette, up to 50 cm (20 in) long, have a pattern of transverse dark green stripes and silver scales.

The leaves of *Aechmea caudata* have toothed edges and a slightly curved spike at the point. Brilliant flowers grow between green bracts.

Aechmea fasciata (often sold as *Billbergia rhodocyanea)* makes a powerful impression, due to the little grey scales on the leaves, which are toothed and have stripes on the underside. It has prickly bracts on the inflorescence of small blue-violet flowers.

Aechmea fulgens is one of the giants of the genus. The leaves of the spreading cup rosette can grow up to 5 cm (2 in) wide and 40 cm (16 in) long. They are dotted with grey up to the middle and have blue-green tips. The variety *Aechmea fulgens* 'Discolor' is particularly colourful, with olive green leaves whose violet-red undersides have a greyish sheen. The coral flowers have blue tips.

Aechmea miniata will take up less room on your windowsill. It is lower growing and has narrower, less spreading leaves.

Cultivation
Aechmea must be kept warm, and at a steady temperature. It does not need a tropical climate, but requires a minimum temperature of 15°C (59°F). While in flower it does best at temperatures around 18°C (64°F).

Aechmea is undemanding. Not even the dry air from central heating distresses it. Its place on the windowsill should be light, but sheltered from the midday glare of the sun. Water with water at room temperature, but give it less in winter. Keep the soil in the pot moist, but not wet, and until the plant stops flowering. Top up the cup formed by the leaf rosette with softened water.

Propagation
As a rule one leaf rosette will produce only one inflorescence, and when it dies off, the whole plant dies. But in the meantime new rosettes will have formed at the foot of the old. You cannot always manage to get these suckers to develop, but it is worth trying. Leave them to grow on where they are, or when they are half the size of the parent detach, allow to dry for a day or two and then plant in an open, lime-free compost.

Aechmea chantinii

AESCHYNANTHUS

Evergreen, flowering hanging plant, very decorative, but rather delicate and difficult to grow.

Position in a hanging pot or basket, very warm, shady, high humidity.
Length up to 50 cm (20 in).
Flowering summer and autumn.
Propagation by cuttings.

In their homeland, the tropical regions of Asia, the various species of aeschynanthus display bright red and often also yellow and orange flowers. The flowers are at the tip of thickish, overhanging tubes with long projecting stamens. They grow in clusters or singly, nearly always at the end of drooping stems with fleshy, leathery leaves. Unfortunately most are difficult to grow. They will flower only at temperatures above 22°C (72°F), and lose their flowers if the temperature fluctuates below this level.

Species
Among the most famous species is *Aeschynanthus pulcher,* with its clusters of red flowers. The closely growing, oval leaves can reach a

length of 5 cm (2 in).

Aeschynanthus marmoratus decks itself with greenish flowers. The lanceolate leaves, up to 10 cm (4 in) long, are light green on top and reddish underneath.

The species *Aeschynanthus speciosus* has clusters of up to twelve flowers. You cannot fail to notice their yellow-red petals with black-spotted borders and protruding stamens.

Cultivation

The species of aeschynanthus do best in peat or sphagnum moss with high humidity. In summer the temperature must not be less than 22-25°C (72-77°F); at other times keep them at 16-18°C (61-64°F). If the plants are kept at the same temperature for the whole year, they will not flower. Water the plants only moderately with lukewarm water, but spray them quite frequently. During the winter it is important to keep the soil almost completely dry.

Propagation

Take shrubby cuttings about 5 cm (2 in) long in spring, and plant them in a loose mixture of peat and sand. At temperatures between 25-30°C (77-86°F) they will form roots within two or three weeks. Plant the young plants in coarse, open soil or peg trailers from spring onwards.

ALLAMANDA

Bushy, climbing evergreen house plant with magnificent flowers.

Position light and sunny with high humidity, away from draughts.
Height with support, up to 2 m (6 ft).
Flowering spring through autumn.
Propagation by cuttings or seeds.

The allamanda comes from Brazil and has a preference for warm positions with high humidity, such as you only find in a hothouse. The allamanda flowers almost without ceasing from spring to autumn.

Almost the only species we find as a house plant is *Allamanda cathartica,* a climbing shrub with leaves like those of the laurel. The golden flowers have a diameter of 5 cm (2 in) and form cymes, generally growing three or four together. The yellow flowers of the variety 'Grandiflora' grow up to 10 cm (4 in) across. Even bigger —some 12 cm (5 in) across—are the flowers of the variety 'Hendersonii', which gleam reddish yellow with light spots over the rather leathery foliage.

Cultivation

While the allamanda tolerates sunlight well in summer when it is in flower, you should shelter it during the resting period in winter. Even then the plant needs plenty of warmth, though less humidity. It is a good idea to support the strong-growing plant with wire or canes so that the flower stems can find room to hang down.

Cut back long stems on weak plants after flowering. It will make the plants bushier and encourage later flowering. Feed the plants every week during the spring and summer.

Propagation

Propagation by seeds is possible, but difficult. Propagation by shrubby cuttings in spring is generally more successful. Keep them under glass at a temperature of about 25°C (82°F).

Allamanda cathartica

ANTHURIUM

Flamingo Flower, Painter's Palette, Tail flower

Perennial house plant with beautiful spathes.

Position light but not sunny.
Height up to 45 cm (18 in).
Flowering at all seasons.
Propagation by division or seeds.

The first specimens of this decorative plant came to Europe from the tropical rain forests of Central and South America in the middle of the last century.

Species
Of the many tropical anthuriums, we have only two of importance: the great flamingo flower (*Anthurium andreanum*) and the little flamingo flower or painter's palette (*Anthurium scherzerianum*).

The great flamingo flower has heart-shaped leaves up to 20 cm (8 in) long and leaf stalks that grow as much as 1 m (3 ft) long. Its striking inflorescence, with a spathe some 10-15 cm (4-6 in) long and a brilliant white to yellowish green spadix with the tiny flowerets growing on it, looks most exotic. The spathe is generally red, but can be orange, white or spotted.

The little flamingo flower has smaller spathes and spirally twisted or curved spadices, usually red.

Cultivation
The anthurium must stand in the light but not in the sun; a north or east window is best. The room temperature should not fluctuate or go below 15° C (59° F). The plant grows best in coarse standard compost or in a mixture of friable leaf mould or coarse peat, with a deep layer of pebbles in the bottom of the pot. Whatever medium is used must be porous and provide good drainage. Anthuriums also do very well in hydroponics.

Water the plants only with tepid, previously boiled water. Since the flamingo flower can produce flowers all the year round, virtually without a break, it must be fed with liquid manure or general fertilizer every 12 or 14 days for the whole year except during winter. The great flamingo flower needs repotting every few years; plant it in its new pot so that the lowest leaves are just above the soil. This is because the species gradually forms little stems. In this way you can completely shake out the soil from the old pot and cut off rotten roots.

Propagation
Old plants can be propagated by division or by separation of rooted side shoots. Propagation by seeds is also possible but very difficult—an operation reserved for the specialist. You need pedicels of different ages, because the flower is bisexual and the stigma ripens before the pollen. The seeds ripen in nine months and are immediately laid on leaf mould, but not covered.

Below: *Anthurium scherzerianum*

APHELANDRA

Zebra plant

Evergreen house plant with strikingly beautiful leaves and flowers.

Position shady, humid, warm place.
Height 20-60 cm (9-24 in).
Flowering summer to winter.
Propagation by cuttings.

Of the many species of aphelandra in the primeval forests of Central and South America we grow only one, *Aphelandra squarrosa,* which is a very popular house plant. Its leaves are oval, pointed and up to 25 cm (10 in) long, and green with silver-white patterns. Little yellow flowers form between the bracts.

Cultivation
The aphelandra is very demanding. It needs a warm, humid atmosphere and a light position, but at the same time it must be kept out of the full glare of the sun. The soil must be porous and rich in humus and must be fed every two weeks until the plant flowers. It does best at temperatures between 18-25°C (59-82°F). It is a good idea to spray it every day. While in flower it must be watered regularly, but not sprayed.

Four to six weeks after flowering the plant needs a somewhat cooler position, less water and no feeding.

After this rest period cut the aphelandra back to about 10 cm (4 in) and repot in new soil after reducing the root ball. Water sparingly at first, then more freely. Begin feeding again four weeks after repotting.

Propagation
The aphelandra is propagated by top cuttings 10-15 cm (4-6 in) long and also by leaf cuttings with a 'latent' bud. Root in a sand-peat mixture, preferably at the beginning of spring. A warm position is essential. To maintain temperature and humidity, enclose young plants in glass.

ARAUCARIA

Norfolk Island Pine

Evergreen house plant with needle-shaped leaves.

Position airy, cool and shady, in sandy soil.
Height in a room, 2 m (6 ft).
Propagation by seed or cuttings.

The ancestors of our Norfolk Island pine were discovered by Captain Cook in the Norfolk Islands in the Pacific Ocean and are magnificent pine trees, growing to a height of 60 m (200 ft). The miniature version became a popular house plant.

The lower part of the upright stem, up to 2 m (6 ft) tall, becomes almost bare after a time unless it is cut back to stimulate new growth. But at the top the needle-shaped leaves, often bluish in colour and growing on horizontal branches, form elegant fronds.

Cultivation
What the araucaria needs chiefly is plenty of air and not too much warmth.

In summer give it a light but not sunny position. Water moderately from spring to the end of summer; feed fortnightly.

From winter on you hardly need water the araucaria at all, though the soil must not be allowed to dry out. In cold weather, keep the temperature between 7-10° C (45-50° F), and keep the room aired.

Normally the araucaria has to be repotted only every few years. Be particularly careful that the soil comes up just to the base of the root.

Propagation
The araucaria can be grown from seed, but it is easier to take young shoots—8 cm (3 in) long—and root them in sand or peat.

ASPARAGUS

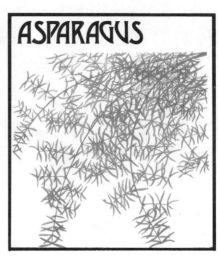

Asparagus Fern

Evergreen house plant, sometimes climbing, sometimes hanging. Certain species grow berries.

Position sunny to half-shady, in porous humus-rich soil always kept moist.
Height up to 2 m (6 ft), both climbing and hanging.
Propagation by division or seeds.

Asparagus is known chiefly as a vegetable, but it has a number of related species that make very popular house plants because they are so little trouble. All these bushes and subshrubs have scaly, quite dull leaves, but grow what are called phylloclades on their branches. These spurious leaves are needle-shaped or leaf-shaped and grow singly or in bunches on the upright or hanging, branching stems. Only a few species will flower as house plants. Pretty red berries develop from the flowers; they are not edible.

Species
Asparagus crispus is a twining or hanging plant. It has very small phylloclades and from winter to early spring bears isolated, strongly scented flowers from which decorative red berries develop. It is a good plant for a basket.

Asparagus densiflorus is a widespread house plant, often still known by its old botanical name of *Asparagus sprengeri.* This species comes from South Africa and has elegant, drooping stems with pointed, needle-shaped phylloclades. A very robust and undemanding species, it can be kept on the balcony in summer.

Another species that can be kept on the balcony in summertime is

Asparagus scandens var. 'Deflexus', a robust house plant, often confused with *Asparagus crispus* on account of its small phylloclades.

Asparagus setaceus, sometimes called asparagus fern, is sold as *Asparagus plumosus.* it is a climbing subshrub which does best in the greenhouse. There it will grow shoots up to 2 m (6 ft) or more long, covered with fine phylloclades.

Cultivation

Asparagus is an ideal basket plant and prefers a light position, though it should not be put in direct sunlight. *Asparagus setaceus* is particularly intolerant of the sun. No species can tolerate a dry root ball, so they must be regularly watered and sprayed, especially in centrally heated rooms.

All species including *Asparagus densiflorus* should be kept at temperatures of 20°C (68°F) in winter.

The plants grow quickly and should be repotted every year, when you can reduce the root ball a little. Plant in good humus-rich soil, and do not use too big a pot or the growth and flowering will be poor.

Propagation

The propagation of asparagus is no problem. Divide the bushes and subshrubs at the beginning of spring, when you are repotting. You can grow the plants from seed, sown in autumn in moist humus at 20°C (68°F).

Below: *Asparagus sprengeri*
Below left and right: *Aspidistra* and *Aspidistra elatior* 'Variegata'

ASPIDISTRA

Cast Iron Plant

Resistant, trouble-free, evergreen foliage plant with insignificant brownish purple flowers.

Position half-shady to shady, cool or warm, in good potting compost.
Height 30 cm (12 in).
Propagation by division.

Nothing can upset the aspidistra. It does just as well in a dark corner as it does on the balcony. It can stand fluctuating temperatures, draughts and dust. Consequently you often see it in entrance halls and corridors and on the counters of shops. This strong constitution has given it the popular name of cast iron plant.

Of the few species that grow wild in the mountains of the Far East, we cultivate only one. *Aspidistra elatior* has lanceolate, leathery leaves that can grow up to 70 cm (28 in) long and 10 cm (4 in) wide. The flowers sprout from an underground pedicel at the lower end of the leaves; they are a brownish purple with a curiously shaped stigma.

More decorative, but more trouble, is the variety 'Variegata', with leaves striped white and yellow.

Cultivation

Do not worry about finding a favourable position for the aspidistra: the cast iron plant is equally content with any kind of light and temperature over 10°C (50°F). 'Variegata', however, needs bright light and temperatures between 10-12°C (50-54°F), or the white and yellow pattern on the leaves will fade.

Propagation

You can divide the rootstock during late winter or early spring into parts each having two or three leaves, and transplant these in new pots.

ASPLENIUM

Bird's Nest Fern, Spleenwort

Decorative pot fern for the hothouse or conservatory.

Position shade or half-shade, in moist soil, with high humidity.
Height up to 80 cm (32 in).
Propagation by division or spores.

The immense genus *Asplenium* —botanists give it over 700 species—occurs all over the world. Among its species are our wall rue as well as huge leaf ferns, epiphytes found in tropical countries on the tops of trees.

Some have been cultivated as house plants for a long time. But generally you can keep them only in a conservatory, as they require a lot of warmth and high humidity.

Species
The bird's nest fern *(Asplenium nidus)* is by far our most popular species. It has a short, erect rhizome and as a young plant has tongue-shaped fronds which grow broader as it matures. In its homeland, the tropical forests of Africa, Asia and

Asplenium nidus

northern Australia, it lives on the branches of tall trees. It needs only a small pot, even when the roots are completely matted. It prefers light humus-rich soil but can get along with an ordinary garden variety.

Less delicate is *Asplenium dimorphum*. Its leaves, up to 90 cm (35 in) long and almost 50 cm (20 in) wide, are triangular and slightly drooping. On the upper side of its leaves it grows adventitious buds—young plants that drop off and grow in the ground.

Adventitious plantlets up to 60 cm (24 in) long grow also on the finely divided, drooping fronds of *Asplenium bulbiferum*. This species occurs naturally in all tropical countries bordering the Indian Ocean. It thrives only in the hothouse.

Cultivation
The spleenworts, which include all the ferns mentioned above, need a shady or half-shady position. Unlike the species *Asplenium dimorphum*, which comes from the Norfolk Islands in the South Seas and is content with normal room temperatures, the bird's nest fern needs temperatures of around 20°C (68°F) and above, as well as high humidity. Water the spleenworts with lime-free warm water and spray them frequently. Put some liquid fertilizer in the water once a month. Repot the plants every two or three years, but do not use larger pots than necessary.

Propagation
The species with adventitious buds can easily be propagated by the indoor gardener simply by keeping the plantlets at air temperature with a bottom heat of 20°C (68°F). Propagate *Asplenium nidus* by spores, sown in the earth at temperatures of about 30°C (86°F).

Aucuba japonica 'Variegata'

AUCUBA

Hardy evergreen shrub with ornamental foliage, kept outdoors in tubs when warm, but indoors when cold.

Position cool and shady place in loamy soil.
Height 1-2 m (3-6 ft).
Propagation by cuttings.

In Japan, its original homeland, the aucuba grows in the open air to make a magnificent evergreen shrub. It is one of our most sturdy house plants, used especially in entrance halls and on landings, as well as for decoration in unheated display windows. The aucuba grows to 1-2 m (3-6 ft) high and has toothed leaves, some yellow striped, some spotted.

A particularly popular variety is *Aucuba japonica,* 'Variegata', whose green leaves have golden-yellow spots. They produce insignificant flowers in spring. Only if you have male and female plants standing near to one another can you expect the red berries after flowering.

Cultivation
The tub plants can overwinter in rooms in which it is no warmer than 6°C (43°F) provided they are not too dark. If you put your aucuba outside in summer, put it in half-shade to start with or the tender leaves will scorch. Later the shrub will even stand the midday sun. The plant needs very little attention: regular watering, and weekly feeding in spring and summer. Repot smaller aucubas every two years. To encourage bushy growth, occasionally cut back selected shoots almost to the ground.

Propagation
Cuttings taken in late winter or late summer will root at temperatures of 12–20°C (54-68°F). The cooler they are kept, the longer they take to root.

BEGONIA

Begonia
Large genus of beautiful flowering outdoor and house plants, which

Begonia **hybrids and others**

includes herbaceous and sub-shrubby annuals and biennials.

Position with few exceptions, semishade and high humidity in humus-rich, porous soil.
Height 15-20 cm (6-9 in); some species up to 2 m (6 ft).
Flowering at all seasons.
Propagation by leaf or stem cuttings, tubers and seeds.

All begonias are by origin shade plants, for they come from the tropical rain forests or subtropical regions of America, Asia and Africa, where even to this day new species or unknown natural hybrids are still being discovered. There are even some species that flourish in mountain forests.

In the tropical forests begonias live either as ground plants or as epiphytes on trees. In the course of

the last two centuries the form of the plants, the shapes and colours of the flowers, have been greatly modified by cultivation. New hybrids and a vast number of varieties have been developed. Consequently even experts have difficulty in finding their way about the genus *Begonia*.

Ornamental-leaved species

These begonias are grown chiefly for their beautifully shaped and coloured foliage, though in certain species you do also get some fine colour from the flowers. The best known species of leaf begonia—its crosses and varieties are almost countless—is *Begonia rex*. It can have either large-toothed leaves of red or violet, often with a green border, or much smaller leaves, often lobed and coloured red, grey or green and generally also speckled with silver-grey.

The shrubby begonias are among the ornamental-leaved species. These subshrubby, upright species come mostly from tropical parts of Central and South America. Many grow as much as 1 m (3 ft) in height. The *Begonia coralina* hybrids can reach a height of 2 m (6 ft) and keep their abundant flowers all year.

All shrub begonias have branching stems, but they do not form wood. The flowers, hanging down in clusters, are very big, generally red or pink, with wonderful leaf shapes and colours. The *Begonia albo-picta* grows really tall. Its green, asymmetrical heart-shaped leaves have a great number of silver-white spots; its flowers are greenish white.

Begonia credneri, a hybrid, produces its pale pink flowers almost all the year round. It too has branching stems, and the leaves are heart-shaped, dark green on top and red and hairy underneath. A good plant for indoor cultivation, it grows 40-50 cm (16-20 in) high.

The fuchsia begonia *(Begonia fuchsioides)*, of shrubby habit, has slightly drooping stems and small leaves of an asymmetrical rounded egg shape. It grows up to 1 m (3 ft) or more high. Its red or pink flowers, rather like those of the fuchsia, appear in the winter months.

The easily grown *Begonia maculata* is a favourite house plant. It is rather like *Begonia albo-picta*, but its leaves are speckled with white, and reddish below. The flowers are white or pink.

Begonia metallica gets its name from the beautiful metallic sheen of the green upper side of its leaves.

The underside is red and the entire surface is wrinkled. The plant can reach a height of 80 cm (32 in), and flowers in thick pinky white clusters. In winter it needs a room with a temperature of between 12-15°C (54-59°F).

The less branching *Begonia scharffiana* is covered with bristly red hairs. Its asymmetrical heart-shaped leaves come to a long point, dark green on top, deep red underneath. Big white-pink flowers grow on long stems.

One of the loveliest of the shrubby begonias is *Begonia serratipetala*. Its leaves are pinnate, each segment double-toothed, bright green with blood-red spots.

Lastly, the ornamental-leaved begonias include those that are particularly suited to growing in hanging pots or baskets. The most attractive of them—the fern begonia, *Begonia foliosa*—has little leaves no more than 1 cm ($\frac{1}{2}$ in) long. Its fern-like shoots are strong and branching, the flowers small and whitish. It needs more warmth and humidity than other species and so is ideal for a conservatory.

The leaves of *Begonia limmingheiana* are a good 10 cm (4 in) long, with deckled edges. The shoots are pendulous; the flowers are light red or orange and white inside.

Cultivation of ornamental-leaved species

Begonias do best in warm rooms, particularly in a north-facing window, for they cannot bear direct sun-

Begonia rex

light. After their strong growth period, they lose some of their flowers in winter but quickly regain their former beauty after repotting the next year.

Water with tepid water and keep the root ball constantly damp. Feed from spring to summer. It is very important to cut back older plants, preferably during vigorous growth.

You need flat pots for all begonias, whose roots spread outwards rather than down. The soil must be rich in humus, porous and nutritious. A mixture of old leaf mould with a generous addition of compost and farmyard manure, peat and sand has proved very successful, but begonias also grow well in standard compost. As the plants grow older you will not need to repot them so often; instead, give them extra manure. Try not to turn the pot or change its position more than necessary. Begonias hate to be disturbed.

Propagation of ornamental-leaved species

Begonia rex particularly, but the basket begonias too, are best propagated by leaf cuttings. Take the fully ripe leaf during the summer and carefully nick the stronger veins on the underside where they branch. Immediately lay the leaves in a bowl one-third to two-thirds full of sterile sand and weight them down with a few pebbles or small pieces of glass so that the ribs or veins of the leaf lie at least partly on the wet sand. After four to six weeks young plants form at the spots where the leaf was nicked, and these you plant in little pots filled with a mixture of sand and soil.

If the leaves are big you can cut a triangular piece out of them, but it must include a vein at the bottom corner. Young plants will develop in the same way within four to six weeks in a mixture of soil and sand.

If there are old plants available, propagation by stem cuttings is also possible. Cut the section of stem into short pieces and powder with charcoal. Then immediately lay the cuttings in the propagation bed, once more with a mixture of sand and peat. Strong plants will develop comparatively quickly.

Shrub begonias can be propagated from top cuttings and similarly planted in a peat-sand mixture. Keep the air moist and the temperature between 20-25°C (68-77°F).

Flowering species

The most beautiful of the indoor

begonias are those grown for their flowers. Flowering begonias have been divided into four groups.

Lorraine begonias
These are available in late autumn and winter. In light rooms—but not in sunny windows—at temperatures of about 18°C (64°F), they are easy to keep. The thick bright pink clusters of flowers complement the light green foliage. Water only moderately, and never on the leaves and flowers, or spots and rot will appear.

Begonia semperflorens

Elatior begonias
Elatior begonias are the breeders' favourites, because their magnificent flowers last so long. They flower white, yellow, pink and light and dark

35

red. Their natural flowering period is autumn, even winter. Elatior begonias are short-day plants: they produce their flowers when the days are shortest. The many different varieties of Elatior begonias vary in size. The pointed leaves grow up to 20 cm (9 in) long, the flowers may grow up to 8 cm (3 in).

Their flowering period may last as long as six months if they stand in a shady but light position and are not watered too much. Remove dead heads immediately and do not let seeds form.

Semperflorens begonias
Unlike other begonias, semperflorens begonias can readily be planted in outdoor beds and are tolerant of the sun. You can also of course keep them as pot plants.

The individual varieties have fleshy leaves and stems, flower very abundantly, and grow from 15-35 cm (6-14 in) high. The leaves are mostly green, quite often dark brown.

They flower until the first frosts, white and pink and sometimes bicoloured. Propagation is by tiny seeds, and is very difficult; it is really best to get your semperflorens from suppliers.

Tuberous begonias
Tuberous begonias are equally well suited for the garden, the balcony and the living room. In the garden they cannot be planted out until after all danger of frost is past. They are best grown in half-shady positions.

Tuberous begonias are divided into various groups: the large-flowered tuberous begonias have flowers that measure 12-16 cm (5-7 in) across, in red, pink, orange and white. The various forms include single, double, deckle-edged, camellia-flowered and bicoloured.

The small-flowered tuberous begonias grow no higher than 25 cm (10 in) and their flowers are from 2-4 cm ($\frac{3}{4}$-$1\frac{1}{2}$ in) across. They are particularly attractive both in bowls and beds.

The size of their flowers puts the 'Bertini' hybrids also into this group. They have small, scarlet or orange flowers with reddish leaves. Unlike the general run of tuberous begonias, they are tolerant of sunlight.

The medium-flowered begonias come from crossing large-flowered and small-flowered varieties. Their flowers may measure 5-7 cm (2-3 in) across.

Basket begonias are branching,

pendulous plants with pointed leaves and flowers averaging 3-6 cm (1-2 in). They do well in baskets by the window or on the balcony.

Propagation of tuberous begonias
Breeding can be successfully carried out from seeds or tubers. Set the tubers out close together in the propagation bed of a greenhouse or in a bowl in a warm room, from midwinter. The depression above each tuber tells you where the shoots will appear. The soil—a humus-rich, nutritious mixture of soil with added peat and sand—must always be kept

BELOPERONE

Shrimp Plant

Abundantly blooming evergreen sub-shrub.

Position in sun and half-shade in moist humus-rich soil.
Height up to 1 m (3 ft).
Flowering at all seasons.
Propagation by cuttings.

The shrimp plant seems to be in flower almost all the year round. Even though the white, tubular flowers with their violet spots fall prematurely, the green to reddish brown bracts can still be admired.

The only commonly found species, *Beloperone guttata*, is grown primarily for its bracts, which really do look like shrimps.

Cultivation

Young shrimp plants should be repeatedly pruned to bring them to a bushy growth. Experts recommend putting the young plants in a half-shady position and pinching off the first flowers to stimulate growth. Later you can put the shrimp plant in a light, sunny window.

Keep these subshrubs moist from spring to autumn and feed regularly. Give the plant less water in the other months, but the root ball must never be allowed to dry completely. If it does, the plant will go for a whole year before producing any more flowers. Repot every year.

Propagation

The shrimp plant is propagated by stem cuttings of half-ripe shoots, which you can take at any time in the year except during the winter, putting them under glass at a soil temperature of about 20°C (68°F). They generally root after two to three weeks, when it is advisable to plant the rooted cuttings in a pot to grow.

moist. Temperatures should range from 18-20°C (64-68°F). When the shoots appear, plant them out in the nursery bed and leave them there until they grow accustomed to the outdoor air. All hybrids must be sheltered from the sun.

In late autumn, shelter those plants

Hybrid tuberous begonias

still in the open from early frosts. After the first real frost, lift the tubers out of the ground, cut off the shoots and lay the tubers out to dry indoors. Clean off the soil and store them in dry peat at 10-12°C (50-54°F).

Beloperone guttata

BILLBERGIA

Angel's Tears, Queen's Tears

Very robust, fine flowering perennial house and greenhouse plant.

Position light, but not in full sunlight, with high humidity and plenty of warmth.
Height 50 cm (20 in).
Flowering spring or summer, according to cultivation and age.
Propagation by suckers or seeds.

The billbergias come from the tropical forests of Central and South America, where they generally live as epiphytes on trees, like orchids. They are hardy plants, popular not only for their flowers but also for their decorative, beautifully coloured elongated bracts. The inflorescence generally droops or hangs down from the stem.

Species
Billbergia nutans, sometimes known as angel's tears or queen's tears, is the species most often seen in Europe. Its narrow, dark green leaves, slightly scaly on the underside, grow from 30-50 cm (12-20 in) long and form rosettes. The nodding inflorescences have finger-long light pink or red bracts. The flowers are green, light red, and tipped with blue. The petals reflex to show golden-yellow stamens.
Billbergia pyramidalis has an upright inflorescence with pink blue-tipped flowers. The long, light green leaves form a deep tube in which to catch moisture. The woolly flower stem is enclosed by pink bracts from which the closely packed globular flower cluster extends.
Billbergia saundersii is notable chiefly for its leaves, the upper sides

Billbergia pyramidalis

of which are bright green, the undersides brownish red and covered with white spots. The lighter the position in which the plant stands, the brighter becomes the pattern on the leaves. There are two popular and pretty varieties of *Billbergia saundersii* obtainable from nurseries: 'Fascinator' and 'Fantasia'.

Cultivation
Once they have reached a certain age, billbergias will flower at any time of the year. If you keep them warm in winter, they will bloom in spring. If kept in a cool place they will not produce their flowers until the summer. They do not like glaring sunlight, but develop especially well in high humidity. Make sure when watering them that some water remains in the funnel formed by the leaves, and that the soil in the pot does not get too moist. Water minimally to prevent rotting. Repotting is best done after the flowering period. Feed about twice a week from spring well into autumn. Provide a humid atmosphere throughout the year.

Propagation
Propagation is by suckers for the hybrids, but billbergias in the greenhouse can also be propagated by seeds. This is a complicated task much better left to professionals.

BOUGAINVILLEA

Decorative shrub with big, colourful bracts.

Position in a sunny room with loam soil.
Height climbs to 6 m (20 ft).
Flowering spring.
Propagation by cuttings.

Bougainvillea is certainly one of the most beautiful plants in the Southern Hemisphere, distinguished not so much for its flowers as for its big, brightly coloured bracts. They are not easy to keep indoors, or to propagate. They need a lot of room and temperatures which vary at different

seasons of the year. Climbing varieties need a framework of wires or bamboo.

Species
The branches of *Bougainvillea glabra* have thorns and oval leaves that come to a point at the tip. The little flowers, tubular and yellow, are overshadowed by striking, brilliant rose-coloured, heart-shaped bracts. This is the best species for growing in a pot as it will flower when quite small. The variety 'Sanderiana' has darker leaves and bracts. 'Alexandra' is lower growing, with purple-violet bracts.

The hairy bougainvillea, *Bougainvillea spectabilis,* has larger bracts in many colours. It climbs to 6 m (20 ft) and looks very well in a big conservatory.

Cultivation
If bougainvillea is really going to flourish, it must have plenty of air, sun and food, and in winter a position with temperatures between 8-12°C (46-54°F). During this time it needs only a little water. Many of the leaves fall in these months.

In spring the plant must be moved to a warmer place, transplanted if necessary, and sprayed in sunny weather. Later the best position is in front of the window in full sunlight, on the balcony, or in a warm spot in the garden. Water the plants once a week with a complete fertilizer solution from spring to autumn. Proper care will usually ensure flowering —but not in cold, wet, sunless years. Rich compost is the most suitable soil.

Propagation
Bougainvillea is propagated by 15 cm (6 in) cuttings of half-ripe, not yet woody, shoots. Winter is the best time, but it must be done under glass and with a bottom heat of 18°C (64°F). They will take about three weeks to root. Or take 8 cm (3 in) cuttings in summer and set them in sandy soil with a bottom heat of 20-25°C (68-77°F).

Browallia speciosa

BROWALLIA

Annual garden and pot plants with pretty flowers or flowering subshrubs for living room and balcony.

Position sunny but as well sheltered as possible from the wind.
Height up to 50 cm (20 in).
Flowering all year, depending on variety.
Propagation by seeds.

Browallia is a botanical curiosity from tropical America. Three of the four species are annuals which will grow equally well in a pot or sheltered place in the garden. The fourth is a subshrub which can flower at any season of the year.

Species
The subshrub *Browallia speciosa* grows to 50 cm (20 in) high. Above its dark green leaves grow its great mauve, white-centred flowers. When grown as a house plant, this species generally bears its flowers in winter. They last until the following autumn.

Browallia viscosa flowers in late summer. Its abundant small flowers are light blue with a white eye. It has a sticky calyx.

Browallia grandiflora, a species we do not often see, grows 50 cm (20 in) high. It forms thick bushes and bears soft blue or white flowers in summer.

Cultivation
Browallia does well in standard compost and needs only moderate watering—rather less in the winter. During its growth period it likes a weekly application of fertilizer.

Propagation
To get flowers in summer, sow the very fine seed in spring at a temperature of 18°C (64°F). Prick out the seedlings later in 12 cm (5 in) pots and grow on. For winter indoor flowering, sow in autumn.

CALADIUM

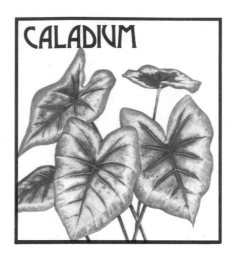

Beautiful perennial tuberous plant with variegated foliage that does best in a conservatory.

Position light to half-shady in loose humus-rich soil.
Height up to 1 m (3 ft).
Propagation by division or offsets.

Caladium comprises magnificent foliaged plants of striking colour combinations. Of some 15 species that grow in the Brazilian forests, we have kept only a few. In their place we have developed sturdier decorative crosses. But even these will only disclose the full glory of their long-stemmed ornamental leaves in a warm environment. In an ordinary room the speckled or marbled patterns can seldom be retained. The darker the plant's position, the more the pattern on the leaves disappears.

Species
Caladium humboldtii is one of the few original species. The little, white-speckled, sagittate leaves grow on slender stems up to 10 cm (4 in) long. This small bushy species is relatively hardy and suited for keeping at normal room temperatures.
Most beautiful of all are the varied green, red, white and yellowish coloured leaves of the *Caladium bicolor.* These hybrids have big leaves and bear insignificant little flowers.

Cultivation
During its growth period caladium needs high humidity and a constant temperature of 20-22°C (68-72°F). The plants cannot tolerate full sunlight or draughts. For the hybrids a warm conservatory or greenhouse is essential. Keep the plants good and moist during growth and give them less water after that. When in autumn the caladium has lost its leaves, store the dry tubers in their pots at 16-18°C (61-64°F). In late winter throw away the old soil, clean the tubers and plant them afresh in rich peat-based compost. Water them sparingly at first and only with lime-free water. As the leaves develop, gradually increase the amount of water.

Propagation
Young shoots about 10 cm (4 in) long can be carefully separated from the tubers and planted in a new pot —preferably in sandy soil. You can also propagate the plants by cutting the tubers or separating offsets. The best time is late winter. Wait till the offsets have formed their own leaflets. If you are dividing the tuber, dust the cuts carefully with finely powdered charcoal to prevent rotting. The divided parts of the tuber will root in a mixture of peat mould and sand. After rooting, plant up.

CALCEOLARIA

Slipper Flower

Annual abundantly flowering pot plant for living room or balcony.

Position half-shady, but light and cool with high humidity, in compost.
Height 20-40 cm (9-16 in).
Flowering spring to mid-autumn.
Propagation by seeds.

The calceolaria originally came from the upper regions of the Chilean and Peruvian Andes, a climate dominated by fog and heavy rainfall. To do well indoors, it must stand in similar conditions.
Of the many species of this genus of the figwort family—some are herbaceous, some subshrubs or shrubs —only the slipper flower has survived as a house plant. It is cultivated only as an annual and thrown away as soon as the abundant, long-lasting flowers are over.

Left: *Caladium*
Below: *Calceolaria* hybrid

Species

Of the many varieties of calceolaria hybrids—which are called slipper flowers because the rather inflated flowers are said to look like shoes or slippers—we can distinguish four groups.

The flowers of the 'Grandiflora' hybrids are up to 5 cm (2 in) across. The plants grow to about 40 cm (16 in) with very little branching.

The 'Grandiflora Pumila Compacta' is described as a dwarf calceolaria. They too have flowers 5 cm (2 in) in diameter, but they grow no more than 20 cm (9 in) high.

Among the commonest are the 'Multiflora' hybrids, freely branching plants 30 cm (12 in) high, with flowers 3 cm (1 in) across growing out of their medium-green, velvety leaves.

Finally there is the group 'Multiflora Nana'. They are fully 5 cm (2 in) shorter than the 'Multiflora' hybrids, and their flowers are somewhat smaller. All slipper flowers have yellow or orange flowers with remarkable red-brown to red spots on the 'slippers'.

Cultivation

The calceolaria is a flower for the north window, as it dislikes direct sunlight. You can keep it best at temperatures of 10-12°C (50-54°F). Water freely if the room temperature rises, so that the evaporation chill will keep the plant cool enough. Do not let the soil dry out completely.

Propagation

Indoor gardeners are advised not to try to propagate calceolarias. You can try with seeds, which are simply laid on standard compost in summer and will—perhaps—begin to germinate at room temperatures around 15°C (59°F). But it is only a slim chance.

Above: *Calceolaria*
Right: *Calceolaria multiflora*

CALLISTEMON

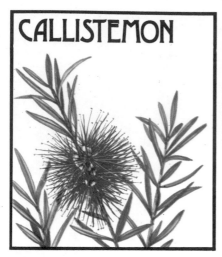

Bottle Brush

Evergreen house plant with ornamental flowers.

Position sunny and airy in standard compost.
Height up to 1 m (3 ft).
Flowering summer.
Propagation by cuttings.

The red flowers of this decorative pot plant are unmistakable. They really do look exactly like the little brushes used to clean the inside of small bottles.

At home in Australia, some species of this genus grow as trees some 3 m (10 ft) high, but elsewhere they are kept as pot plants or in tubs. The erect stems have hard, lanceolate leaves up to 5 cm (2 in) long. The bristly inflorescence, some 10 cm (4 in) high, grows at the top of the stem. The fine, purple-red stamens grow close together, almost horizontally, from the middle of the stem. The red flowers with their yellow stamens cluster thickly.

Cultivation
Try to put your bottle brushes outdoors during the summer. They need a lot of light and air. Water them plentifully and feed them once a week. In winter give the plants a light place at a temperature of 6-8°C (45-46°F).

Propagation
You can take cuttings at any time in autumn or winter. Plant them in sand under glass at 18°C (64°F). After about four weeks, when roots have formed, put the young plants in lime-free soil and in the first period prune them fairly often.

Callistemon

CAMELLIA

Evergreen shrub with particularly lovely flowers.

Position half-shady and cool, in well-drained, lime-free soil.
Height up to 60 cm (24 in).
Flowering winter to spring.
Propagation by cuttings.

The transitory beauty of the camellia is almost proverbial. But unfortunately it almost always gives the indoor gardener endless trouble. Many species of the shrub grow wild in South Asia, where some are trees of over 15 m (50 ft) high. The most famous member of the camellia family, the tea plant, is now grown commercially.

Species
The most common domestic species are *Camellia japonica* and *Camellia williamsii,* which after some three years can grow up to 60 cm (24 in) high. The dark green of the shiny, leathery leaves makes an attractive

***Camellia japonica* hybrid**

46

Camellia japonica 'Apollo'

contrast with the delicate, rose-like flowers. This decorative appearance has encouraged breeders over the years to produce endless new varieties, so that now we can get camellia flowers in white, pink, and bright and deep red. They include single, semidouble and double varieties, some of which are as much as 6 cm (2 in) across. The most famous is 'Chandleri Elegans', a speckled pink and white variety.

One thing is common to all varieties of every colour and shape: camellias are very sensitive to any change in their position, temperature, humidity and moisture. They drop their buds easily, especially if they do not get enough water when they are forming flower and leaf buds.

Cultivation
Camellias are at their best in the garden in warm weather. Bury the flowerpot in soil in a half-shady and airy but not too draughty corner of the garden. A place on the balcony will do as well, but do not keep them indoors.

Until late summer the root ball should be kept reasonably moist with lukewarm water in porous, limefree soil which is mixed with peat and sand. After that, you should water more sparingly so that the buds develop well, and five weeks later normal watering can be resumed. During the late winter and spring, feed the plant once every two or three weeks.

Camellias cannot stand the dry warmth of central heating. They must be kept relatively cool, at 10-12°C (50-54°F), or the flowers will not open and the buds will fall. After flowering, the plants should be kept even cooler until they are planted out in the open.

Propagation
Camellias are propagated by cuttings. But the procedure poses many problems and is rarely successful. For this reason it is best left to the professional gardener who would possess the necessary specialized equipment.

Camellia japonica 'Donation'

CAMPANULA

Bellflower

Very beautiful, mostly blue perennial or annual. Good basket plant. Only a few species are suitable for growing as house plants.

Position a sunny place out of draughts, in porous soil.
Height indoors 30 cm (12 in).
Flowering summer and early autumn.

Propagation by seeds, division or cuttings.

More than 300 different species of bellflower—which gets its name from the shape of its delicate flowers —bloom in the meadows of Europe, tall annuals and low-growing carpet plants, wood plants and mountain plants, and also annual and biennial summer flowers. Most species are grown out of doors and can be planted out in the garden as soon as warm weather arrives. Two species predominate as house plants, and both originally grew wild in the Mediterranean countries.

Species

Campanula fragilis, which can be trained as an espalier or used as a basket flower, produces its blue flowers with a white centre at the end of the shoot. It flowers in early summer, grows up to 30 cm (12 in) high, and is propagated by seeds.

Quite different from it is *Campanula isophylla,* with its pendulous stems and light blue flowers. The variety 'Alba' has white flowers and grows 30 cm (12 in) high. This variety, and this species, go equally well as climbers and in baskets. In cold weather they must be kept cool and given plenty of air. Both species have very fragile, prostrate stems, which exude a milky juice if damaged.

Cultivation

Bellflowers like a light, warm position in summer, but must not be put in direct sunlight. After the last frosts are past, towards the middle of spring, you can also put them out on the balcony or the terrace. But they will scarcely flower at all if they are in a draught. Remove old shoots carefully in early spring to stimulate a strong new growth.

It is advisable to repot them every two or three years. Clean off the old soil, but do not put the plant into too large a pot or it will use all its strength to develop its roots.

The plants cannot tolerate dry soil, so you must water them regularly. During their winter rest period, cut down the watering a little. Give a little liquid fertilizer twice a month during the growth period.

Propagation

Just before or after the growth period, sow seeds, take cuttings of nonflowering basal shoots to insert in peat or sand, or divide plants with more than a single crown. When roots form, transplant to compost.

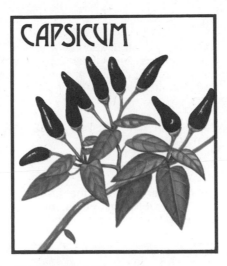

CAPSICUM

Chillies, Red Pepper

Annual decorative plant with beautiful, brightly coloured pods.

Position half-shady and cool.
Height 20-50 cm (9-20 in).
Flowering summer.
Propagation by seeds.

Most people probably think of the pepper as a spice or a vegetable, but they can be cultivated as ornamental pot plants with small, brightly coloured fruits. There are more than twenty species in Central and South America, where pepper comes from, but we cultivate only one species for ornamental purposes, *Capsicum annuum.*

This annual plant grows as a small bush to a height of 50 cm (20 in). Insignificant, circular flowers, white or reddish in colour, grow between the little, ovate leaves, but you will see them only if you grow the plants yourself. Larger ornamental pepper plants are generally offered for sale in late autumn or winter with the brilliant fruits already ripe. You can now also get cut and dried branches which will last a long time in a vase.

There is a very small-growing variety, 'Wolbeck Gnom', which grows no higher than 20 cm (9 in), but which fruits as luxuriantly as the full-size variety.

Cultivation

You cannot go far wrong with capsicums. With regular watering and a cool, half-shady position, the fruits will retain their splendid appearance for a long time. They shrivel a little earlier in a warm room than they would outside, but even then they do not look unsightly.

Propagation

If you want to grow ornamental peppers yourself, you can buy seeds. Sow them in seed compost in spring, cover with glass and keep them in a warm place. Prick out the developing plantlets, pinch out the growing tip to make plants bush out, and plant in pots. It is best to put them in an airy position outdoors while they are in flower.

Capsicum annuum

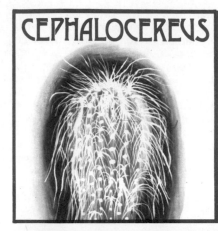

CEPHALOCEREUS

Old Man Cactus

An immense columnar cactus, which never flowers when it is kept as a house plant but is immensely popular for its truly extraordinary appearance.

Position in full sun, very warm, in poor, porous soil.
Height up to 4 m (12 ft).
Propagation by seeds.

It is not their great age that gives the old man cacti their name, but the white, fluffy down, up to 12 cm (5 in) long, that grows at the top of their stem and, allegedly, resembles the sparse and snowy hair of an extremely old man. This head of hair protects the slow-growing, many-ribbed, green plants from the fierce sun of their native Mexican mountains.

Species
Not until the old man cactus (*Cephalocereus senilis*) reaches a height of 6 m (19 ft) does it begin to flower. It then develops a sort of

Cephalocereus senilis

peruke on the top and upper sides of its stem, out of which grow pink flowers about 5 cm (2 in) long. In this form it is hardly suitable as a house plant, but even if the plants are not able to flower in the house, they still look very decorative.

Another uncommon species is *Cephalocereus chrysacanthus,* which differs from *Cephalocereus senilis* in having wavy yellow hair and, in addition, it has yellow thorns, which grow sideways and downwards. This species has reddish-coloured flowers that open up only at night. It grows up to a height of 4 m (13 ft).

Cultivation
The old man cactus does well on a sunny windowsill in poor and porous soil mixed with small limestone chippings. Do not water too often or the plant begins to rot, but spray the plants now and again. The 'old man' should be kept at temperatures of about 15°C (59°F) in winter. Like real old men, it is rather sensitive to draughts, so never put it by an open window.

Younger specimens should be repotted every spring. Be careful not to damage the root system. The repotted plant is sometimes glad of some support, but do not stick the canes into the soil or you may easily damage the roots and the plant will begin to wilt.

Propagation
Propagation is for the enthusiast. Seeds can be sown in slightly sandy soil, but the results are fairly unpredictable and may prove a disappointment for the amateur gardener.

Chamaedorea elegans

CHAMAEDOREA

Mountain Palm

Evergreen, flowering miniature tree.

Position light places, but must be protected from direct sunlight from early spring to autumn.
Height up to 2 m (6 ft).
Flowering the whole year.
Propagation by seeds.

The attractive, evergreen mountain palm has become increasingly popular as a house plant over the past decade. Originally it came from the mountains of South and Central America.

Species
The most common is *Chamaedorea elegans,* sometimes sold as *Neanthe bella.* Its leaves grow to 1 m (3 ft) in length and are pinnate, with 14 leaflets. It begins to flower as a very small plant, male and female flowers appearing on different plants. Less common is *Chamaedorea metallica,* which has large, incised leaves.

Cultivation
The mountain palm needs a fairly light position, but dislikes direct sunlight. It needs plenty of water in summer, so water it complete with the pot once a week. Spray the leaves now and then, or leave it out in the warm rain.

In winter, its rest period, it needs only a little water and no feeding at all. Sponge the leaves every week with soft warm water, and if the air in the room is dry, spray the leaves regularly or the tips of the leaves will turn light yellow.

Propagation
To propagate, sow some seeds in a mixture of sand and peat. They will germinate comparatively easily in a moist heat, and grow quickly.

CHLOROPHYTUM

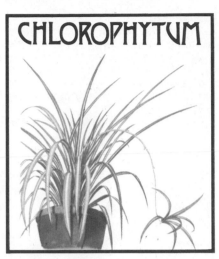

Spider Plant

Trouble-free house plant with tiny insignificant flowers and striking pendulous scapes. Good basket plant.

Position light, but not in direct sunlight, in ordinary potting compost. Should not stand in water.
Height up to 20 cm (9 in). Hanging scapes up to 1 m (3 ft).
Propagation by side shoots or division.

The spider plant is a rewarding house plant. It will tolerate the dry air in offices as well as the steam of the kitchen, it comes to no harm if you sometimes forget to water it, and it is so helpful in producing side shoots for propagation that even a complete beginner at gardening will have absolutely no trouble with this South African member of the lily family. It will survive in poorly lit positions but will not produce side shoots.

Species
The most common spider plants are almost without exception the variety 'Variegatum' of the species *Chlorophytum comosum.* The narrow lanceolate leaves, growing up to 40 cm (16 in) long, are light green with creamy white stripes and white edges. The true species, often referred to as *Chlorophytum capense,* has only green leaves. The insignificant little flowers develop in early summer on long scapes, on which young rooting plants also appear and can be potted up.

The spider plant has a short earth stem and thick, fleshy, tuberous roots with which the plant anchors itself firmly in the ground so that it can bear the considerable weight of the young hanging shoots.

Cultivation

In the growth period, the spider plant should be watered regularly and fertilized once a week. On the whole it is better to water too little rather than too much, since the plant is not particularly fond of standing water and acid soil.

In winter, its rest period, you can stop feeding altogether and cut down the watering, depending on what sort of position the plant has. If it is in dry air, you should water it more than you would in a cool summer. The spider plant can usually tolerate temperatures of 10°C (50°F) and below for quite a time without ill effect.

The plant grows quickly and so should be repotted every two years. Use a mineral-rich, fairly loamy soil in a wide but not too deep pot.

Propagation

The simplest way to propagate the spider plant is to separate the rooted runner from the scape and put it in a pot, keeping it fairly warm at first. After only a few days you can put the new plant in its final position. Young plants should be fed often.

Chlorophytum comosum **'Variegatum'**

CISSUS

Kangaroo Vine

Evergreen climbing shrub with unremarkable flowers.

Position half-shady to shady, in loamy, humus-rich soil.
Height climbing up to 3 m (10 ft).
Propagation by cuttings.

These shrubs, which originally grew in Australia and the tropical parts of Africa and South America, presumably got their name because many species are outstanding climbers. There are also quite a lot of succulent species of cissus, both climbers and nonclimbers. But they are rarities as house plants.

Species
The most widely distributed species is called the kangaroo vine, *Cissus antarctica*. It is a rapidly growing evergreen shrub which climbs with tendrils. It has broad, pointed leaves with a toothed edge on which the veins are distinctly marked. This slender, green plant is so popular because it is completely undemanding and can also tolerate considerable fluctuations of temperature. You can keep the kangaroo vine just as well in a heated room as in a cool entrance hall where the temperatures may sometimes drop to around 5°C (41°F).

Cissus discolor boasts leaves with all sorts of designs on them in red, silver-grey or yellowish green. This decorative semievergreen climber should be kept at a steady temperature of 20°C (68°F). It is beautiful as a hanging basket plant.

Cultivation
The cissus must have no direct sun and above all must not 'get their feet wet'. Certainly you should water them well, but never let water collect at their base, especially in winter, or they will get yellow spots on their leaves. The splendidly coloured *Cissus discolor,* with its pointed leaves up to 15 cm (6 in) long, can be made to flower and then produce small blue berries if the temperature of the room is kept constant. From spring to autumn the cissus must be fed once a week. Repotting in the spring is recommended but is often very difficult if the plants are trained up a trellis. If they are not, you should put a few bamboo canes in the bowl for the tendrils to climb along.

Propagation
The propagation of cissus is simple. Take cuttings in spring and keep them under glass or plastic foil where they will soon root. Cuttings of *Cissus discolor* must be kept at at least 20°C (68°F) while those of the kangaroo vine grow well at 15°C (59°F).

Cissus antarctica

CITRUS

Evergreen tree or shrub with scented flowers.

Position in direct sun or in half-shade. Keep cool and dry during the winter.
Height 30-120 cm (12-48 in).
Flowering in spring.
Propagation by seeds and half-ripe cuttings.

The citrus shrubs and trees have dark evergreen foliage, and the white or yellowish flowers have a penetrating, bittersweet scent. The small fruit of these highly attractive house plants—limes, lemons, oranges or mandarins—cannot of course compare with the citrus fruits in the shops. They are grown for purely decorative purposes, not as a food source for they have no flavour at all, but their scent is lovely.

Species
We have cultivated the orange *(Citrus sinensis)* for a long time. The low trees or bushes, which originally came to Europe from eastern Asia, often have thorns, and oval, scented leaves up to 10 cm (4 in) in length, on long stalks. The white, sweet-smelling flowers are traditionally worn or carried by brides in many European countries. The fruits are round and, not surprisingly, orange-coloured.

The lemon *(Citrus limon)* is a small, thorny tree with light green, oval leaves. The oval yellow fruits are pointed. The commonest house plant of this family is the dwarf orange or calamondin *(Citrus mitis).* Its orange-coloured fruits hang down in bunches between the rather leathery leaves, often beside new flowers. The dwarf orange takes nearly a year to ripen and has a faintly limey flavour.

Citrus mitis

Cultivation

If the citrus trees like plenty of light during the summer, they are just as keen in winter to have a cool, dry position. The winter temperature must not exceed 5°C (41°F) or the plant will immediately shed its leaves. Even the root ball must be allowed to get quite dry then.

You can put citrus trees outdoors or on the balcony in summer, or by an open window. Give them plenty of fertilizer and water until mid-summer; for best results the water should not be too hard. Spray when you see flower buds and when in flower to help set fruit.

Repot the little trees or shrubs in winter only every four to six years as they do not like root disturbance. Choose pots that are not too big, and reduce the old root system a little with a knife. The crown can also be cut back in spring if necessary, but you should wait for at least a year after repotting.

Propagation

You can propagate by seeds, which generally germinate very easily in a mixture of leaf mould and turf, or by half-ripe cuttings. But do not expect too much. You will raise only 'wild trees', as they are called, which hardly ever flower or fruit.

Citrus sinensis

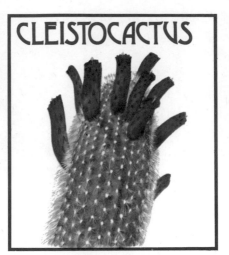

CLEISTOCACTUS

Attractive columnar cactus with many decorative flowers.

Position light to sunny, warm or cool according to the season.
Height up to 2 m (6 ft).
Flowering spring or summer, according to species.
Propagation by cuttings or seeds.

The slender, profusely flowering cleistocacti make popular show pieces in any collection. The genus comprises a number of species that come from the mountainous regions of South America. The columns rise directly out of the ground. In time they grow to as much as 2 m (6 ft) high and have tubular flowers.

Species

The bright red, slightly curved tubular flowers of the species *Cleistocactus baumannii* appear early in the spring. This species grows up to 2 m (6 ft) tall and is densely covered with whitish thorns.

Connoisseurs rate *Cleistocactus strausii* as one of the most beautiful cacti. Its great charm lies in the striking contrast between the snow white spines and the glowing dark red flowers, which can grow as much as 8 cm (3 in) long.

Cleistocactus wendlandiorum (also known as *Cleistocactus flavescens*) is smaller, and the spines are creamy yellow. It has orange-coloured flowers, bent at right angles.

Cultivation

In summer the cleistocactus must be kept as warm as possible. Even direct sunlight does it no harm. The important thing is to give it plenty of water. In winter bring the plants indoors to a light and cool place, watering only a little so that the soil does not dry out.

Propagation

Take cuttings or sow seeds.

Cleistocactus strausii

CLIVIA

Evergreen house plant with magnificent flowers.

Position light, but not in direct sunlight, in fairly loamy soil.
Height up to 60 cm (24 in).
Flowering spring or autumn.
Propagation by offsets or by seeds.

Clivia was once a popular house plant, but now we see it less often. It needs a great deal of attention all year round if you want it to flower. Clivia has still not abandoned the lifelong habits of its native South Africa. But the plants are long-lived and can, with the right treatment, often be persuaded to flower twice a year.

Of the three species of clivia we grow only one, *Clivia miniata*. The evergreen leaves, growing at ground level, are slightly broadened at the base and form a funnel with a light throat. Up to twenty orange flowers, of very different sizes, can grow in a single cluster. Clivia does not have a real bulb but a bulbous stem surrounded by dense leaf sheaths.

Cultivation

Clivia is very fussy about its position. Year in, year out, it must stand in the same place and with the same side facing the light. The best place is in a window that only gets direct sunlight first thing in the morning or in the evening. It wants temperatures of about 15°C (59°F) and tolerates dry air well.

If you really want to enjoy clivia flowers, you must be careful about watering. Clivia dislikes standing water. In its rest period, from autumn to winter, it must stand in dry earth. Wipe the leaves with a wet cloth from time to time during this period. Feed every ten days from late winter through summer. Young plants

Clivia miniata

should be repotted every year, but old plants only seldom—particularly if you want a dense display.

Do not begin feeding and watering until the flower stem has reached the height of the leaves. At this period you should keep the plant warm at 18°C (66°F), or the flowers will appear inside the funnel of leaves and never blossom fully.

Propagation

A second growth from the seeds that form in the flowers of clivia is unlikely, but you can buy seeds to sow. Or use the abundant suckers. Choose those with four or five leaves and plant them in a mixture of sand and peat.

COCOS

Small, decorative indoor palm with attractive pinnate leaves.

Position shady and warm, in slightly sandy garden soil.
Height up to 150 cm (59 in).
Propagation by seeds.

Even in its natural habitat in Brazil the cocos palm grows no higher than 150 cm (59 in).

Species
Of the two species, we cultivate only one, *Cocos weddelianum,* as a house plant. The plant takes 20 years to reach its maximum height and is usually seen as a small plant about 30 cm (12 in). The short stem is often enveloped by brownish fibres. The flexible leaf stalks bear opposite, narrow pinnate leaves. There will often be as many as 200 of these to a frond. The upper surface is dark green and the underside is whitish.

Cultivation
The cocos palm must stand in a shady, warm place in the window all year round. Even in winter the temperature should never be below 18°C (64°F). Always keep the plant moist and, if possible, keep some water in a dish under the pot. Keep out of draughts.
 The cocos palm thrives best in a high, narrow palm pot. Take the greatest care not to damage the roots when repotting, or the plant will quickly die.

Propagation
Propagation by freshly imported seeds is possible but difficult for the amateur gardener. You must have very high bottom heat and humidity. It is easier to buy young plants from a nursery than to try and raise from seed yourself.

CODIAEUM

Croton, South Sea Laurel

Evergreen house plant with splendidly coloured leaves.

Position in half-shady and warm places with high humidity.
Height up to 1 m (3 ft).
Propagation by cuttings.

Croton is a plant grown exclusively for its foliage. Remove the flowers at once, for they only take strength from the plant. At home in tropical Southeast Asia and the Pacific Islands it reaches a height of 3 m (10 ft). Elsewhere it reaches 1 m (3 ft).
 Codiaeum variegatum, the only species, has endless hybrids of disparate appearance. The leaves of the varieties are quite different both in shape and in colour.
 The colours range from whitish to dark red, and the patterns on the leaves from patches and spots to fine linear designs. The only common

Codiaeum variegatum

factor is leathery surfaces of the leaves.

Cultivation
The croton can safely be put on the ledge of a south-facing window. It needs protection only against glaring sunlight; but a lot of light is necessary if the leaves are to keep their colour and patterns. Also, the humidity must be kept constant. Spray the leaves frequently, and keep the soil ball moist. Feed once a week. In winter the croton needs a room where the temperature is not below 18°C (64°F). Give it a little less water at this time.

Propagation
The chances of successful propagation are not great. But if you want to try, take strong, ripened cuttings in the greenhouse in early spring, dip the tips in powdered charcoal to stem the flow of latex, and insert them in a mixture of peat and sand with high bottom heat and humidity.

Codiaeum variegatum

Codiaeum variegatum

COFFEA

Coffee Plant

Undemanding and rewarding evergreen house plant. Established plants have scented flowers and decorative fruits.

Position half shady and moderately warm, in loamy soil.
Height 80-200 cm (32-72 in).
Flowering summer.
Propagation by seeds and cuttings.

Many flower lovers have no idea that the coffee plant can flourish not only on a plantation but in the living room. You cannot buy them as pot plants, but you can grow fine specimens from fresh seed.

Grown commercially, they reach a height of 5 m (16 ft), but the house plants you grow yourself will rarely grow more than 1 m (3 ft) high. They

Coffea arabica

can reach twice that height after a few years.

Of the 50 or so species, the best known is *Coffea arabica*. Widely distributed as a commercial and ornamental plant, it has shiny sinuate leaves that grow transversely on horizontal branches.

After three or four years the first little white, stellate flowers appear in summer. They smell like jasmine. After the flowers the tiny red berries ripen, each one containing two seeds. Commercially these are harvested as coffee beans; the amateur gardener can use them as seeds for sowing.

Cultivation
The coffee plant must be sheltered from strong sunlight at a steady temperature. It feels best in summer at 16-20°C (61-68°F) and in winter at 14-16°C (51-61°F). Water generously during the hot seasons, less later on, but never let the loamy soil dry out. If the air in the room is dry, spray frequently. Also, in spring and summer, put some fertilizer with low lime content into lukewarm water for watering.

Propagation
The seeds of the coffee plant must be put in moist sand as soon as they are ripe and kept under glass at a temperature of 25°C (77°F) until they germinate. When little plantlets have formed, pot them and treat them the same as older plants. If you already have a coffee plant, you can take stem cuttings in the spring, let them root in moist sand and plant them later.

59

COLEUS

Flame Nettle

Very popular house plant with magnificent ornamental leaves. Generally a perennial.

Position in a sunny room or in a box on a balcony facing south.
Height according to species, from 15-70 cm (6-28 in). Flowering mid- to late summer.
Propagation by cuttings or seeds.

The charm of the flame nettles lies not in their quite insignificant blue or mauve flowers but in their magnificently patterned, brilliantly coloured leaves. Only young plants have these pretty leaves; the leaves of older plants are crumpled and wrinkled and their coloured patterns already faded. The flame nettle has many species of quite different appearance. Some of them are only annuals, some are subshrubs that can form fine bushes.

Species
The *Coleus blumei* hybrids are grown mainly for their wonderful foliage. Different varieties reach heights of from 30-60 cm (12-24 in) and all are perennial. They have angular stalks, woody at the lower end, and oval leaves that come to a point, with all sorts of colour patterns. Since these plants are grown primarily for their foliage, it is best to take off the flowers, which would otherwise weaken the growth. *Coleus fredericii,* from Africa, forms a shrub 1 m (3 ft) high with light coloured leaves. This annual produces dark blue flowers.

Cultivation
The flame nettle needs a light room, but not too warm. In summer it also does well in a windowbox or on the balcony and can even be planted outdoors in the full sun; but in rainy summers a disaster is inevitable. The flame nettle should be put in a fairly rich potting compost and watered and sprayed frequently with tepid, previously boiled water. It easily wilts if it does not get enough water. It should have liquid fertilizer once a week from spring to autumn. Pinch out growing tips regularly to make the plant bushy.

The flame nettle passes the cold weather best in a kitchen window in moist air. Otherwise keep the plants fairly dry, at a temperature of about 10°C (50°F), and cut them back firmly after flowering. Occasionally spray lightly in the morning and put them out in the sun.

Propagation
Do not let flame nettles grow too old.

Right: *Coleus blumei* hybrid
Below: *Coleus blumei* hybrids

It is best to propagate them before they get unsightly. Take cuttings of your favourites, which will grow readily in a mixture of peat and sand kept constantly moist. It is even enough to put the cuttings with their lower ends in a glass of water. They will form roots in as little as 14 days.

Seedlings can be raised from seed in a warm room. But you may get some surprises—hardly any two of the plants coming up will resemble each other.

Plant both cuttings and seedlings separately in small pots with peat-based or standard compost, and pot out gradually until they stand in a 15 cm (7 in) pot. Prune them once or twice to get shapely branching.

Coleus blumel hybrid

Coleus blumei

COLUMNEA

Evergreen, abundantly flowering basket plant.

Position light to half-shady, out of direct sun and draughts.
Height up to 120 cm (48 in).
Flowering at all seasons, according to species.
Propagation by cuttings.

The *Columnea* species, which are at home in the tropical rain forests of Central America, have become quite robust hanging plants, with their leathery thickly growing leaves and brightly-coloured profusion of flowers.

Species
Magnificent red flowers with a yellow spot gleam from the dark green foliage of *Columnea gloriosa* from autumn to spring. The little, hairy, almost round leaves grow on long

Columnea gloriosa

stalks that hang down at an angle. This species must be kept in a conservatory.

Columnea hirta has a long flowering period but is very sensitive to light. The pale red flowers grow on long stems covered with reddish brown hairs.

The *Columnea vedrariensis* hybrid is very robust, flowering at temperatures around 17°C (62°F). You most often find them in nurseries under the name of *Columnea kewensis*. Its narrow, rounded leaves with a little point are brownish green on top and reddish underneath. The bright red flowers bloom from late winter to early spring.

Cultivation
The columnea is intolerant of direct sunlight and especially sensitive to draughts. When the buds begin to form, the plants want temperatures around 20°C (68°F) and high humidity; but after this they want rather lower temperatures. Do not get water on the plant or it will cause yellow spots. Use only softened water and lime-free food. Repot into flat pots after flowering. Like many plants that like a high humidity, columnea may be attacked by the soft-skin mite. Young plants are in particular danger and should be kept from other plants till you have examined them and ensure that they are free from pests.

Propagation
Cut a shoot into several pieces about 5 cm (2 in) long and plant them in a propagator at 20-22°C (68-72°F). Propagation by seeds is difficult and not recommended for the amateur gardener.

CORDYLINE

Cabbage Palm, Flaming Dragon Tree, Scarlet Aspidistra

Difficult indoor shrub with colourful, ornamental foliage and insignificant small flowers that appear only on older plants.

Position half-shady and warm, with high humidity, in sandy soil.
Height up to 2 m (6 ft).
Propagation by cuttings.

In tropical parts of India and Australia some 15 species of the cordyline grow as trees or shrubs. Outstanding examples will sometimes grow to over 4 m (13 ft) in height. They are popular elsewhere as ornamental plants with pretty, brightly coloured leaves. These leaves, narrow and sword-shaped, grow on a small stem and branch out just above the ground to make a

Below: *Cordyline* **(right) and its relative** *Dracaena* **(left)**

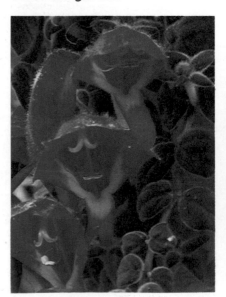

dense crown. The small, insignificant flowers are found on older plants.

Species

Cordyline terminalis is one of the most beautiful ornamental house plants. Long, stalked leaves grow on the slender stem to a length of 50 cm (20 in). Their original colour is green, but breeders have produced many varieties with particularly beautifully coloured leaves—most of them multi-coloured—in shades of green, red and white.

The white to reddish flowers of the older trees grow in panicles and are succeeded by little red berries. In greenhouses with tropical conditions the shrubs can be grown to 2 m (6 ft). The lower-growing, red-leaved varieties are better suited for a living room.

The fragrant white-flowering *Cordyline australis* with leaves up to 1 m (3 ft) long and the violet-flowering *Cordyline stricta* with broader, shorter leaves are easier to grow and just as attractive as the more temperamental species.

Cultivation

If you want to get lasting pleasure from *Cordyline terminalis,* you must have a warm conservatory with very high humidity. The plants must stand in a light but not sunny place at temperatures between 22-28°C (72-82°F). Keep the soil pretty moist and feed once a week.

The species *Cordyline australis* and *Cordyline stricta* particularly like a half-shady place on the balcony during the summer. Shelter them carefully from draughts, and give them plenty of water. Water them less in winter and keep them away from frost at temperatures of up to 10°C (50°F).

Propagation

You should propagate cordyline only if you have a conservatory or a greenhouse. Top cuttings need very high bottom heat—about 35°C (95°F)—and moist air to make them take root in humus-rich soil under glass.

Crossandra infundibuliformis

CROSSANDRA

Charming, abundantly flowering, subshrub.

Position very light, but not in direct sun.
Height up to 1 m (3 ft).
Flowering spring and summer.
Propagation by cuttings.

Although the crossandra came to Europe from the tropical forests of India and Sri Lanka as long ago as the beginning of the 19th century, it was quickly forgotten again, and it is only in the last few years that interest has revived in it, the main reason being that it was long looked on as a very difficult plant.

Species

Crossandra infundibuliformis is a low-growing plant with dark green leaves that flowers in spring and summer. Its salmon-pink flowers have a distinctly one-sided corolla. The flower stems, 10 cm (4 in) long and growing in the axils, carry green bracts.

'Mona Wallhed' is a particularly easy, robust and compact variety. *Crossandra subacaulis* is still quite rare. It has yellow-white flowers which do not appear until midsummer.

Cultivation

A first essential for cultivation is enough moisture in the soil and in the air. After the rest period in autumn and early winter feed once a week until late summer. Plants that have filled their pots with their root system should be repotted in standard compost.

Propagation

Take cuttings in winter and keep them under glass; plant them out in summer.

CYCLAMEN

Sowbread

Tuberous plant, one of the most popular and rewarding house plants.

Position in a light, cool room.
Height 10-20 cm (4-9 in).
Flowering in spring.
Propagation by seeds.

The cyclamen is one of the most popular house plants. There are so many different forms of flower among the 14 or so species that a whole battery of cyclamens could never get boring or monotonous.

Species

The famous indoor cyclamen—*Cyclamen persicum* (otherwise *Cyclamen puniceum, Cyclamen latifolium*), a tender plant suitable for potting—is a relative of wild flowers that grow in the mountain woods of Iran, Greece and Asia Minor. It has rounded leaves and produces large, attractive rose, salmon pink or white flowers.

There is also a great range of cultivars. You can choose between strangely patterned leaves, large or small, scented or unscented flowers, smooth hoods or fringed heads on the flowers, single or double, bordered and striped blooms.

Cyclamen persicum

Cultivation

When you buy cyclamens, make sure that all the flowers are not already out. There ought to be a good number of buds still hidden among the leaves.

Too much warmth, and an oppressive, dry position are bad for the cyclamen. It likes temperatures around 14°C (57°F), with plenty of light and air.

Water cyclamens carefully with softish water. If possible, water them so that the corm stays dry, or it may rot. Feed with liquid fertilizer every week or two.

Faded, yellowing leaves can be removed by twisting them away from the corm. If you cut them off, the corm easily begins to rot.

Propagation

The corms of cyclamens do not divide or produce others so propagation is possible only by seeds, but it is not too difficult. They should bloom within 12 to 15 months.

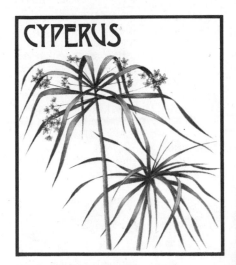

CYPERUS

Umbrella Grass, Galingale

Very tough, moisture-loving, freely growing perennial ornamental grass with pretty flowers.

Position half-shady, cool or warm according to species, in normal or very moist, loamy soil.
Height 30-150 cm (12-60 in).
Flowering spring to autumn, according to species.
Propagation by division or cuttings.

Cyperus is a house plant as unusual as it is long-lasting, notable for the abundance of its graceful leaves. Over 500 different species occur in the tropical and subtropical regions of Africa and America. Some of the species can grow to 5 m (16 ft) in height.

The low-growing species are widespread as house plants. The narrow leaves clustered at the top of the thin, flexible stalk look like a feather duster. Amid these strong heads of foliage small whitish flowers grow in spring and summer in ears, or umbels.

Species
The best known species of cyperus, the umbrella grass (*Cyperus alternifolius*), comes from swampy areas in the Malagasy Republic. It grows to a height of 150 cm (60 in) and has long, pointed leaves, 20 cm (9 in) long and never more than 1 cm ($\frac{1}{2}$ in) wide.

Very similar, but only about 30 cm (12 in) high, is the dwarf species, *Cyperus gracilis*.

Cultivation
Cyperus alternifolius is among the most versatile of house plants. Being a true swamp grass, it grows well in an aquarium or at the edge of a pool. If you want to put it on the window ledge, you must put its pot into a high-sided container filled with water and spray the plant regularly. The same applies to *Cyperus gracilis*.

All species of cyperus can tolerate temperatures up to 25°C (77°F) but should be kept out of the full glare of the sun. In winter they can do with less warmth, the lower limit being about 10°C (50°F).

Propagation
Cyperus is easy to propagate by division. Divide the plants carefully at the roots and replant. With *Cyperus alternifolius* and *Cyperus gracilis* you can also take cuttings—the head of a leaf with about 5 cm (2 in) of stalk. Plant them in damp sand or lay them in water. When they root, plant them in small pots.

Cyperus gracilis

Harry Smith

DIEFFENBACHIA

Dumb Cane

Extremely poisonous evergreen house plant with attractive ornamental leaves.

Position in light, but not sunny, places with high humidity.
Height up to 1 m (3 ft).
Propagation by cuttings and air-layering.

Dieffenbachia, which comes from the forests of tropical America, is among the most popular house plants in the world on account of its beautifully patterned leaves. It is named after Josef Dieffenbach (d.1863) who was the head gardener at the Vienna Botanical Gardens for many years. Its little flowers, rather like those of the arum lily, are not particularly attractive and can only be seen on older or greenhouse plants.

Take great care with this plant, however, as it is· extremely poisonous. Biting any part of it causes intense pain and prevents speech for several days. Keep hands away from eyes when handling it, and wash hands well afterwards.

Species
Dieffenbachia bausei, a robust species and very widespread, has yellow-green leaves of up to 25 cm (10 in) long, with a lot of dark green spots and rather fewer white ones. There is a narrow green stripe round the edge of the leaves, which tend to darken as the plant grows older.

Dieffenbachia macrophylla has no pattern on the leaves. It is a strong grower, forming a green stem on which the dark green, rather leathery leaves grow. This species does best in deep shadow.

Dieffenbachia maculata (also called *Dieffenbachia picta*) comes from Brazil. It grows a powerful stem sometimes as much as 1 m (3 ft) tall. The oblong leaves are patterned in white and yellow. Many varieties of this species have been grown. The best known are 'Jenmannii', 'Mag-nifica' and 'Julius Roehrs'. Even experts are sometimes hard put to tell the difference between them.

Flat, only slightly arched leaves distinguish *Dieffenbachia seguine,* the original dumb cane. Its leaves and leaf stems are stripy and spotted with white. The best known varieties are 'Irrorata' and 'Nobilis'.

Cultivation
Unfortunately dieffenbachia generally loses its lower leaves when kept

in an ordinary room where constant humidity and room temperature are difficult to ensure. Protect the plants from direct sunlight, and from spring on, when they begin to shoot, feed them well and give them plenty of water—a dry root ball results in brown edges on the leaves. In winter the plant can do with a temperature of about 16°C (61°F). The rest period

Left: *Dieffenbachia seguine*
Below: *Dieffenbachia*

starts in autumn, when you should water sparingly and feed hardly at all. Repot every spring.

Propagation
Top cuttings are the best method of propagation, because with the same operation you can rejuvenate older plants that have grown bare at the bottom of the stem. You can also plant or lay stem cuttings, preferably with a leaf on them, in heat of 30°C (89°F). A humus-rich soil is best.

DIPLADENIA

Profusely flowering, creeping ever-green house plant.

Position warm and sunny places with high humidity.
Height on supports, up to 120 cm (47 in).
Flowering spring to autumn.
Propagation by cuttings.

In the last century dipladénia was a favourite house plant, but later became a rarity found only in botanical gardens. Its renewed popularity is due to Danish gardeners, who have succeeded in reducing the luxuriantly climbing plants to a more compact growth.

Species
Dipladenia boliviensis bears white flowers with a yellow throat, growing in clusters, three or four of them together. Bright green leaves, 8 cm (3 in) long, grow on slender stems.

The striking flowers of *Dipladenia sanderi* grow together in pairs. The flowers are up to 7 cm (3 in) across, pink with a yellow throat. You can now buy pretty hybrids of this species, notably 'Amoena', bright pink, and the salmon-coloured 'Rosea'.

Dipladenia splendens produces flowers that are pink inside and white outside; they bloom in summer. The leaves of this species grow up to 15 cm (6 in) long. In cultivation it is usually twined round cane supports as a pot plant or trained on strings or wires against a greenhouse wall. It will flower only when about 20 cm (9 in) high.

Cultivation
These shrubs and subshrubs, which originated in tropical America, need a lot of water but cannot tolerate standing in continuous damp. So

you must ensure that the soil is well drained. Feed them once a fortnight. They have a rest period from autumn through winter, when they should be watered only a little, just enough to prevent the plants from flagging.

It has always proved best to spray the plants from time to time, even in winter. Repot in spring in medium-sized pots to ensure they flower readily.

Propagation
Take cuttings of young lateral shoots in spring or older stem cuttings with two leaves in summer and insert in peat and sand at 16-18°C (61-64°F). When rooted, pot in potting compost. The leaves of the rooted cuttings will be pale at first but take on colour during subsequent months.

Dipladenia splendens

DRACAENA

Dragon Tree

Tropical tree or shrub, kept as foliage plant. It seldom flowers.

Position half-shady and warm, with high humidity.
Height 2 m (6 ft).
Propagation by cuttings or seeds.

Tourists in the Canary Islands who buy little green foliage trees in the market are usually unaware that these will grow into trees 20 m (65 ft) high. Part of the characteristic scene of the Canary Islands, *Dracaena draco*, the dragon tree, can grow at an astonishing rate. Of course that happens only in the tropics. But with proper care dragon trees indoors will grow to a height of 2 m (6 ft) and live for years. There is a specimen in the Canary Islands said to be over 1000 years old.

Green-leaved species
The true dragon tree · (*Dracaena draco*) is a tall-stemmed tree with grey-green leaves growing close together. They grow to a length of 50 cm (20 in) and come to a sword-shaped point. *Dracaena hookeriana* has a short, often branched stem. The narrow, leathery leaves grow up to 70 cm (28 in) long and have lighter borders. A favourite is the variety 'Latifolia', with leaves up to 8 cm (3 in) wide, as well as the brightly leaved 'Variegata'.

Coloured-leaved species
Dracaena deremensis has long, pointed, shining dark green leaves about 50 cm (20 in) long. At first the leaves stick straight out, but later they hang down a little. This species from East Africa is not so often seen in the nurseries as its bright-leaved varieties 'Bausei' and 'Warneckii', whose dark green leaves have white-green stripes.

Dracaena fragrans develops tall stems; its dark green leaves reach a length of 75 cm (30 in) and are very narrow and drooping, hanging rather crookedly. All the varieties have foliage with white or yellowish stripes or edges.

The shrub-like *Dracaena godseffiana* comes from Zaire. It is an abundantly branching bush. Its bright green leaves grow together in groups on the upright branches and display curious white spots. This species comes into flower when quite young. The yellow-green, strongly scented flowers give way to pretty red berries. Well known varieties are 'Florida Beauty', with large white spots on the leaves, and 'Kelleri', with marbled leaves.

The smallest species, *Dracaena*

sanderiana, has lovely white-patterned foliage and is popular among flower lovers, because it is easy to look after. This species has narrow leaves up to 20 cm (9 in) long growing horizontally from a thin, short stem; the leaves have stripes of white and silver-grey.

Cultivation

In a normal living room only the green-leaved species and the variety *Dracaena fragrans* 'Rothiana' can be kept without special equipment. They need light and winter temperatures at 12-14°C (54-58°F). The other species and varieties are more awkward to cultivate, because of their temperature and humidity requirements. One exception to this, however, is the shrubby *Dracaena godseffiana*.

Put dragon trees in a light, warm place but remember that they do not like direct sunlight. Rich soil and regular watering and spraying does a lot to make them grow well. During the autumn and winter give them less water. Apart from the species mentioned above and the variety 'Rothiana', do not keep the plants in rooms under 18-20°C (64-68°F). These plants really need to live in the conservatory if they are to be successful.

The dragon tree should be repotted into a medium-sized container every two or three years. Be careful not to damage the root systems during this operation; the plants are very sensitive to root damage. The best soil is a mixture of leaf mould, peat and loam, but you can also use standard rich compost. Larger plants need weekly feeding.

Propagation

Only experts should try to propagate the dragon tree. *Dracaena draco* is grown from seeds. The other species are propagated from stem cuttings put in a propagator at 21-24°C (70-75°F) in a half-peat, half-sand mixture. Enthusiasts with few technical resources are advised against propagating this plant.

Dracaena draco, **full size**

ECHEVERIA

Succulent annual or shrub, with very decorative flowers.

Position in full sunlight in a rather loamy soil.
Height up to 150 cm (60 in).
Flowering late winter to autumn, according to species.
Propagation by leaf cuttings or shoots, offsets and seeds.

Above: *Dracaena godseffiana*
Below: *Dracaena sanderiana*

In southern Europe you often see echeverias used as ground-cover plants. Their thick, fleshy leaves, arranged in rosettes, are sometimes white and yellow, and sometimes green, or even violet. Certain species have leaves dusted with powder, which protects the plant from the sun's heat. They are easy to grow, spreading to form a thick carpet.

Species

The common species *Echeveria agavoides* is stemless and has light green leaves with rusty brown points. The short, broad, sharply pointed leaves form thick rosettes from which yellow-red, short-stemmed flowers with yellow tips protrude, generally in spring.

Similarly stemless is the *Echeveria carnicolor* with its flesh-coloured flowers and loose rosettes of up to 7 cm (3 in) wide. This attractive plant has small, pointed, blue-grey leaves which occasionally exhibit a red gleam. The yellow-red and bell-shaped flowers appear from late winter to early spring.

Echeveria derenbergii has red-edged leaves covered with bluish powder. In drought the rosettes, some 6 cm (2 in) across, fold up to practically form a sphere. This short-stemmed species remains very small; its bell-shaped, yellow-red flowers are yellow inside and seldom grow higher than the rosettes. It flowers from spring to summer.

Echeveria elegans is a little shrub about 40 cm (16 in) high, whose branches are covered with soft hairs.

The small green leaves form rosettes of about 7 cm (3 in) across at the tips of the shoots. This species produces big, pink bell-like flowers from spring to summer.

Echeveria gibbiflora forms thick rosettes at the tips of its strong branches. The greeny-blue leaves have a red sheen and grow up to 15 cm (6 in) long. This species bears red flowers which look as if they are frosted. More common than the true species is *Echeveria gibbiflora* 'Metallica'. It has blue-green leaves, rather broader and rounder than those of the species and generally covered with a mat of light red-brown hairs.

Echeveria gigantea, a subshrub of about 30 cm (12 in) high, has inflorescences as tall as 150 cm (60 in). Its leaves often have a red border and grow to 20 cm (9 in) long. The inflorescence of many yellow flowers does not appear until the autumn.

Echeveria setosa is thickly covered with white bristles. This fine down is even found on the lovely yellow-red flowers, which appear from spring to summer. The thick, green leaves form tight rosettes and often have a waxy sheen.

Cultivation

Echeveria needs a light position both in winter and summer. In winter, except for the winter-flowering species, they must be kept at temperatures of about 8°C (46°F) and only watered a little. Even in summer

Echeveria gibbiflora 'Metallica'

these plants need little water; too much water causes rot. Feed them once a month during their growth period. The plant does best in rather loamy soil with a mixture of sand. Young plants should be repotted every year; established plants are best left alone.

Propagation

Even beginners will be able to propagate echeverias with no trouble. Old stems that have been cut down will usually send out new shoots from the leaf scars. After letting them dry off for two days, simply plant leaf cuttings or even leaf stalks in the ground and they will root. Use sandy compost and keep them slightly moist.

Propagation is also possible by offsets from the rosettes and by seeds.

Echeveria gibbiflora

EPIPHYLLUM

Orchid Cactus

Perennial house plant with lovely flowers.

Position light place in chalk-free soil; in summer, half-shade outdoors.
Height up to 1 m (3 ft).
Flowering spring to summer.
Propagation by cuttings or seeds.

Orchid cacti grow on trees in the tropical rain forests of Central and South America.

We cannot keep these original species on our window ledges, but we have many splendid hybrids which will almost always grow and thrive. These large-flowering cacti will survive at a minimum winter temperature of 5°C (41°F), but their large showy flowers are produced more frequently if the plants are kept warmer.

Cultivation

During the winter rest period orchid

Below: *Echeveria setosa*

cacti need a light, cool place at temperatures of about 8-10°C (46-50°F) and should only be watered sparingly. After that the plants like a warmer temperature and rather more water of the lime-free, tepid kind. Outdoors from spring to autumn, orchid cacti feel best in a warm, sheltered place in the garden, but out of direct sunlight. There they should be watered freely, sprayed and fed with high-potassium cactus fertilizers.

Do not repot too often or they will not flower readily. Repot only after flowering or, better still, replace the top layer of soil in the pot.

Propagation
Side-shoot cuttings, surfaces thoroughly dried before planting, normally grow well in new soil. Or sow seeds in spring at 21°C (70°F).

Epiphyllum 'London Glory'

EUONYMUS

Flowering shrub with ornamental leaves and small, decorative fruits.

Position sunny to half-shade and airy, in loamy soil containing peat.
Height up to 150 cm (59 in).
Flowering spring and summer.
Propagation by cuttings.

The dark green, leathery leaves of some species look like laurel leaves. Growing wild, they often reach a height of 8 m (26 ft), but the hard, angular branches of the cultivated species grow only to a maximum of 150 cm (59 in). The ovate leaves, coming to a point at the tip, with slightly toothed edges, are dark green, or in some breeds green with yellow and white patterns. Small white flowers are followed by bright red berries.

The only pot plant is *Euonymus japonicus,* from Japan. Many varieties of this species have been bred, notable mostly for their beautifully patterned leaves. Best known are 'Aureomarginatus', with dark green, yellow-bordered leaves, 'Albo-marginatus' with white edges to the leaves, and 'Microphyllus' with leaves in shades of green, yellow and white.

Cultivation
During the summertime the euonymus enjoys the open air of the balcony or terrace. It must have a sunny to half-shady position with plenty of air. In winter return it to a light room at about 5°C (41°F). From spring to autumn give it plenty of water and feed it every fortnight.

Propagation
Take top cuttings in early spring or late summer and root them in warm, moist sand. Then plant them in pots of loamy earth mixed with peat.

EUPHORBIA MILII

Crown of Thorns

Popular and trouble-free semisucculent shrub with showy spurious flowers.

Position light, sunny and airy, in good humus-rich soil.
Height up to 150 cm (59 in).
Flowering winter and spring.
Propagation by cuttings.

Since the crown of thorns was first brought to Europe from the highlands of the Malagasy Republic in the early nineteenth century, this succulent indoor shrub has won countless friends. The plant is ideal for dry indoor air and, with the right handling, will last for decades. The branches, which are as hard as pencils, are brownish green and bear many thorns. Between the thorns lanceolate-obovate, light green leaves occur.

The crown of thorns, like all species of its genus, contains a poisonous sap. From late winter to early summer—occasionally earlier —it produces small flowers, insig-

Euphorbia milii

nificant in themselves but distinguished by very decorative, crimson, kidney-shaped bracts. The plant is inclined to climb.

Cultivation
The crown of thorns needs a sunny place by the window. Above all it is intolerant of humidity. It does not need a cool spot, even in winter, when you can keep it in the living room, but give it rather less water. As a young plant it should be repotted every two years or so.

Propagation
Propagation by cuttings in spring is easy. But you must remember to wear gloves all the time to avoid the thorns. Lay the young shoots in tepid water to draw off the milky sap, or dip in powdered charcoal to stem its flow. Then let the cuttings dry and plant them in a mixture of sand and peat.

EUPHORBIA PULCHERRIMA

Poinsettia

Evergreen indoor shrub with striking red or cream bracts and insignificant yellowish flowers.

Euphorbia pulcherrima

Position light and half-shady, in porous humus-rich soil.
Height up to 1 m (3 ft).
Flowering autumn to early spring.
Propagation by cuttings.

The poinsettia is an evergreen house plant originally from Mexico with striking bright red or creamy white bracts. Its relatively recent popularity is largely due to the intensive breeding carried on, especially in America, which has succeeded in overcoming its original awkwardness as a house plant. Its pointed, slightly curved, white-veined green leaves are totally overshadowed by the bracts. These are grouped round the tiny and insignificant yellowish flowers which appear in winter.

Cultivation
Poinsettia can stand in a room all year round, in a light but not sunny place and at temperatures of 20°C (68°F) or less. During the growth period, spring to autumn, water freely and spray with tepid water. After flowering, water only moderately and cut the plant back. To make the plants flower again, they must be allowed to stand in light rooms for only ten to twelve hours a day for some eight weeks before the autumn flowering period. During this period even street lighting and the occasional switching on and off of electric lights will hold up the formation of flowers. The temperature at this time should be kept constantly at around 17°C (63°F).

Propagation
You can take leaf cuttings in summer. When they stop exuding their milky, poisonous sap, plant the cuttings in flat pots of standard compost, with a bottom heat of at least 25°C (77°F). The cuttings should root in about three weeks.

Right and below:
Euphorbia pulcherrima

FATSHEDERA

Evergreen indoor shrub with light green leaves.

Position light place in a cool room.
Height up to 2 m (7 ft).
Propagation by cuttings.

Fatshedera, a cross between hedera (ivy) and fatsia (an indoor aralia), has only one species, *Fatshedera lizei*, which is an upright shrub with an inherited tendency to climb—but just a little. The stem of the young plant has rust-coloured hairs and the evergreen leaves resemble those of the fatsia but are harder, smaller and more hairy. Only occasionally in late summer does it decide to flower.

Fatshedera lizei

Then it produces close round clusters of green flowers. There is a very pretty ornamental-leaved variety, 'Variegata'.

Cultivation
Fatshedera does not care for the sun, but likes bright light in a cool room. Fresh air suits both the green-leaved and the coloured-leaved variety. The soil—a standard compost—must be moderately watered and manured. The leaves should be carefully washed down each week. A room temperature of 10-12°C (50-54°F) is enough during the winter, when the plants need less water and no food.

Propagation
Propagation is possible only by cuttings. You can use the head, with three or four leaves, and you can also cut up a shoot and plant pieces on which one leaf remains. Plant the cuttings in little pots filled with sand mixed with leaf mould—the top cutting by itself, the stem cuttings three to a pot. Cover them with an inverted glass cover or a plastic bag to ensure the required humidity. Whatever you do, do not let the pots stand in the sun. At moderate temperatures of about 18°C (64°F) rooting and the formation of buds at the leaf shoulders will go ahead quickly. You can propagate at any time except in winter. Growing three cuttings in one pot will produce particularly healthy and bushy plants.

FATSIA

Fig Leaf Palm

Evergreen indoor shrub with big, impressive leaves.

Position shady and cool, in loamy earth.
Height up to 2 m (6 ft).
Propagation by seeds or cuttings.

The fig leaf palm is one of the best known of all foliage plants. (You will often hear it called the castor oil plant, but this is not correct.) With due care it will grow many years old, and in the course of time will form strong, slender stems. These, together with the huge palmate leaves, give it a most attractive appearance. At home in Japan these shrubs quite often grow 5 m (16 ft) high. As house plants, however, they seldom grow more than 2 m (6 ft). Their great virtue is that they do well in dark corners of the room or entrance hall without losing any of their beauty.

There is only one species of fatsia, *Fatsia japonica*. But many attractive varieties have been developed from it. The stems of young plants are thin and flexible. Dark green palmate leaves, not unlike maple leaves, grow on smooth stalks; they are deeply lobed and can develop up to nine 'fingers'. The young leaves are about 15 cm (6 in) across, brown, with a rough upper side. Later they grow as much as 40 cm (16 in) wide and are smooth and leathery.

When the fatsia matures, umbels of greeny white flowers appear in mid-summer and autumn, forming thick little clusters. Quite often small black decorative berries grow from them.

The most popular variety, 'Variegata', has whitish or yellow patterns on the leaves. 'Moseri' is compact and low-growing.

Cultivation
The fatsia gives very little trouble. It can stand in the cool and dark, indoors or (in summer) outdoors.

Fatsia japonica

Water it well and feed once a week, from spring to autumn. Give less water from then on, and let the plant overwinter at about 8°C (46°F). Wash the great leaves down with a damp cloth once a month.

Propagation
There is no difficulty in propagating from imported seed, which you must sow at a warm room temperature in ordinary seed compost as soon as it ripens. With coloured-leaved varieties you can also propagate by cuttings, but the new plant will most probably do less well than the parent. If you are propagating by cuttings, a minimum bottom heat of about 25°C (77°F) is best. The cuttings will usually strike in wet sand at this temperature.

Fatsia japonica 'Variegata'

FICUS

Indian Rubber Tree, Weeping Fig, Fiddle Back Fig, Creeping Fig

Evergreen shrub or tree with leathery leaves. Some species are climbers.

Position in a not too light place.
Height 2-4 m (7-13 ft).
Propagation by cuttings or air layering.

Indian rubber trees divide open-plan offices into individual rooms, break up our living rooms and cheer up our entrance halls, staircases and corridors. In the tropical regions of Asia at least two thousand species grow wild to reach a height of 30 m (100 ft).

Species
Ficus benjamina (weeping fig) is a pretty ornamental shrub. It has slightly drooping branches and oval, pointed leaves 6-10 cm (2-4 in) long.

A rather more spreading shrub is

Ficus elastica 'Decora'

Ficus cannonii, which can grow as tall as 4 m (13 ft). Its short-stemmed bronze foliage, red on the underside, is very striking. This plant grows quickly, and if you want to confine it in a heated room, you had better prune it back severely every year. If you plant the pruned-off pieces in warm soil, they will root like cuttings.

The leaves of *Ficus deltoidea* are only a little smaller. The charm of this species lies in its greeny yellow fruit, only 1 cm (½ in) long. You often get a lot of fruit even on young specimens. This plant comes from the Azores, and grows 50 cm (20 in) high.

Ficus edulis, a shrub with hardly any branches, from New Caledonia, bears edible fruits about the size of peas. Its leaves are bright red when they first appear, later turning brownish green. It needs a rather warm spot and will not bear fruit until well established.

The best known of all is *Ficus elastica*, the true rubber tree, whose

Right: *Ficus elastica* 'Doescheri' (front) and *Ficus benjamina*
Below: *Ficus elastica* 'Variegata'

brilliant, oval and pointed green leaves grow up to 40 cm (16 in). Young leaves are often covered by red stipules, which soon fall. The commonest are the cultivar 'Decora', with shining, dark green leaves and brightly coloured stipules, and the 'Variegata' varieties, with whitish, yellowish or even greyish spots on the leaves.

Ficus lyrata or *pandurata* (the violin case rubber tree or fiddle back fig) has even bigger leaves of up to 50 cm (20 in) long. They are dark

green with light veins. This species is a really high- and wide-growing plant.

If you have a trellis partition in your room, *Ficus pumila* (also called *repens* or *stipulata*) will easily climb up it to a height of 4 m (13 ft). This plant, the creeping fig, has strong tendrils which enable it to climb brick, even concrete, walls. It also makes a good hanging plant. Its leaves are narrow, kidney-shaped and arched. The form 'Minima' has white-green, rather smaller leaves.

Besides the climbing variety, another fine species for decorating a trellis is *Ficus radicans*. This has long, pointed leaves some 5 cm (16 in) long, and roots growing at the leaf nodes with which the shrub clings to the frame.

Ficus rubiginosa (also called *australis*) will thrive even in cold rooms. Its leaves, some 10 cm (4 in) long, are rusty red at first, hairy on the underside and dark green and leathery on top. The form 'Variegata' has yellowish white patches.

Cultivation

Ficus benjamina likes a warm environment—even in winter the room temperature should not fall below 18°C (64°F). In summer it must be shielded from the sun and liberally watered, and it must be sprayed in high temperatures and dry air to prevent the leaves drying out. Fertilize it twice a week, except in winter.

A moist atmosphere in a warmish room is what *Ficus deltoidea* needs; it can tolerate a good deal of sunlight but should be sheltered from the sun in the middle of the day. Spray the plant regularly and from spring to autumn feed it with house plant fertilizers every two months.

Ficus elastica cannot stand cold

water and the other species also prefer being watered and sprayed with tepid water. *Ficus elastica* must also be kept out of draughts. Its ornamental-leaved varieties particularly like a light position. Do not let it get cooler than 10°C (50°F) in winter. It needs plenty of food during the growing period, but little water.

The violin case rubber tree or fiddle back fig can be kept in any normally warm room, but since it does best in a humid atmosphere, spray it often. Maturer plants need fertilizer every fortnight, but not in winter. Their position should be light but not sunny.

The climber *Ficus pumila* will tolerate full sun—though not in the middle of the day. It will also thrive in a dark place. It must have plenty of water in summer, with a tepid spray once a week, and some manure. In winter, it requires less water and no manure at all. It will still require spraying.

All species of the genus *Ficus* grow well in loamy, nutritious soil.

Scale insect and red spider can be a threat to them, and leaf spot diseases can appear as a result of too low a temperature, fluctuating temperatures or draughts. Yellow patches on the edges of the lower leaves are due to excessive cold or damp.

Propagation

Propagation is difficult. Propagation by seeds is more or less out of the question because the seeds will not become fertile, and propagation by cuttings is dubious because of the excessive care required. In the spring, take a cutting from a runner, stem or side shoot, with from two to four leaves, and keep it in a bottle of water in front of a sunny window until it roots. You can also plant the cutting in a mixture of peat and sand and keep it in a bowl on the radiator until it strikes. Put a plastic cover over the top so that the cuttings can root in a constantly humid atmosphere. *Ficus benjamina, elastica* and *lyrata* can also be propagated by air layering.

Left: *Ficus pumila*
Below and right: *Fuchsia*

FUCHSIA

Shrub with very lovely flowers. Popular plant for the balcony.

Position half-shady, in light humus-rich soil with no lime.
Height between 15 cm (6 in) and 5 m (16 ft).
Flowering all seasons, according to species.
Propagation by cuttings.

The fuchsias are shrubs—in rare cases small trees—that come from the upland forests of South and Central America.

We grow only very few of the many species, but experts have reckoned that just those must contain over two thousand varieties. We differentiate between upright and hanging varieties. The upright varieties may be grown as bushes, standards or against walls, as pot plants in a cool greenhouse, or outdoors, the latter as plants for hanging baskets.

Fuchsias are chiefly grown for their attractive pendulous flowers, which consist of a tube ending in four spreading sepals and four overlapping petals forming a bell.

Species
This splendid little tree with a magnificent scent, fuchsia or lilac fuchsia tree (*Fuchsia arborescens*), produces a great many little rose-coloured flowers in hanging panicles from winter to spring. This plant, which looks very attractive growing in a tub, needs unheated rooms during its flowering period, with temperatures of between 8°C and 12°C (46 and 54°F). During the summer it should be planted out in the garden, where it needs nutritious soil.

A rarity among the fuchsias is *Fuchsia corymbiflora*, which blooms on half-shady balconies from mid-summer to autumn. The widely opened flowers, like the reflexed bracts, are brilliant carmine red.

Even in cool climates you can grow *Fuchsia magellanica* in the garden, in the shade of deciduous trees. Even if the upper parts of the plant are killed by frost, they will produce new shoots next season. This species will grow to 1 m (3 ft) high and has long, pointed leaves with reddish veins. The deep red flowers grow on long stems in the leaf shoulders. Seedsmen have developed some lovely varieties of this species. 'Gracilis' is a thin-stemmed, soft-haired plant, not more than 80 cm (32 in) high, with very long purple flowers. 'Madame Cornelissen', which grows to 50-60 cm (20-24 in), has dark green leaves; strange white flowers grow above its brilliant red bracts. 'Riccartonii' has drooping branches with beautiful red pendulous flowers under dark violet bracts.

The dwarf among the fuchsias is the variety 'Tom Thumb', which grows to only about 25 cm (10 in) and is to be found everywhere in the rockery and on the balcony.

Fuchsia procumbens has a low, almost creeping growth; it is one of the few species of this shrub that come from New Zealand. Exceptionally, its flowers have no petals. The long, bluish corolla makes an attractive contrast with its yellow-brown bracts.

Fuchsia triphylla has dark, bronze-coloured leaves and striking orange-red tubular flowers. It is from this species that the racemose fuchsias (*Fuchsia triphylla* hybrids) have been developed. They do well in sunny positions. They bloom from mid-summer to autumn in many combinations of colours, but must be brought indoors before the first frost.

You can enjoy the fuchsia hybrids —also called garden fuchsias—all year round. They are characterized

Below: *Fuchsia procumbens*

as having upright or hanging growth, and as bearing robuster single or double flowers.

Cultivation

Outdoor fuchsias should always have a half-shady place and be mulched in winter to protect the stem and roots from severe frost. Fuchsias on the balcony and indoors also need a half-shady place in summer, but a little morning sun will do no harm. Keep them in light positions in unheated rooms in winter, but do not let the temperature fall below 10°C (50°F) for any length of time. Fuchsias want dry soil in winter, and you should not begin to water them liberally until they begin to shoot. It is a good thing to syringe them frequently in their growth period and flowering period. All fuchsias, indoors or on the balcony or in the garden, are glad of a powerful dose of mineral fertilizer or organic manure in spring.

Propagation

Fuchsias are propagated by cuttings which should be taken six months before you want flowering plants. The cuttings should be kept at about 20°C (68°F).

GREVILLEA

Silk Bark Oak

Evergreen indoor tree.

Position light and cool, in lime-free soil; outdoors in summer.
Height up to 2.5 m (8 ft).
Propagation by seeds or cuttings.

As a house plant, grevillea does not have a particularly silky bark; the

Grevillea robusta

common name really applies more to the mature trees in their natural habitat in Australia. Its leaves, astonishingly like fern fronds, have a silky sheen on the underside, especially when young. They grow about 20 cm (9 in) long, doubly pinnate, green and smooth on top and having silvery hairs below.

Grevillea robusta grows as high as 50 m (164 ft) in Australia, and even in the Mediterranean region there are 20 m (66 ft) specimens. We think of it as no more than an elegant, undemanding pot plant, reaching a height of 2.5 m (8 ft).

Cultivation

A silk bark oak growing in a bowl or tub in the living room or hall during the winter will do best in temperatures between 12-20°C (56-68°F). It likes a light position, but not direct sun because its fern-like leaves fade very easily. If you keep it at temperatures below 15°C (59°F), it will become stunted, but with high temperatures will simply shoot up. If you do not prune it, it will not grow new shoots.

You can stand this decorative, elegantly shaped plant outdoors in the summer in half-shade. Water it

regularly and spray it with the syringe all year round. Repot young plants every year. The ideal soil consists of a mixture of three parts leaf mould, two parts old cow manure, one part coarse sand and some loam. Or simply use a lime-free potting compost.

Propagation
Grevillea is propagated by seeds or cuttings. Sow them in the spring in sandy leaf mould with some peat. Young side shoots are planted in sandy soil in summer.

GUZMANIA

Foliage and flowering evergreen perennial for the conservatory.

Position shady and warm, high humidity, in loose, humus-rich porous soil.
Height up to 60 cm (24 in).
Flowering all seasons.
Propagation by suckers or seeds.

Guzmania comes from the tropical

Left: *Grevillea banksii*
Below: *Guzmania lingulata*

rain forests of South and Central America and cannot normally be raised as a house plant. It has green coloured, elongated and pointed leaves that form a funnel-shaped rosette. One inflorescence grows from each funnel, and according to species it may form a head, a cylinder or a spike. The bracts are often bright red.

Species
During the last decades a number of very beautiful guzmania hybrids have been developed by crossbreeding.

The most common form other than hybrids is *Guzmania lingulata,* which forms leaf rosettes up to 80 cm (32 in) wide. The leaves, 5 cm (2 in) wide, have undersides with reddish brown lines. This species has an erect shape bearing dark red bracts and white flowers.

Guzmania minor has small rosettes made from a large number of narrow green leaves which come to a point and often have a reddish tinge. The white head of flowers is surrounded by bright red bracts.

Guzmania monostachya has an upright inflorescence which grows straight up from the thick, rather spreading rosette of narrow, greeny yellow leaves. The bracts are dark red to blackish at the bottom, becoming bright red further up with pure white flowers which last only a few days.

Guzmania musaica, a native of Colombia has many-leaved rosettes of up to 50 cm (20 in) high. The foliage has a pattern of fine, red-brown lines on the upper side and brown dots underneath. It bears yellow-white flowers enclosed within orange bracts.

Cultivation
These natives of tropical forests need moist, warm air, light without sun, plenty of water and plant food once a fortnight, room temperatures that never fall below 18°C (64°F) even at night, and high humidity.

Guzmania needs to be sprayed frequently, and the pot, containing broken crocks, should stand in a 'footbath'. Before the flowers develop, top up the leaf funnel with water, but stop when the flowers begin to develop.

Propagation
Detach the rooted suckers which will root only in high room temperatures and great humidity. Enthusiasts with few technical resources are advised not to try to grow plants from seed.

GYNURA

Subshrub with decorative foliage and pretty fruits; one climbing species.

Position as light as possible and warm, in nutritious humus-rich soil.
Height up to 1 m (3 ft).
Flowering in autumn, or sometimes in late winter.
Propagation by cuttings.

Gynura comes from the tropical rain forests of Africa and India. Its purple foliage—found only on young plants —has made it very popular, though when in flower it has a disagreeable smell. Gynura is a composite with

Gynura scandens

Harry Smith

angular stems on which large, toothed, velvety leaves grow opposite one another.

Species
Gynura aurantiaca is a subshrub of up to 1 m (3 ft) high, thickly covered with purple hairs, especially on the underside of the leaves. The clusters of yellow flowers do not appear until late autumn.

Gynura scandens, a climbing and hanging subshrub, looks lovely trailing over a bamboo frame. It has dentate leaves on which violet hairs and orange flowers appear.

Cultivation
Gynura prefers as light a position as possible and can even be put out on the balcony in summer. In winter the plants need temperatures of between 15-18°C (59-64°F) with a minimum temperature of 12°C (54°F) at night. Give them plenty of water, and from spring to autumn a generous feeding once a month will ensure lively growth. If they get too much warmth and not enough light, the plants will begin to lose their violet colouring. Make them bushy by repeated cutting back.

Propagation
Cuttings will root easily at any time. Since older specimens lose their colour, it is best to plan for a second growth each year.

HEDERA

Ivy, Pot Ivy, Persian Ivy

Evergreen climbing shrub, ornamental on walls and tree trunks.

Position in half-shade or shade.
Height climbs up to 30 m (98 ft).
Propagation by cuttings.

The ancient Greeks and Romans used to look on ivy as a symbol of gaiety, friendship and fellowship. Even today the darkest, dullest wall looks more friendly with ivy climbing over it, and for this reason this climbing plant has become very popular.

Species
Persian ivy *(Hedera colchica)* has bright triangular or oval leaves 10-25 cm (4-10 in) long, with a dull green, leathery upper surface. The berries are black and round.

The common ivy *(Hedera helix)* has a profusely branching stem. It creeps along the ground or prefers to climb up trees, walls or fences with the aid of aerial roots. As long as the ivy climbs with youthful vigour, its lobed leaves, dark green, and often with

Hedera colchica **'Dentato-variegata'**

white veins, will have from three to five points. Its size ranges from 4-10 cm (1-4 in). As soon as climbing ceases, the leaves will change to their alternative form and become larger and fuller. On the flowering shoots the leaves are oval or diamond-shaped, and duller in colour on the sunny side. These shoots have no aerial roots which will not appear until the plant is eight to ten years old.

There is a wide selection of pot ivy varieties. They include climbing or trailing varieties of the young *Hedera helix*, with leaves between 3-7 cm (1-3 in) long. There are as many leaf patterns as there are varieties: yellow or white spots, or even all-white or yellowish white on a background of green or grey-green.

The white-flowering form of *Hed-era canariensis*, 'Gloire de Marengo', is among varieties suitable for fairly large conservatories.

Cultivation

In the open air ivy creeps along the ground to form a thick carpet. If it meets an obstacle, it simply climbs up it with the aid of its aerial roots. It is easily satisfied. Any soil is suitable as long as it is not too dry. It must have damp soil if it stands in the full sunlight. Ivy grown in a room will thrive even in a shady position.

Leggy plants must be cut back every year at the beginning of the growth period.

As a house plant, ivy makes a good plant for the conservatory, but it also does well in a darker room. If the air

Hedera helix

is dry, you must look out for two pests to which ivy is most susceptible—aphids and red spider.

The ornamental-leaved forms of indoor ivy need rather more warmth than the green. Water them moderately as soon as the soil is dry. Spring to autumn, feed them every three weeks. Pot ivies will overwinter at about 12°C (54°F) in a dryish environment and need only be watered from time to time.

Propagation

You can propagate by planting cuttings from tips of shoots in ordinary garden soil. For a climbing plant take cuttings from the runners, for a bush, cuttings from adult growth. They grow very quickly. Cuttings from pot ivy are more delicate. Keep them under transparent polythene at first.

HIBISCUS

Rose Mallow

Profusely flowering tender evergreen shrub.

Position sunny to half-shady and warm, in loamy soil.
Height up to 2 m (6 ft).
Flowering spring through autumn.
Propagation by shrubby cuttings.

Hibiscus rosa-sinensis **hybrids**

Of all the hibiscus species, *Hibiscus rosa-sinensis* has won a special place among our house plants. A native of South China, it is a rather spreading, evergreen shrub with pointed, bright green leaves and abundant, large trumpet-shaped flowers. Usually these last for only a day, but since the plant goes on producing new buds endlessly, a hibiscus remains in flower from spring to autumn.

Countless hybrids have been bred from *Hibiscus rosa-sinensis,* differing mainly in the shape and colour of the flowers. You can get them with white, yellow, orange, red and pink flowers, and some in double forms. The variety 'Cooperi' is especially well known; its leaves are variegated with dark green, cream, and crimson.

Cultivation
Shelter young hibiscus shrubs from

Hibiscus rosa-sinensis

the full glare of the sun, but let the older specimens enjoy full sun and great warmth, without which they do not flower long. Give them plenty of water and spray them frequently from spring until well into autumn. You can also put them out on the terrace in the rain. During the growth period, from late winter on, feed them every week or their bud formation will be affected. Repot older plants every two or three years, younger plants every year in late winter.

Propagation
You can propagate the hibiscus in early spring by shrubby cuttings, which must be kept under glass with air and soil temperatures at around 25°C (77°F). But be careful to take cuttings from stems that have not yet become completely woody. In autumn you can also begin to propagate by stem cuttings. Take only cuttings without buds.

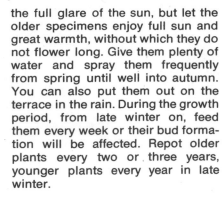

HIPPEASTRUM

Amaryllis, Barbados Lily

Bulb plant with impressive flowers.

Position light and sunny during the growth period, outdoors in summer.
Height 30-60 cm (12-24 in).
Flowering according to species, mostly winter or early spring.
Propagation by offsets.

Flower lovers know the hippeastrum as Barbados lily or more commonly amaryllis, which is incorrect. Hippeastrum comes from America, growing wild in the tropical and subtropical regions, but the house plant is the result of years of breeding.

The result can be seen in *Hippeastrum reticulatum* 'Stratifolium' and in *Hippeastrum vittatum* hybrid which blooms more abundantly than its American ancestors and bears new, bigger, but neater flowers. But in one respect it resembles its American forebears: once a year it must have its rest period, without which the plant will not yield its magnificent flowers. The growth period that follows must also be strictly observed, when it needs plenty of feeding. Each bulb should produce two scapes with four flowers on each. The flowers should point straight out.

Cultivation

During the rest period in autumn, the plant should not be watered, and it needs a warm place where the temperature does not fall below 16°C (61°F). As soon as the first flower shoots appear on the bulb, in winter, put the pot in a light place in the window with a temperature of about 22°C (72°F), but do not start watering until the scape is some 25 cm (10 in) high. By then the hippeastrum can tolerate a rather cooler position,

17-18°C (63-64°F). During or after flowering, the plant produces tall, narrow leaves. The number of scapes produced the following season depends on the number of leaves.

After flowering, cut down the flower scapes just above the bulb, and then you can repot. Do not sink the bulb too deep in the soil; it is best to leave the top half of the bulb uncovered. Whether it is on the window ledge or out of doors, the plant needs a light and sunny position with at least 12°C (54°F) of warmth during the growth period. Water regularly until late summer and, as soon as enough roots have formed, feed twice a week with a complete fertilizer solution. Keep feeding after the flowers have gone and until the leaves begin to yellow and die. Only after this should you stop feeding and gradually reduce watering in autumn. When the three-months-long rest period begins, the plant will have lost its leaves.

Propagation

There is only one method of propagation that can be recommended to the layman, and that is by offsets. New bulbs often form on the bulbs of old pot plants, which, when rooted, can be separated and planted out.

Hippeastrum reticulatum 'Stratifolium'

HOWEA

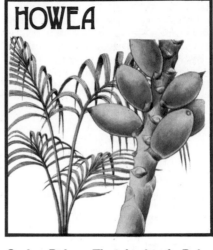

Curly Palm, Thatch Leaf Palm, Kentia Palm

Undemanding indoor palms with bushy pinnate leaves growing close together.

Position shady and moderately warm, in loamy garden soil.
Height up to 3 m (10 ft).
Propagation by seeds.

Howea is a native of the Lord Howe Islands in the Pacific Ocean where it sometimes grows as a mighty tree 15 m (49 ft) high. But the howeas we see in pots and tubs do not generally grow more than 2 m (6 ft) high and rarely as much as 3 m (10 ft). Their orderly, narrow, pinnate leaves grow on slender stems and attract attention by their symmetrical, thick growth. Howeas growing wild develop long flower stems after a number of years, but indoor specimens hardly ever flower.

Species

We know two species of the genus *Howea* which at first glance aren't easy to distinguish. There is probably some interbreeding. *Howea belmoreana* has strongly ribbed pinnate leaves, straight or slightly curved, on short stems.

Howea forsteriana—the curly palm or thatched palm—has a slender stem and long-stemmed leaves. At the bottom of the stem the leaf segments hang down, but farther up they grow out sideways. Their underside is slightly scaly.

Cultivation

The howeas do not need much light

Howea forsteriana

and will thrive even in deep shadow. You can keep them in a room all year round, young plants at about 20°C (68°F), older at 18°C (64°F). In winter the temperature should stay at about 15°C (59°F).

Water liberally, especially in summer, when you must also feed once a week. Give less water from autumn through winter, but do not let the soil dry out. The fronds should be regularly cleaned with a damp cloth and sprayed from time to time.

Propagation

Experts regard raising howeas in a room as difficult. If you want to try, buy some freshly imported seeds in late winter or early spring. Soak them in water at 30°C (86°F) and after two days lay them in a flat bowl of seed compost at a room temperature of 30°C (86°F). When the plantlets are about 5 cm (2 in) long, insert them in small pots and keep them shady, humid and warm. From mid-summer on repot them in bigger pots, but accustom them slowly to the sun. Never water with alkaline water.

IMPATIENS

Busy Lizzie, Touch-Me-Not

Perennial, abundantly flowering pot plant. Very popular for the balcony.

Position light, but not in direct sunlight, in slightly sandy humus-rich soil.
Height up to 50 cm (20 in).
Flowering the whole year.
Propagation by cuttings.

Impatiens walleriana

Impatiens glandulifera

Busy lizzie gets its name from its ability to flower abundantly all year round. In summer you see this tireless plant in boxes on the balcony and bowls in the garden, but do not fail to bring it indoors in winter, for it is very sensitive to cold and will suffer damage from temperatures below 12°C (54°F).

Busy lizzie is the bushy shrub *Impatiens walleriana,* a species of touch-me-not. It has much-branched, fleshy and rather translucent stems and pointed, slightly toothed, light green leaves. Many varieties—and busy lizzie has a great number—have leaves with white patterns. The flat-shaped flowers, which have the spine found in all species of *Impatiens,* for example *Impatiens glandulifera,* grow densely above the foliage and shine in every shade of red.

Well known varieties are 'Firelight' with orange flowers, 'Petersiana' with bronze foliage, and 'Variegata' with white-bordered leaves.

Impatiens walleriana varieties

Cultivation

Busy lizzie likes a warm position but not direct sun. Half-shade is best for it in winter too, when the plant must be kept at temperatures of about 20°C (68°F). If it gets cooler, it will shed its leaves and stop flowering. You should water it liberally, but the root ball should be moist rather than wet or the stems will rot. Despite its continual flowering, the plant needs feeding only during the main growth period, from spring to autumn, and even then only once a week. Repot when it seems to be necessary in light humus-rich earth. Discard the plants when they get too leggy, using the best part of the existing plant to make new plants.

Propagation

You can propagate busy lizzie at any time of the year by cuttings, about 10 cm (4 in) long, which root easily in water or sandy soil. Replant them separately in pots and within four months you will have a new young plant. Pinch out the growing points to encourage bushy growth.

KALANCHOË

Succulent annual or subshrub with abundant flowers.

Position sunny to shady, airy, in loamy garden soil.
Height 10-50 cm (4-20 in).
Flowering winter through spring.
Propagation by seeds or cuttings.

Tropical shrubs or annuals, kalanchoë are notable for the unusual shape and colour of their leaves and flowers. The thick, fleshy leaves mostly grow opposite each other along a strong stem. The white, yellow or red flowers are only small, but they grow in crowded clusters, which gives the impression of luxuriant growth. The species we keep as pot plants grow no more than 50 cm (20 in) high, but become very bushy.

Species

A most popular species is the profusely flowering *Kalanchoë blossfeldiana,* a subshrub some 30 cm (12 in) high with bright red clusters of flowers that grow on such a long stem that they are often used as cut flowers. You can also get a number of

Kalanchoë tomentosa

Kalanchoë blossfeldiana

varieties with yellow, orange and deep red flowers, of which the best known are 'Compacta Liliput' and 'Orange Triumph'.

The abundantly growing *Kalanchoë marmorata,* an annual about 50 cm (20 in) high, flowers in great snow-white clusters. The big, ovate leaves have brownish spots and a jagged edge.

The tiny leaves of *Kalanchoë rhombopilosa* also have red-brown spots. It grows to a maximum of 10 cm (4 in).

The subshrub *Kalanchoë tomentosa,* up to 50 cm (20 in) high, has particularly attractive foliage. The very fleshy leaves, about 6 cm (2 in) long, are covered with a silvery green-grey down, and the jagged edges are speckled with dull red.

Cultivation
The plants must have a light, warm place at a temperature of about 20°C (68°F). They need an airy position and must be kept good and moist. Water them less in winter and keep them at about 10°C (50°F), though *Kalanchoë blossfeldiana,* exceptionally, must overwinter at 15°C (59°F). Between spring and autumn feed the plants every fortnight.

Propagation
The plants can be propagated by seeds in early spring; let them germinate under glass at about 20°C (68°F). You can also take cuttings in the spring or summer; let them dry for a day or two before putting them to root in moist sand and later plant in loamy garden soil.

Bay Laurel, Sweet Bay

Evergreen ornamental shrub, with occasional tiny flowers.

Position sunny and warm, in sandy soil.
Height 2-3 m (6-10 ft).
Propagation by cuttings.

You will find laurel trees all over the world: in gardens, on terraces, in halls or rooms. It is generally cut to form a pyramid or sphere or a tall-stemmed bushy crown.

The bay laurel grows wild in most Mediterranean countries, where it reaches a height of 15 m (49 ft). As a pot plant it will grow to only 2-3 m (6-10 ft). It has decorative, thick, shining foliage. The yellow-green clusters of flowers are insignificant.

Laurus nobilis

Species
Our commonest species is *Laurus nobilis.* Its short-stemmed, oval leaves come to a point at both ends, feel leathery to the touch and have a shiny, dark green surface. The whitish clusters of flowers appear on older specimens in spring.

Laurus azorica, a native of the Canary Islands and the Azores, has bigger, broader leaves. Its foliage is more yellow and less thick.

Cultivation
Laurel trees flourish if they get plenty of air and warmth, so it is best to put them in the garden or on the balcony in late spring and summer. Keep them moist, and spray frequently or the shining leaves will become yellow and dull. In spring and summer feed once a week.

In winter the plants must stand in a light room at about 5°C (41°F). Water meagrely to ensure that they do not form any shoots.

It is usually enough to cut laurel shoots that are growing too long back to the right length at any time, but if, after some years, the plant gets too big for the room, you can cut it back to the desired height in early spring.

Propagation
Laurel trees can be propagated by cuttings; put them to root in moist sand at about 18°C (64°F), autumn to spring. After about a month you can plant the young plants in a pot of sandy garden soil. It will be several years before you get a tree worth looking at.

MARANTA

Arrowroot, Prayer Plant

Difficult luxuriant perennial house plant with strikingly beautiful patterns on the leaves.

Position shady and warm, with high humidity, in porous garden soil.
Height up to 30 cm (12 in).
Propagation by division or cuttings.

Marantas are among the most popular indoor foliage plants because of the extravagant range of colours found on their leaves. Found mainly in the rain forests of Brazil, they bear broad, oval leaves either spread flat over the ground or standing upright. Like its hybrid relatives, the maranta seldom grows to more than 30 cm (12 in).

Only two species are found as house plants, but many attractive varieties have been bred from them. The short-stemmed leaves mostly have strong ribs and are spotted or striped with every conceivable shade of green, red and brown.

Species
The pretty, oval, short-stemmed leaves of *Maranta bicolor* grow up to 15 cm (6 in) long and as much as 11 cm (4 in) broad. The dark green surface is patterned on both sides of the prominent midrib with as many as six dark brown spots. In between, a light green stripe runs along the leaf. The underside of the leaf is coloured red-brown to violet.

Maranta leuconeura has rather narrower leaves, though they still grow up to 15 cm (6 in) long. The upper side of the light green, white-veined leaves has spots of white and dark green. The underside has a bluish green to reddish sheen. The variety 'Kerchoveana' has leaves with

striking patterns: the sea green upper side has regular dark spots on each side of the midrib. The underside is greenish blue spotted with red. The white-ribbed leaves of the variety 'Massangeana' are rather smaller and less pointed, brown spotted on top and red underneath.

Cultivation
A true plant of the tropics, the maranta needs as high a humidity as possible and a constant temperature of 18-22°C (64-72°F) in winter. Always keep the plants moist with tepid water and feed once a fortnight from spring to autumn. Spray frequently.

Propagation
You can separate the rhizomatous roots of luxuriant marantas with a sharp knife at the beginning of spring, and plant them in peat-based compost. Propagation by cuttings is also possible; cut young shoots with two or three leaves from the base of the plant and let them root in damp sand and peat.

Maranta leuconeura 'Fascinator'

MIMOSA

Sensitive Plant, Humble Plant

Decorative subshrub with small flowers.

Position sunny to half-shady, in constantly moist, standard compost; cannot tolerate draughts.
Height 40 cm (16 in).
Flowering in summer.
Propagation by cuttings or seeds.

What florists sell you as mimosa is usually a species of acacia. Mimosa is a decorative, but short-lived, subshrub kept all too seldom as a house plant. The leaves of these easy-to-

care-for plants from South America droop at a touch, and assume the so-called sleeping position. They resume their former position after a short period if left undisturbed. This characteristic will occur only if you keep the plant at a room temperature of 20°C (68°F) and is a daytime only phenomenon.

Mimosa pudica, the humble or sensitive plant, a subshrub just 40 cm (16 in) tall, is the only species in general cultivation. Other varieties need greenhouse care. This attractive plant bears clusters of small, tufted ball-like violet to reddish flowers in summer. Its light green leaves are bipinnate, composed of numerous narrowly elliptic leaflets.

Left and below: *Mimosa pudica*

Cultivation
Mimosa should be kept at temperatures around 20°C (68°F) in summer and some 15°C (59°F) in winter. Water it regularly. It is also sensitive to draughts and smoky rooms. Give it some weak liquid fertilizer about once a week from spring through autumn.

Propagation
Mimosa is propagated by cuttings, which you put under glass in spring, or by seeds, which you lay in little pots in spring and keep at about 20°C (68°F). The seedlings must be kept under glass until established, which should be by about the beginning of summer. Do not prune seedlings, as is often recommended; feed them well instead.

MONSTERA

Swiss Cheese Plant, Shingle Plant

Resistant, evergreen climbing house plant.

Position light, warm but not in direct sunlight, in humus-rich soil.
Height up to 10 m (33 ft).
Propagation by top cuttings or air layering.

The Swiss cheese plant, so called because its leaves are perforated like Gruyère cheese, is perhaps the commonest of all house plants. You will hardly ever see an office or conservatory that does not have one of these semiepiphytic climbing shrubs with evergreen, deeply lobed, perforated leaves standing out on long stalks. This robust and graceful house plant comes from the rain forests of South and Central America, where it generally grows on the branches of trees. It will not grow so big as a house plant as it does in its natural environment, but you will see occasional specimens in botanical gardens, in halls and on landings which are as much as 10 m (33 ft) high.

Mature specimens form smooth, rope-like aerial roots, whose outer layer, the velamen, consists of a spongy tissue that stores up water, and with which the plant can absorb moisture from the air at any time.

You must not on any account cut off the aerial roots. You should either lead them back to the soil in the same pot or lead them into another, where they will immediately turn into ground roots. Or pack damp moss around them to encourage the plant to grow more vigorously. Or simply leave them alone.

Species
Monstera deliciosa grows very strongly. The stem of this shrub very quickly forms wood. The big, dark green, rather leathery leaves grow on long, bare stalks of up to 60 cm (24 in) long. Older plants bear decorative clusters of flowers almost every year; they are surrounded by a creamy spathe almost 20 cm (9 in) long. When the flowers ripen, they produce large numbers of violet, strongly scented, hexagonal berries, which are edible.

The variety 'Borsigiana' grows more quickly than others, and is rather more delicate. Its leaves are not so deeply lobed and less perforated.

Monstera obliqua has long, pointed leaves which have a continuous chain of holes along the border.

Cultivation
Monstera likes warmth, humidity and a light position, but not direct sun. Ideally the room temperature should be between 12-20°C (54-68°F), but brief fluctuations will not do the plant any harm.

If you put the plant in too dark a

Monstera

position, or if the temperature rises too high, the leaves will not develop their characteristic shape. Also, if the highest leaves on a plant are in constant rising warm air, they will not produce the lobes and holes. To restore them to this characteristic shape, transfer the plant to a cooler place.

Water the plant according to its size and give it a frame to climb up in good time. Do not give it much water in winter but feed well in summer. It is a good idea to wipe the big leaves with a damp cloth.

Propagation
If you want to have a fine, bushy indoor plant, remove the top shoot. You can then propagate the plant by air layering. Alternatively you can remove the top cutting, about 1 m (3 ft) long, and plant it in a fairly large pot of garden soil. Do not cut the aerial roots off even the cuttings. The soil should be rich and very coarse and kept good and moist. Stem cuttings laid in damp peat and kept at a temperature of about 30°C (86°F) will quickly root.

MYRTUS

Myrtle

Evergreen ornamental shrub with beautiful, scented flowers and aromatic foliage.

Position sunny and airy, in loamy, lime-free soil.
Height 20-50 cm (9-20 in); rarely, as much as 2 m (6 ft).
Flowering summer and autumn.
Propagation by cuttings.

Myrtle has been a symbolic plant from time immemorial. In olden days it stood for fertility, later for chastity and purity. You may still see brides carrying sprigs in their bridal bouquets.

Most species are natives of the Mediterranean countries where they

Myrtus communis

reach as high as 5 m (16 ft). The only species at all common as a house plant is *Myrtus communis*, common myrtle, whose lanceolate, leathery leaves grow opposite each other on erect branches. They have a shiny, dark green surface and a slightly spicy smell. Large numbers of pretty, short-stemmed flowers appear in the leaf axils in summer and autumn. Numerous yellowish white stamens stand out above the white petals. On older specimens, which can reach 2 m (6 ft) high, little blue-black berries appear in the autumn.

Cultivation

Since myrtles should stand in a sunny, airy, but not too warm place, they do very well in the open air in summer. In winter bring them in to a cool room, with temperatures between 2-10°C (37-50°F). Feed established plants with weak liquid manure at fortnightly intervals during the summer. Water freely in summer, less in winter according to room temperature, giving them just enough to stay moist. Do not let them stand in water or let the root ball dry out. Prune only straggly shoots from the base in spring.

Propagation

You can take cuttings of lateral non-flowering shoots in summer and put them to root in sand under glass. Pot on first in small pots with sandy soil, then in larger pots with loamy soil the following spring. Frequent nipping out of the tips of shoots ensures bushy growth.

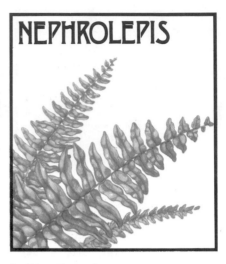

NEPHROLEPIS

Ladder Fern, Sword Fern

Bushy indoor fern with decorative pinnate leaves.

Position half-shady and airy, in humus-rich soil.
Height up to 80 cm (32 in).
Propagation by runners or by spores.

Ferns have always been popular as house plants. Still among the favourites is nephrolepis, the bushy ladder or sword fern with its filigree pinnate leaves. This tropical and subtropical perennial bears light to dark green leaflets on more or less curved fronds which are generally wavy or even crinkly. In older plants they often grow over 1 m (3 ft) long.

Species

The most attractive varieties have been developed from the species *Nephrolepis exaltata*. The individual breeds are mainly distinguished by the variously formed pinnate leaves, which can either be quite smooth or heavily wrinkled.

The best known variety, 'Bostoniensis', has dark green, lanceolate leaves which are simply pinnate. 'Boston Dwarf' has leaves of the same shape but considerably shorter. 'Rooseveltii' has long, wavy leaves, strong and lasting. The bushy variety 'Whitmannii' attracts attention by its prettily crinkled, compound pinnate, light green leaves.

At first sight the species *Nephrolepis cordifolia* is hard to tell from *Nephrolepis exaltata*, but you can recognize it by the tiny storage bulbs growing on long runners. The slender, crowded leaves are generally dark green and have a particularly large number of leaflets in the pinnate leaf.

Cultivation

From spring to autumn the ladder fern must stand in a half-shady, airy place. A north window is ideal. The temperature should not exceed 20°C (68°F), and in winter should not fall below 15°C (59°F). Water freely in summer, less in winter. To prevent the root ball from drying out, put the pot from time to time up to its rim in a basin of water and leave it there for a few hours. Take off dead leaves.

Young plants grow very strongly and must be repotted every year. Repot older plants only every two or three years, preferably in spring. Take great care not to damage the delicate root system when repotting.

Propagation

Detach strong runners from luxuriantly growing ferns and plant them in humus-rich soil. The best periods are spring or early autumn. Or, to ensure strong growth, separate nascent plantlets from the runners (stolons), and pot in peat and sand at greenhouse temperatures of 13°C (55°F).

Many ladder ferns can also be propagated by spores, but this is best left to professionals.

NERIUM

Oleander, Rose Bay

Tender evergreen house plant with fascinating flowers.

Position sunny and airy, in sandy loam.
Height growing wild, up to 4 m (13 ft).
Flowering in summer.
Propagation by cuttings.

If you have ever had a holiday near the Mediterranean, you will know the abundant, scented flowers of the wild oleanders. These bushy shrubs grow up to 4 m (13 ft) high in their own country. They bear white, yellow, pink or red clusters of flowers between shining, bright green, long, pointed leaves.

Indoors, the oleander grows less abundantly. Nor does it flower often, and in rainy summers it scarcely flowers at all.

If you take cuttings for a second growth, be careful! All parts of it are poisonous.

Of the three species, we can grow only one as a pot plant, *Nerium oleander*. When young, its lanceolate-leaved stems are flexible, but later become woody. The delicate clusters of flowers, which appear in summer, are generally pink, but there are also white, yellow or red varieties, some of which bear large double flowers.

Cultivation

The best guarantee of a good show is an airy position in full sun, so in spring and summer you should keep your oleander on the balcony or terrace as much as possible. But the plants cannot tolerate heavy rainfall or the first night frosts. The oleander needs a lot of water and must be fed once a week.

Put the shrubs in a light, airy place all through the winter. Minimum room temperature is 7°C (45°F). Water less in autumn and winter, but do not let the plant dry out.

Propagation

Take stem cuttings in summer, which will root in water or moist sand if protected from the light. Pot on in small pots with sandy loam. Prune flowering shoots frequently to encourage bushy growth.

Left: *Nephrolepis exaltata*
Below: *Nerium oleander* hybrid

Nerium oleander

NERTERA

Bead Plant, Fruiting Duckweed

Creeping, mat-forming perennial herb with striking berries.

Position half-shady, airy and cool, in sandy loam.
Height up to 10 cm (4 in).
Flowering in spring.
Propagation by division.

The bead plant is one of the few house plants grown purely for its ornamental fruits.

The genus includes only a few species, and of those we grow only the South American *Nertera granadensis*. It forms a dense cushion up to 10 cm (4 in) high. The stems are some 20 cm (9 in) long, with tiny oval leaves growing closely along them. This carpet is covered in spring with tiny greenish white flowers.

The bead plant really comes into its own in late summer, when it produces round, scarlet berries which often last well into the winter.

Cultivation
The bead plant will get through the summer unharmed as long as it stands in a light, half-shady, cool and—above all—airy position. A place by an open window, or on the balcony, suits it best. The temperature should not be higher than 16°C (61°F). In winter the plants need a light room with a temperature of about 8°C (46°F). Water regularly, but not too much, in summer, and rather less in winter. Spray frequently, except when the plant is in flower.

Propagation
The plants can be cut into several pieces in late summer or early autumn. Plant these cuttings in small pots with sandy loam. A bit more bottom heat next spring will stimulate abundant fruiting.

NIDULARIUM

Bird's Nest Bromeliad

Low-growing perennial with beautifully coloured leaf rosettes.

Position half-shade and warm, in loose humus-rich soil.
Height up to 30 cm (12 in).
Flowering spring to autumn.
Propagation by offsets.

In its Brazilian homeland nidularium grows in the forks of trees. Indoors it is grown as a hanging or basket plant. The species we cultivate are comparatively small. The narrow leaves of the widely fanned-out rosette seldom grow longer than 30 cm (12 in). The middle of the rosette is often red, and forms a little nest in which the white, blue or reddish flowers grow closely together.

Species
Nidularium fulgens has marbled dark green leaves with brown edges. The inner leaves of its erect rosette range from white to red, and between them a cluster of up to 40 small blue flowers can gather together.

The loosely arranged leaves of *Nidularium innocentii* gleam blue-black but become red at the centre of the rosette. They have toothed edges, and their underside is reddish. The flowers are greeny white.

Cultivation
The rosettes form well in a humid hothouse atmosphere, but will also thrive in a half-shady place in a warm room with high humidity. In summer they need temperatures of at least 22°C (72°F), in winter of at least 15°C (59°F). As with many bromeliads, the soil needs only moderate watering, but some water with the chill off should always stand in the funnel of the rosette. Spray in summer.

Propagation
Older specimens form offsets at the foot of the rosette. To propagate you can cut these with a sharp knife and plant them in loose humus-rich soil. Growth takes place best with some bottom heat and very moist air.

Nidularium innocentii **'Lineatum'**

OPHIOPOGON

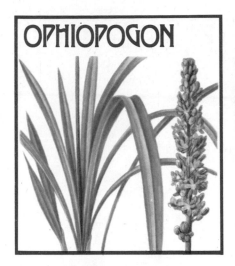

Undemanding indoor perennial with grass-like evergreen leaves.

Position shady, in loamy soil.
Height 15-80 cm (6-32 in).
Flowering in summer.
Propagation by division.

Perhaps the most striking feature of the ophiopogon is its thick, luxuriantly growing, grass-like leaves.

Species
The evergreen leaves of the species *Ophiopogon jaburan*, which comes from Japan, grow up to 40 cm (16 in) long and about 1 cm (½ in) broad. Above the thick heads of older specimens there sometimes appear in summer as many as nine racemes of white or violet flowers. There are several varieties with firm, yellow foliage or with leaves striped and spotted with white and yellow.

Ophiopogon japonicus grows more bushy but considerably lower. Its dark green leaves grow only 15 cm (6 in) long. They are hard and stand erect and close together. The variety 'Variegatus' has white and yellow-striped leaves. Both species and varieties flower white or violet. Small blue-green berries quite often occur.

Cultivation
Ophiopogon does equally well in cool rooms or in warm. Even dry air does it no harm. All that matters is that you should protect it from the full glare of the sun. Water regularly in summer, but just keep the soil slightly moist in winter.

Propagation
The plants of the ophiopogon can be easily divided in late winter or early spring. Plant in small pots of loamy soil.

OPUNTIA

Prickly Pear

Cactus with pretty flowers. Some are hardy.

Position hot and sunny, on rich, open soil.
Height between 5 cm and 5 m (2 in and 16 ft).
Flowering spring and summer.
Propagation by cuttings and seeds.

Even the real cactus experts have not yet managed to classify the immense number of prickly pear cacti or even to make an estimate. There are too many species, too different in size, in appearance, in flowers and in the conditions they need for growth. But they do have one troublesome characteristic, and that is their glochids—tiny spines with a sort of hook at the tip, which break off at a touch and stick in the skin.

The prickly pears originated in America. Today they grow wild in every warm part of the world. The stems are branching and of different shapes—flat, circular stems, for instance, cylindrical stems and globular stems, some erect, some prostrate.

Species
Even as a young plant, *Opuntia azurea* produces a marvellous, fiery red flower. The stems of this species have very few glochids and vary in colour between blue-grey and rusty brown. They have a remarkable long, dark central spike, with a white tip growing from the areoles at the ends of the joints.

Opuntia bergeriana has a red flower 5 cm (2 in) wide that blooms in summer. This plant will grow up to 2 m (6 ft) high in a tub and has broad joints up to 25 cm (10 in) long.

Opuntia microdasys often produces branching shrubs up to 1 m (3 ft) high. The joints are rounded, about 15 cm (6 in) long. The pale yellow flowers, 5 cm (2 in) across, are not so striking and often fail to appear in cultivation.

Cultivation
The prickly pear needs a porous, preferably sandy, loamy soil and a sunny position. Water freely while the plants are growing in spring and summer, and on hot summer days spray as well as water. In the rest period—it generally begins in autumn when the flowers have fallen—reduce watering or even stop it altogether. In winter put the house plants in light, airy, but always cool places at about 8°C (46°F).

Propagation
All species of opuntia can be propagated by cuttings without trouble. Cut a side shoot off in the spring, let the cutting dry a little, then put it in a pot of very sandy soil. Propagation by seeds is possible but calls for a lot of patience as the seeds take a long time to germinate. Soak them in water a day or two before planting.

Opuntia

OXALIS

Perennial for the room and balcony with abundant flowers.

Position half-shady, moist and cool, in sandy, loamy humus-rich soil.
Height up to 20 cm (9 in).
Flowering autumn or, if forced, also in winter.
Propagation by offsets.

A popular plant, because of the superstition that a four-leaved clover brings luck. *Oxalis deppei* looks rather like a four-leaved clover. It is a bulbous perennial with a long, juicy root, originally from Mexico. Its leaves grow on a stem 20 cm (9 in) long and have a brownish patch on each of the four leaflets; the underside of these 'clover leaves' is a silvery grey-green. If you just let the plant grow normally, it will flower in a room or on a balcony in early autumn.

Gardeners have managed to get this 'lucky' flower to bloom in winter. To obtain these flowers, put several offsets in small flower pots in autumn and cover them with about 1 cm ($\frac{1}{2}$ in) of sandy loamy humus-rich soil. Given a temperature of 8°C (46°F) and moderate watering, they soon root, and by early winter the rapidly growing plant will have produced tubular, yellow-throated flowers.

Cultivation
Oxalis deppei is generally kept too warm. You should put it on the north side of the house, preferably in an unheated room or an entrance hall, but in the light. Water regularly in growing and flowering periods. The plant has its rest period in spring, when, if you want to grow it as a normal indoor foliage plant, you can detach the offsets and replant them. After flowering, store the detached suckers until next spring at a temperature just under freezing point.

Propagation
Divide the plants after flowering.

PACHYSTACHYS

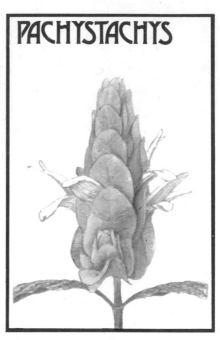

Bushy indoor perennial with abundant flowers and brilliant bracts.

Position half-shady, but light and airy, in ordinary garden soil.
Height up to 50 cm (20 in).
Flowering spring to autumn.
Propagation by cuttings.

These shrubby perennials are about 50 cm (20 in) high, with long, pointed leaves on which the veins are distinctly indented. Growing up from the leaves are a number of erect flower stems, of up to 15 cm (6 in) long. The white flowers last only a short time and then fade, but the golden bracts shine on for weeks.

Cultivation
Pachystachys lutea, the yellow beloperone, needs a light and airy position, but one that is sheltered from the summer sun. Keep the ordinary garden soil moist, and water with lukewarm water.

During the growth and flowering periods, from late winter through autumn, the plants need liquid fertilizer every fortnight. During the rest period give no fertilizer and hardly any water.

Propagation
You can take cuttings 8-10 cm (3-4 in) long in spring and summer. First put them in water, then plant them in sandy soil. Keep the shrubby cuttings under glass or protect them with plastic foil. Repot the young plants in loose garden soil.

Oxalis deppei

PANDANUS

Screw Pine

Evergreen house plant with adventitious roots and attractive leaves.

Position light and warm, in loose, humus-rich soil.
Height up to 150 cm (59 in).
Propagation by seeds, suckers or offsets.

You cannot fail to recognize the screw pine by its long narrow leaves growing spirally up the stem. After about five years the plant lifts itself up out of the ground on strong adventitious roots or aerial roots.

Of more than 500 wild species, some of which grow as high as 20 m (66 ft), only three are common as house plants. They have sword-shaped, variously patterned leaves, some of them growing erect, others bending over to a greater or lesser extent.

Species
The dark green leaves of the shrub *Pandanus sanderi* have white, yellow or light green stripes, and their edges have little red spines. They grow up to 1 m (3 ft) long and 6 cm (2 in) wide.

The spiral growth shows particularly clearly in the leaves of *Pandanus utilis*, which grow 150 cm (59 in) long and 8 cm (3 in) wide. The stiff, blue-green leaf-swords of this indoor tree bear long, red prickles on their edges.

The shrub *Pandanus veitchii* grows equally bushy. The leaves, dark green in the middle with silver margins towards the edges, have only a few spines.

Cultivation
The screw pine needs plenty of light all year round, but no full sun, and high humidity. The right temperature for its position in summer is between 20° and 25°C (68° and 77°F). Water freely in spring and summer, and feed once a week. Give it less water in autumn and winter, and a minimum temperature of 13°C (56°F). Repot mature plants in spring.

Propagation
You can get freshly imported seeds for all species to germinate at 28°C (82°F). *Pandanus sanderi* and *Pandanus veitchii* can also be propagated by offsets. Take cuttings about 20 cm (9 in) long in spring and let them root in sand at 22°C (72°F) until they are well established.

Paphiopedilum callosum

PAPHIOPEDILUM

Slipper Orchid

Evergreen orchid, also suitable as cut flowers and hardy enough to thrive in a temperate room.

Paphiopedilum insigne

Position light and airy, in peat.
Height up to 30 cm (12 in).
Flowering according to species, autumn to spring.
Propagation by division.

While most orchids are hothouse plants, paphiopedilum will often thrive in a temperate room. There are 50 wild species and a number of hybrids.

One part of paphiopedilum's attractive flower, the lip, stands out like a little slipper. Behind this there is a big, vertical spathe, from which two smaller inner spathes grow down sideways. The flower stands at the top of a long scape between leathery, spear-shaped leaves.

Species
The big, brightly coloured flowers of *Paphiopedilum callosum* appear in early spring, growing at the top of a slender scape 30 cm (12 in) high. Behind the rust red lip there is a white spathe with red stripes along it. The side spathes are green, turning to red in the middle and spotted with black at the edges. The blue-green leaves have spots of dark green.

The especially hardy species *Paphiopedilum insigne* will flower throughout the winter if properly looked after. These brilliant orchids, up to 10 cm (4 in) across, have a greeny yellow lip speckled with brown. The vertical spathe, green with a white point, is covered with reddish brown spots. The narrow side spathes are light green, the veins marked out in brown. A number of cultivated varieties have been developed from this species, among which are 'Chantinii' and 'Harefield Hall'.

Cultivation
Paphiopedilum must stand in an airy, light spot, but not in the sun. Night temperatures for *Paphiopedilum callosum* must not fall below 25°C (77°F) in summer or 18°C (64°F) in winter. Cold-house species like *Paphiopedilum insigne* need night temperatures of only 18°C (64°F) in summer and 12°C (54°F) in winter. Always keep the plants well moistened with lukewarm water, and syringe them every day in summer. Water sparingly for three weeks after flowering.

Propagation
Plants that are growing well can be divided in the spring. Plant in loamy leaf mould and in the early stages spray them several times a day.

PARODIA

Globe cactus with brightly coloured spines and magnificent heads of flowers.

Position sunny and warm in loamy soil.
Height up to 20 cm (9 in).
Flowering spring and summer.
Propagation by seeds.

The parodias, which come from South America, have coloured spines, and even as young plants often flower with unusual abundance. There are numerous species, some globular, some growing as straight or twisted columns. Their ribs bear a number of tubercles, from which curved spines often grow. In spring and summer red or yellow flowers, mostly star-shaped and often in groups of two or three together, grow from the top of the cactus.

Species
Parodia aureispina is a globe, 6-8 cm (2-3 in) across, with tubercles on the ribs, which have soft white bristles at the edges and curved yellow spines at the centre. The bright yellow flowers grow to 3 cm (1 in) in diameter.

The species *Parodia chrysacanthion,* 10 cm (4 in) high, grows globular at first but elongates later. The soft, covering spines are golden-yellow and grow to 3 cm (1 in) long. Little yellow flowers grow on the white, downy top of the cactus.

Parodia maasii grows 20 cm (9 in) high and 15 cm (6 in) wide. The yellow-brown spines grow in all directions, with a sharp curve in the middle. The flowers, up to 5 cm (2 in) across, are red brown, red or salmon pink.

A common species is *Parodia microsperma*, a globe cactus 10 cm (4 in) across. Between the light-coloured thorns at the edge of the tubercles grow red-brown central thorns, some of which are long and hooked. This species blooms yellow or orange.

Parodia sanguiniflora is certainly among the loveliest species. The big globe, up to 8 cm (3 in) in size, is covered all over with little tubercles, from each of which grow a great many border spines and four red central spines. The flowers are of various colours—orange, scarlet, red.

Cultivation
Parodia cacti must be kept sunny

and warm in summer, and in winter the temperature must not fall below 10°C (50°F). Water freely in the warm season, preferably with lime-free water. Keep very dry in winter.

Propagation
The parodias can be propagated by seeds, but not with ease. The tiny little seeds must be kept completely in the dark until they germinate. Transplant the seedlings in loam. Keep them under glass at first.

Right: *Passiflora caerulea*
Below: *Parodia aureispina*

PASSIFLORA

Passion Flower

Splendidly flowering, evergreen climbing shrub with twining stems.

Position sunny and airy, in sandy soil.
Height up to 2 m (6 ft).
Flowering spring to autumn.
Propagation by cuttings.

The passion flower is popular for its twining foliage and fascinating flowers. There are over 400 tropical species in the wild and some cultivated species which, when grown as house plants, must be supported by a trellis.

Species
The wide-open stellate flowers of *Passiflora caerulea* have a dense central corona of blue filaments. An extraordinary feature is the protruding triple, dark red style. The broad, stalked leaves have five or seven lobes. Well known varieties are the ivory 'Constance Elliott', and 'Empress Eugénie' with big, reddish or violet flowers.

The big, red flowers of the Brazilian species *Passiflora racemosa,* 10 cm (4 in) wide, grow in loose clusters. The filaments, growing like a wreath, are in shades of blue and white.

Cultivation
After early spring, the best place for a passion flower is in the light and sun of a windowsill. From late spring to autumn you can even put the plants out on the balcony, and during this

time you must water freely and feed once a week. Spray frequently. In winter the soil should be only slightly moist. *Passiflora caerulea* should then be kept as cool as possible, at about 5°C (41°F), but *Passiflora racemosa* needs an overwintering temperature of some 18°C (64°F).

Propagation
Take top cuttings in early spring, and let them root in warm sand under glass. After about eight weeks pot on in sandy soil.

Far right and right: *Pelargonium grandiflorum* **hybrids,** *Pelargonium zonale* **hybrid**
Below: *Passiflora caerulea* **fruits,** *Pelargonium*

PELARGONIUM

Geranium

Perennial shrub or subshrub for house and balcony, as popular for its foliage as its flowers.

Position airy and warm in sun and half-shade, in fairly moist humus-rich soil.
Height up to 2 m (6 ft).
Flowering spring through autumn.
Propagation by cuttings.

There is hardly a hanging basket, window box, or balcony in which geraniums do not appear. With their many quite different species and abundance of cultivated varieties, the geranium can be kept as a cold-house plant, a plant for the living room and as a half-hardy garden plant.

The name 'geranium' is botanically incorrect. What we insist on calling a geranium is a pelargonium in correct botanical terminology.

The genus has too many species, varieties and hybrids to sort out here. Our common house and balcony

plants are not true species but hybrids or crosses.

Regal species

The *Pelargonium grandiflorum* hybrids, also known as regal pelargoniums, are kept indoors all year, though they can summer on the balcony if well sheltered. They have light green, kidney-shaped leaves as big as a hand and slightly toothed at the edges. Plants with a single shoot and usually woody stem, they bear flowers of up to 5 cm (2 in) across, which form dense clusters of pink, red or white with dark spots. Older specimens, from say the fourth or fifth year, slacken their flowering and should be exchanged or renewed from cuttings.

Cultivation of regal species.

These geraniums like moist soil but no standing water. Feed about twice a month as long as they are growing.

THey need light positions both in summer and winter, but should be kept out of the full sun at midday. Keep them cool in winter, at about 12°C (54°F), but do not put them in the cellar as you would with geraniums from the window box.

Propagation of regal species

When the flowers begin to wilt, propagate the hybrids by ripened cuttings, put into sandy soil broken up with peat. Not until then do you give the young plants a warmer position —if possible at temperatures not exceeding 15°C (59°F).

Ivy-leaved species

The *Pelargonium peltatum* hybrids, with their trailing or drooping stems, are ideal for flower baskets or for boxes on the balcony. You can keep them in the open air in summer. They are called ivy-leaved geraniums or pelargoniums on account of their rather thick, smooth and shiny leaves, which look a bit like ivy leaves. They grow on long brittle stalks and are green to greeny brown. They range in colour from white to violet, and in some species the flowers are double. All share a long-lasting inflorescence, usually from spring through autumn.

Cultivation of ivy-leaved species

During their growth period the ivy-leaved geraniums need plenty of water and should be fed about once a fortnight. Remove dead flowers immediately. After the flowering period, cut these subshrubs back a little and then store them dry in a light cellar until late winter. Be care-

ful not to damage the root ball when you come to repot them.

Propagation of ivy-leaved species
Propagate ivy-leaved geraniums in late summer by cuttings; plant them in slightly sandy humus-rich soil and keep them in the shade. They only need very little water. The young plants must be kept light and cool during the winter at about 10°C (50°F).

Zonal species
Most of the geraniums you find on balconies and in gardens are *Pelargonium zonale* hybrids or, otherwise, zonal geraniums. They get their name from the semicircular, brownish mark on their leaves. These little subshrubs have upright, succulent stems which grow woody in older specimens. The little bushes are strongly branched and have round leaves with slight indentation. The characteristic geranium scent is unmistakable; you get it when you rub the leaves between your fingers. Zonal geraniums bear round clusters of flowers in all shades of red, from rose pink to fiery red or violet. Famous varieties include the light pink 'Jean Billis'.

Cultivation and propagation of zonal species
As for ivy-leaved geraniums.

Succulent species
Among the 250 or so species of geranium there are a few succulents, which laymen would hardly expect to see classified as such. They are grown less for their tiny flowers than for their dense foliage. Of these, good examples are *Pelargonium crassicaule,* with a thick, short stem, on the upper half of which grow needle-like leaves, and *Pelargonium ferulaceum,* whose many leaves have silky hairs.

Cultivation of succulent species
Both species are true house plants, preferring a light position and temperatures of between 10° and 15°C (50 and 59°F). During the rest period after flowering, these species should be kept quite dry.

Propagation of succulent species
They are readily grown from seed in sandy, loamy soil.

Nonsucculent species
The rose geranium *(Pelargonium*

Pelargonium peltatum

graveolens) is grown for its scented leaves. This sturdy shrub has five-lobed, hairy blue-green leaves, which smell like roses. This species is kept as a house plant, like the species *Pelargonium radens*, also known as rose geranium. The leaves of *Pelargonium odoratissimum*, the lemon geranium, give off a marvellous scent of lemons. Their attractive, velvety leaves grow on long stems. The light pink flowers of this species, like those of the rose geraniums, are very small.

Propagation of nonsucculent species

The best way to propagate these nonsucculent species is by cuttings, taken in the spring. They develop quickly and soon can be put out in sheltered positions on the balcony. Although they are really house plants, they can be planted out, but must be brought inside in autumn and left to overwinter in a cellar.

Right: *Pelargonium peltatum* **hybrid**
Below: *Pelargonium* **'Mac Mahon'**

Pelargonium **'William Walker'**

112

Pelargonium zonale (upright),
Pelargonium peltatum (hanging),
Petunia, Lobelia

PEPEROMIA

Pepper Elder

Evergreen, sometimes epiphytic indoor plant with beautiful leaves of varying contours.

Position half-shady and warm in sandy garden soil.
Height up to 20 cm (9 in).
Propagation by cuttings.

The pepper elder has become one of the most popular foliage plants. The genus originates in the tropical forests of South America where many of the 400 or so species live on the branches of trees.
   Their fleshy leaves, ornamental or green, smooth or wrinkled, are heart-shaped, round or lobed and grow on a long stalk.

Species
The rounded leaves of the *Peperomia argyreia* grow on red stalks 12 cm (5 in) long. They are greeny brown on top with silvery stripes, and reddish underneath.
   Peperomia caperata has small, heart-shaped wrinkled leaves, marbled light and dark green on top. It bears thin clusters of yellowish white

Peperomia argyreia

flowers on long, red speckled stalks. *Peperomia glabella,* with its twining branches, is often used as a hanging plant. The green leaves are oval.
   The long, white leaf stems of *Peperomia griseo-argentea* have a striking red pattern. The densely growing leaves, roundish to heart-shaped, are irregularly cambered with wavy edges. The upper side gleams silver-grey, the underside is greeny white.
   The broad, oval leaves of *Peperomia obtusifolia* are particularly stiff and leathery. They have a short, red-spotted stem and white flower spikes.

Cultivation
The pepper elder needs a light, warm position out of the sun. Ornamental-leaved species must overwinter at a minimum temperature of 18°C (64°F), the others at about 15°C (59°F). Water regularly but not too much in the summer growth period, feed once a fortnight, and keep the atmosphere moist. In the winter rest period give the plant just enough water to keep the root ball from drying out.

Propagation
You can take stem or leaf cuttings all year round—but only stem cuttings for the ornamental-leaved species. Let them root in peat and sand under glass at 20°C (68°F), and later put the young plants in peat-based compost.

Peperomia griseo-argentea

PHILODENDRON

Sweetheart Vine

Evergreen, climbing foliage plant.

Position half-shady to shady, but light and warm in nourishing humus-rich soil.
Height up to 5 m (16 ft).
Propagation layering or cuttings.

We have many cultivated species of philodendron which differ from one another widely in appearance and in the shape of the leaves. Moreover, these shrubs and trees acquire quite different features as they mature. Many can only be kept as young plants, because later they get too large to keep in a room or to climb. They rarely flower as house plants, but the inflorescence and the brightly coloured surrounding spathe are very attractive.

Species
Philodendron bipinnatifidum needs plenty of room. It has broad, slightly heart-shaped young light green leaves with long stems. Later the leaves become irregular in shape. These are not climbing plants. They have a short, upright stem dotted with the scars of fallen leaves.

Enormous, thin leaves, deeply lobed, and growing on long, spotted stems, distinguish the quick-growing *Philodendron elegans*. This climbing plant from the rain forests of Brazil has aerial roots which you must in no circumstances cut off.

The red-stemmed *Philodendron erubescens* has a great many small aerial roots. This climbing plant has leaves of an elongated heart shape, which on the young plant are reddish. As the plant grows older, the underside of the leaves remains reddish while the upper side changes to dark green. The flowers are particularly beautiful. The characteristic spadix is snow white with a rusty brown spathe behind it.

Philodendron martianum, a non-climbing species with leathery, dark green, shiny leaves, soon grows too big for an ordinary room, but you can often see it as a splendid foliage plant in a conservatory.

The easily cultivated *Philodendron scandens,* or sweetheart vine, is a climbing plant with long, thin stems bearing dark green leaves that are heart-shaped at first and round out as the plant grows older. This plant will quickly twine up a stake padded with moss. Without such support it makes a pretty basket plant.

Cultivation
Philodendrons need positions that are light to half-shady, warm and giving maximum humidity. During their rapid growth they need feeding once a week and plenty of lime-free water. Spray the big leaves frequently and wipe them with a wet cloth once a week. When the plants are resting in winter they do not need much water. Repot younger plants every two years, putting them in open humus-rich soil. Older plants can be repotted at longer intervals.

Propagation
You can propagate older specimens by air layering, which is easier than trying to raise the plants from imported seeds. Propagation by cuttings is difficult, because you have to keep the cuttings under glass, preferably in late spring, for weeks at a temperature of around 30°C (86°F).

PHLEBODIUM

Evergreen perennial fern.

Position shady and warm with high humidity, in coarse compost.
Height up to 150 cm (59 in).
Propagation by division.

When botanical nomenclature was rearranged, one species was withdrawn from the old fern genus *Polypodium* and established as a genus on its own.

Right: *Phlebodium aureum*
Below: *Philodendron erubescens, Philodendron scandens*

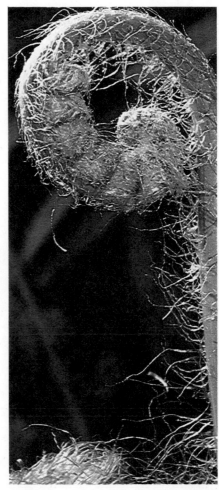

Species
This huge fern, *Phlebodium aureum*, from the Brazilian rain forests has remarkable blue-green leaves. They grow on stalks 50 cm (20 in) long and themselves reach a length of 1 m (3 ft) or more. The evergreen plants grow well in baskets, especially when young.

Besides the true species, there are also two varieties: 'Glaucum crispum' with dark blue, very wrinkled leaves and 'Manalanum' with wavy, deeply lobed pinnate leaves.

Cultivation
Phlebodium plants thrive best in warm rooms or a conservatory. They like high humidity and winter temperatures of not below 20°C (68°F). Always water them with previously boiled water at room temperature.

Propagation
For the indoor gardener the best method is to divide the plants when repotting.

PHOENIX

Date Palm

Evergreen house palm, grown in tubs on the balcony or terrace.

Position sunny and airy, in nutritious, loam-rich soil.
Height outdoors, up to 5 m (15 ft).
Propagation by seeds.

Date palms are easily-cared-for tub plants which do as well indoors as on the balcony or terrace. But keep them away from frost in winter, for these trees from the tropical and subtropical parts of Asia and Africa can only tolerate temperatures of under 10°C (50°F) for a short time. Of the numerous species, including those in botanical gardens, we only keep three. Their stems are covered with the scars of fallen leaves. The evergreen, irregularly pinnate leaves fold inwards and curve backwards and give the trees bushy tops.

Species
Tourists visiting the Canary Islands and seeing the trees of the *Phoenix canariensis* growing up to 15 m (49 ft) tall might not believe that these were the very same plants that they had growing on the balcony at home. This species generally has thick, short trunks and dark green, curved fronds, whose pinnules are folded and somewhat twisted. It needs an airy position in summer so that it can ward off a patchy fungus.

The true date palm, *Phoenix dactylifera,* has a tall stem and blue-green fronds with stiff, strongly folded pinnules. The dwarf date palm, *Phoenix roebelinii,* is a convenient house plant, with short stem and dark green leaves. Its soft and narrow pinnules are arranged on the

Phoenix canariensis, **full size**

fronds in two rows. This species cannot tolerate direct sunlight and needs high humidity all year round.

Cultivation
Apart from the dwarf date palm, all species need sunny positions, with some shade in summer, and plenty of fresh air. Water freely with softened water during the growth period from early spring through summer, and once a week add liquid fertilizer to the water. Wipe the fronds with a damp cloth fairly often, and do not

allow the root ball to dry out. In the rest period in winter give the plant less water and either move it somewhere cooler or arrange for higher humidity in a warm room. The dwarf date palm, exceptionally, needs no cool place to overwinter.

Repot younger specimens every two years into loamy soil, older plants every four. Do this in the spring, and scarcely water at all for a week afterwards.

Propagation
If you really want to grow a date palm yourself, put fresh imported seed to soak in warm water for two days and then sow them in a flat bowl under very little soil, keeping the bottom heat at 25-30°C (77-86°F). When the seedlings appear, lift the seed out carefully and put in small pots, pressing the seedlings down firmly; then put them in a warm, damp place out of the sun. Plants sown in late winter will have advanced far enough by late summer to be transplanted into a tub.

Phoenix dactylifera

Phyllitis scolopendrium

PHYLLITIS

Hart's Tongue Fern

Strong, evergreen perennial fern.

Position half-shady and shady, in moist soil.
Height 20-40 cm (9-16 in).
Propagation by spores, division or leaf cuttings.

The hart's tongue fern is so robust that you can safely keep it in an unheated hall, and it can even overwinter on the balcony. It does equally well in a moderately heated room, but dislikes direct sunlight.

A great number of varieties have been developed from *Phyllitis scolopendrium*. All have blunt leaves, some 40 cm (16 in) long and 5 cm (2 in) wide. The different surfaces of the leaves distinguish the varieties: 'Undulata' has a wavy surface; 'Crispa' has very wrinkled edges to the leaves; and on 'Marginata' the borders of the leaves are patterned. Dark lines of spores can be seen on the underside of the fronds.

Cultivation
The soil for the hart's tongue must always be moist, and in summer the plant should be sprayed frequently. During the growth period add some liquid fertilizer to the water once a month. Give less water in winter. In spring repot in garden soil.

Propagation
Propagate by division in spring. Only the true species can be propagated by spores, and it is a difficult task. The best method of propagating is by leaf cuttings. Tear the bottom ends of leaf stalks from the rhizome and keep them at a constant temperature of about 20°C (61°F). They will not strike for eight or ten weeks.

Left: *Phyllitis scolopendrium*

PILEA

Artillery Plant, Aluminium Plant, Gunpowder Plant, Pistol Plant

Evergreen house plant with patterned leaves but dull flowers.

Position half-shade to shade, in ordinary garden soil.
Height up to 30 cm (12 in).
Propagation by cuttings.

Pileas get their popular names from a curious characteristic: when the small flowers are watered, the ripe buds of the male flowers discharge a cloud of fine pollen all round them. The many species belong in the tropics. They are kept as house plants for their beautiful, oval leaves, which grow transversely on long stems. The plants look prettiest when they are young and bushy. By the time they are three years old they have lost their profusion of leaves.

Species
Pilea cadierei, the aluminium plant, can grow as high as 30 cm (12 in). The dark green upper side of the leaves is speckled with silver; the underside is light green. Insignificant white flowers grow in the leaf shoulders.
Pilea microphylla, the gunpowder or artillery plant, grows 15 cm (6 in) high. Its bright green, elongated leaves grow on branching stems, the light coloured flowers in umbels.

Cultivation
This foliage plant thrives in the half-shade or shade; it can go on the balcony in summer. Let it overwinter in cool or warm rooms at between 8°C and 20°C (46° and 68°F). Keep moist in summer and feed it each week. Give it less water in winter.

Propagation
Put top cuttings about 5 cm (2 in) long into moist warm sand at about 20°C (68°F) to root.

PIPER

Pepper

Undemanding evergreen climber.

Position half-shady and warm, in ordinary garden soil.
Height climbing, up to 2 m (6 ft).
Propagation by cuttings.

Everybody knows about the spice, but the pepper plant is also an attractive house plant. Some species are especially suitable for climbing up walls or for growing in hanging baskets on account of their lengthy, twining shoots, and big, sometimes colourfully patterned leaves.

Species
Black pepper, *Piper nigrum*, is grown commercially in the tropical regions of Asia. Black peppercorns are the round berries of this plant dried while they are still unripe, and white peppercorns the same berries, ripened and peeled. We can grow this species only as an ornamental house plant: it seldom produces its insignificant flowers, and never fruits. The bright green leaves, growing opposite each other on twining stems, are up to 15 cm (6 in) long.
The ornamental pepper, *Piper ornatum*, has heart-shaped, stalked leaves, spotted pink and white on the upper side, red below.

Cultivation
Pepper cannot tolerate full sun, but does well in even a shady place at ordinary room temperatures. *Piper nigrum* must overwinter at not less than 12°C (54°F), *Piper ornatum* at not less than 16°C (61°F). Water normally, but cut down a bit in winter. Feed once a fortnight from spring to autumn, and spray frequently.

Propagation
Group several cuttings together under glass in very light soil in spring and summer. The temperature must be around 25°C (77°F).

PITYROGRAMMA

Gold Fern, Silver Fern

Very ornamental indoor fern.

Position light and half-shady, in humus-rich soil, not too damp.
Height up to 50 cm (20 in).
Propagation by spores.

Pityrogrammas do not need much moisture. They secrete a gold and silver powder which prevents excessive transpiration, and this makes them particularly suitable for keeping in heated rooms. The powder forms only on the underside of the fronds, but drops down on to the other fronds until the whole plant is covered with the resinous dust.

Species
Pityrogramma argentea, a native of South Africa, forms a silver-white powdery deposit under its leaves. These plants, of bushy habit, have red-brown leaf stalks 15-20 cm (6-9 in) long, with fine dark green leaves.
Pityrogramma calomelanos has fronds up to 60 cm (24 in) long, dark green on the upper side and tinged with gold underneath; the triangular leaves grow on black stalks.
The commonest is *Pityrogramma chrysophylla* which has triangular, dark green leaves powdered with golden-yellow underneath. They grow on dark green to black stalks of up to 50 cm (20 in) long.

Cultivation
Pityrogrammas like a lot of light but dislike direct sun. They keep best in a room with temperatures at between 12-15°C (54°-59°F). Only water them if the soil feels dry. Feed every week in summer, every four in winter.

Propagation
Propagation is a job for the experts.

PLATYCERIUM

Stag's Horn Fern, Elk's Horn Fern

Exotic fern with big antler-like leaves. A basket plant.

Position a shady place in the room or conservatory, with a constant temperature and air that is not too dry.
Height 40 cm-2 m (16 in-6 ft).
Propagation by spores or division.

Characteristic of the 20 species of platycerium is the cushion formed by its sterile fronds, which grow in great numbers at the base of the fertile fronds. They die and create a cushion of humus where roots form, fed by the water stored there. The long, narrow, strap-shaped antler-like leaves first stand erect, but later hang down. They are much forked, with a leathery surface, and carry the store of spores.

Species
Platycerium bifurcatum or *alcicorne* comes from Australia. The species which has been subdivided by botanists nowadays appears as *Platycerium bifurcatum, Platycerium stemaria* and *Platycerium vassei.* The fern is covered with a fine white and light grey down which partly disappears as it grows older. The round, sometimes overlapping, sterile fronds, called scale leaves, have a diameter of up to 40 cm (16 in). The antler fronds are doubly or trebly forked; those lowest down grow erect, while those at the top hang down. Spores are stored at the ends of the leaves, which can grow as much as 70 cm (27 in) long.

Platycerium grande grows much bigger. The scale leaves reach a length of 60 cm (24 in). The antler-like leaves hang down as much as 2 m (6 ft) and are many times divided. The spores are found in a big, kidney-shaped area at the base of the first fork.

Cultivation
You can plant stag's horn ferns in baskets or wooden tubs; also in a hole in the side of a biggish bit of moss-filled cork. It is best to hang the containers up with copper wire. Important requirements are porous soil (cow manure, peat, moss, even standard compost), and regular spraying, watering and feeding with a complete fertilizer. The stag's horn fern needs a lot of feeding; you should even push little bits of lightly-manured peat under the scales.

What suits the plants best is a firm position in shade or half-shade, away from draughts, in a normally heated room where the temperature does not fall below 15°C (59°F). It likes humid air, but will tolerate dry temperatures.

Propagation
Propagation by spores is difficult and calls for expert knowledge. Propagation by division is much easier and can be successful at any time of year.

PLECTRANTHUS

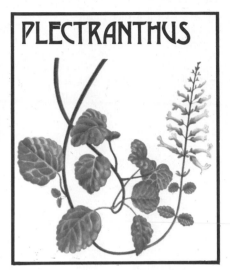

Perennial house plants for cool or warm rooms.

Position sunny or half-shade, in rooms, staircases, offices or entrance-halls.
Height 60-100 cm (24-40 in).
Flowering according to species, early spring or autumn.
Propagation by cuttings.

It is not easy to get hold of a plectranthus. A relatively easy way is to arrange a swap with another enthusiast. There are 120 species growing in Africa and eastern Asia, but only two are common in Europe.

Species
The Germans call *Plectranthus fruticosus* the moth king, not because it attracts moths but because its smell is said to drive them away. Its heart-shaped, toothed leaves give off a strong smell when rubbed. *Plectranthus fruticosus*

Left: *Platycerium bifurcatum*
Below: *Plectranthus oertendahlii*

flowers in light blue panicles in early spring.

Plectranthus oertendahlii is of lower, drooping habit and so makes a good basket plant. The leaves are oval or round, light green and white-veined. Violet flowers appear in short clusters in autumn.

Cultivation

Plectranthus fruticosus will do well in any nutritious soil and grows throughout the year. It flourishes particularly in places such as halls, landings and corridors, where the temperature may drop to about 5°C (41°F). If you wish, though it is not essential, you can put it out on the balcony or the terrace in summer. *Plectranthus oertendahlii,* however, should stay in warmer rooms in the shade. Water freely during spring and summer, but keep the plants just moist in winter.

Propagation

Both species are easily propagated by cuttings: shoots 6-10 cm (2-4 in) long are put in a little bottle of water. They will produce roots in just a few days.

Below and right: *Plumbago auriculata, Plectranthus oertendahlii*

PLUMBAGO

Leadwort

Flowering ornamental shrub which must overwinter in the warm.

Position light, sunny, as sheltered as possible.
Height about 150 cm (59 in).
Flowering in summer.
Propagation by cuttings or seeds.

It is not too easy to grow plumbago, but the plant will repay your care with endless flowering. In summer, even longer in mild, sunny years, the five-petalled, plate-shaped flowers will go on growing together in clusters. Depending on its size, you can grow the plants in pots, baskets, tubs, window boxes or beds. Plumbago is naturally bushy and branching, but by cutting back the side shoots you can train it to grow as a shrubby plant which will take two years to form a crown.

Species

The commonest species grown is *Plumbago auriculata* or *capensis,* which comes from South Africa. It is an upright shrub, but also a climber, with leaves of up to 5 cm (2 in) long. Its weak, floppy stems usually need tying to supports. Its sky blue flowers, with long, viscid calyxes, occur from spring to autumn. The variety 'Alba' bears white blooms. *Plumbago indica* has pink clusters of flowers as does *Plumbago rosea.*

Cultivation

Until they get too big, plumbagos should be kept indoors all year round. Even in winter, when it has lost its leaves, it should stay in the light. You can then cut back and repot in early spring.

In spring and summer it can go out in the open air—on the balcony or terrace—or can be planted out in a flower bed. It does particularly well in the sun, so long as it is well sheltered from the wind. Water it freely at this time and feed once a week with liquid fertilizer. In autumn you must bring the plumbago back into the house to overwinter at 6-8°C (43-46°F). During the winter keep the plants just moist.

Propagation

Propagation is long and wearisome, both by seeds and by cuttings. Amateur gardeners expecting quick results in return for their efforts are advised to leave this plant to those with much greater reserves of patience.

POLYSTICHUM

Shield Fern

Evergreen, hardy fern with luxuriant filigree fronds.

Position half-shady and airy, in moist garden soil containing peat and sand.
Height up to 1 m (3 ft).
Propagation by division or cuttings.

The numerous species of the shield

Polystichum setiferum

fern are at home in almost every part of the world. Most grow as evergreen, hardy outdoor plants, but some are grown as pot plants. The erect fronds of the polystichums, up to 1 m (3 ft) long, grow closely together from thick, scaly roots, and branch out to form compound pinnate leaves with a filigree effect.

Species
The species *Polystichum aculeatum* has hard, lanceolate leaves up to 80 cm (32 in) long, growing on short stalks with brown-red hairs, mostly double pinnate and bright green.

The luxuriant, ovate leaflets of *Polystichum setiferum,* with finely toothed edges, are outstandingly beautiful. There are several varieties with particularly fine, shaped leaflets. Best known are the dark green 'Plumosum Densum', with very delicately constructed, feathery leaves, and 'Proliferum', with very narrow, compound pinnate leaves on which grow small suckers.

Cultivation
Besides a half-shady position in the window, as airy as possible, the shield fern needs a lot of water. Never let it dry out. In winter the temperature must not fall below 10°C (50°F).

Propagation
Propagation is very simple: divide older plants with a sharp knife in autumn and replant. You can take cuttings in autumn from varieties with suckers. Let them root in warm, moist peat at about 20°C (68°F).

Below, left and right: *Primula obconica*

PRIMULA

Fairy Primrose, Chinese Primrose

Perennial house plant with many species, all flowering abundantly.

Position half-shady and cool, in porous soil.
Height up to 40 cm (16 in).
Flowering all the year.
Propagation by seeds.

Primula means 'first' and gets its botanical name because some of the outdoor species, like *Primula auricula*, are among the first plants to flower in the year. While most species are garden or wild flowers, a few can also be kept as pot plants in the living room or on the balcony.

Because one species, *Primula obconica,* contains the hormone primin, the entire genus is regarded with some reserve. Primin induces an allergic reaction in many people, in the form of a skin rash. Although varieties without primin have been bred from *Primula obconica,* they are not as beautiful as the other cultivated forms or as the true species.

Primulas have leaves that form rosettes at ground level, while the shape and colour of the flowers vary. Four species are grown exclusively as house plants but many outdoor species can be grown in pots.

Species
The fairy primrose, *Primula malacoides,* is an annual with many varieties which flower in winter and early spring. The flowers grow in whorls at different heights on long, thin stems. It has mid-green leaves with deckled edges; those by the ground are heart-shaped, while those growing higher up are round. This species flowers in white, pink and crimson and in shades of red to purple violet.

Primula and other spring blooms

Primula obconica can be cultivated to flower at any time of year. It has long-stemmed, soft leaves with a slight down (the source of primin). Umbels of colourful flowers grow on scapes of up to 25 cm (10 in) long. The many varieties have mostly red or blue flowers.

The Chinese primrose *(Primula praenitens* or *sinensis)* has a great many varieties with widely varying flowers. Breeders have even raised Chinese primroses with pink blooms like carnations, but mostly they are cup-shaped with an inflated calyx. The long-stemmed, big, round leaves are toothed at the edges. An outstanding feature is that the whole plant is covered in soft hairs.

Primula × kewensis, an annual obtained by crossing *Primula floribunda* with *Primula verticillata,* bears flowers of plain canary yellow, which grow on long scapes. The plants are covered with a white powder.

Cultivation
Indoor primulas like light but not full sun. The fairy primrose and *Primula obconica* want winter temperatures of not more than 12°C (54°F), the Chinese primrose and *Primula × kewensis* should be kept at about 15°C (59°F). All of them are susceptible to overwet soil and to the root ball drying out. Water them every day. Once the flower stems start to lengthen, give regular weekly liquid feeds. If primulas are kept too warm in winter, they will only flower for a short time. *Primula obconica* should be discarded after flowering, although they can be grown on.

Propagation
Primulas are propagated by seeds. Sow them under glass in seed compost during the growth period, and maintain a temperature of about 16°C (61°F).

Reinwardtia trigyna

REINWARDTIA

Tender evergreen subshrub with many short-lived flowers.

Position half-shady and airy, in sandy garden soil.
Height up to 80 cm (32 in).
Flowering autumn to spring.
Propagation by cuttings.

This subshrub makes no great demands as a house plant. Its display of yellow flowers is charming during the winter. The little flowers grow in clusters in the leaf axils of the upper branches. Although the individual, delicate, stellate flowers last only a few days, the flowering period lasts for several weeks. As soon as one flower withers, the next begins to open.

Species
Reinwardtia tetragyna flowers from autumn to spring. Its bright green, ovate leaves grow opposite each other on the stems.

The light yellow flowers of *Reinwardtia trigyna* reach a diameter of 3 cm (1 in). They grow in the axils of the lanceolate leaves from winter to spring.

Cultivation
The plants must be protected from glaring sunlight and should stand in as airy a position as possible. In summer you can put them out on the balcony. In winter the room temperature must not fall below 10°C (50°F). Water and spray regularly.

Propagation
Take cuttings in early spring, to root in a mixture of peat and sand at 14°C (57°F). Put the plantlets in sandy soil in summer. Pinch out tips in first growing season to make plants bushy.

RHAPHIDOPHORA

Evergreen climbing plant with ornamental leaves.

Position light to half-shady, in porous, humus-rich soil.
Height on a frame, several metres (feet).
Propagation by cuttings.

Botanists have only recently made up their minds about some species of rhaphidophora, and classified the gold-flecked climbing plant.

Whatever the botanists may have called it in the past, this evergreen climbing shrub has long been a popular foliage plant. The rhaphidophoras are very good climbers on a trellis and have pretty, golden-yellow spots or stripes on their leaves, which on older specimens can attain a breadth and length of 50 cm (20 in). Despite intensive efforts, the plants cannot be made to flower—why, no one knows.

Cultivation
Rhaphidophora aurea needs a light position away from direct sun, with plenty of warmth and high humidity. From spring through autumn water moderately and syringe the leaves frequently; occasionally wipe down the leaves of older specimens. During rapid growth the plant will be glad of plenty of fertilizer. In the winter rest period water little and do not feed at all.

Repot young specimens in spring each year, older plants less often. They need good porous soil and a layer of broken crocks in the pot.

Propagation
Rhaphidophora is propagated by cuttings of ripe growth, which will grow best if cut in spring and planted under glass at temperatures of over 20°C (68°F).

RHIPSALIDOPSIS

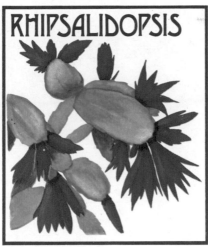

Easter Cactus

Abundantly flowering cactus with leaf-like joints.

Position half-shady, but light and warm, in porous, humus-rich soil.
Height up to 40 cm (16 in).
Flowering spring.
Propagation by cuttings.

The Easter cacti have pendent stems with flat, broad joints which mostly have bristles in their indentations. The little flowers have no crown tube, but radiate fringed petals. In its Brazilian homeland it grows on the branches of trees. Elsewhere it is cultivated mostly as a pot plant.

Species
Rhipsalidopsis gaertneri really forms tiny trees. It is much branched, and its joints are 5 cm (2 in) long and just 2 cm (1 in) wide. It generally flowers in spring, with bright red flowers of up to 4 cm ($1\frac{1}{2}$ in) long growing from areoles at the ends of the joints. There are generally several flowers at a time.

Rather more decorative than *Rhipsalidopsis gaertneri* is its hybrid, *Rhipsalidopsis* × *graeseri*, which bears stiff bristles on the areoles at the ends of its leaf joints. The flowers, which appear in spring, are edged with brilliant red and pink in the middle.

The third, smaller, species, not often grown, is *Rhipsalidopsis rosea,* whose flowers are all pink. It has short, flat leaf joints and at 20 cm (9 in) tall is only about half as big as the other species.

Cultivation
The Easter cactus has a resting period from the fall of its last flower until late summer—or even later for late-flowering plants. During this period put the plant in half-shade and give it little water. The rest period begins when the joints begin to shrink. When these plump out again, begin to water freely and to give the plant repeated doses of cactus fertilizer. The plant will want a warm place at 24-28°C (75-82°F) from now until early winter. Then, until the first buds begin to form in mid-winter, keep the plants cool, preferably on the windowsill in an unheated room, and give them less water. As soon as buds begin to form, water freely again and take the plant back into a heated room. Make a light mark on the plants and do not change their position again. It is quite normal for some buds to fall if a lot of them are forming. Instead of repotting, take up the top layer of soil from the pot and put new soil over the uncovered roots.

Propagation
Unless you are a real cactus expert you should stick to the tried and true method of propagating by cuttings. Plant strong joints in very sandy standard compost and keep the pots under glass at a temperature of around 25°C (77°F). Pot on the plantlets after two months, put them in a warm place and do not give them too much water.

Rhipsalidopsis gaertneri

Rhipsalidopsis rosea

RHODODENDRON

Indoor Azalea, Indian Azalea

Popular evergreen shrub which can be made to flower continuously.

Position until late spring in a cool, light room, then outdoors in a half-shady place, in lime-free soil.
Height 1-2 m (3-6 ft).
Flowering winter or spring.
Propagation by cuttings.

Botanists no longer call these plants azaleas, but prefer rhododendron. Amateur enthusiasts, however, can be expected to stick to the old name.

Indoor azaleas are a special breed. They generally cast their leaves like an old dress, although they are soon replaced. But there are pot azaleas that also do well in the open and will even survive a winter outdoors if planted in a sheltered position. Belgian and German breeders have been especially successful in breeding azaleas as pot plants.

The original plant came from eastern Asia, where it grows in areas of heavy rainfall, covering mountain slopes with great areas of blossom.

The vast number of cultivated hybrids and varieties are known under the general name of 'Indian Azaleas', although the ancestors of our present-day pot plants come from Japan and China. Even the plant's namesake, the true *Azalea indica* (now called *Rhododendron indicum*), came not from India but from Japan, though that was not known when the plant was named.

Cultivation
The azalea needs an acid, damp and porous soil. A good mixture is light,

The rich hues of rhododendron blossoms make it a rewarding house and terrace plant.

lime-free compost and peat. During the flowering period, in winter or spring, the azalea can stand on a window ledge in a living room. But it will thrive only if it is regularly watered with lime-free water.

After flowering, they must go into a cool, light room in which the temperature never exceeds 10°C (50°F). In spring, the plant can be put outdoors in its pot. A few hours of sun during the day will not do it any harm. On very hot days azaleas must be sprayed several times. Take them indoors again in cooler weather into a light, cool room with temperatures of about 5-10°C (41-50°F), and move them back into the living room before they flower.

Repot after flowering every two or three years, but only if the plant is becoming pot-bound. After flowering, feed once a week until the middle of summer, and start again when the plant begins to form its new buds, usually in autumn.

Propagation
After flowering, take half-ripe cuttings and insert in peat and sand at 16°C (61°F). Keep humidity high. The cuttings are often slow to root.

RHOEO

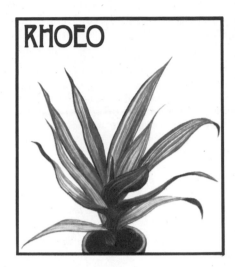

Boat Lily

Evergreen house plant with erect-growing leaf rosettes and insignificant flowers.

Position shady, airy and warm, in ordinary garden soil.
Height up to 30 cm (12 in).
Propagation by seeds or cuttings.

Only one species of this plant from tropical America is at all widespread.

Rhoeo spathacea has narrow lanceolate leaves that grow up to 30 cm (12 in) long and 6 cm (2 in) wide. They grow closely together to form an erect rosette; after a time the lowest leaves bend down a little. The shiny upper sides of the leaves are olive green, the undersides shine reddish violet.

The leaves of the particularly beautiful variety 'Vittatum' are also striped with light yellow. Clusters of little white flowers, framed by slender bracts, grow in the lower leaf axils from late spring to early summer.

Cultivation
The plants are at their best in a shady, warm place. In spring and summer they need comparatively high humidity and very moist soil, and require feeding once a week. In winter they need very little water, otherwise they easily begin to rot. The room temperature in the cold season must be at least 15°C (59°F).

Propagation
You can propagate rhoeos by seeds, which germinate quickly in warm soil at 18-21°C (64-70°F). Propagation by top or stem cuttings is also simple; plant them in moist, warm sand to root and then pot on in standard compost.

RHOICISSUS

Grape Ivy

Evergreen climbing plant with shiny leaves.

Position half-shady and light, in loamy humus-rich soil.
Height climbing 2-3 m (6-10 ft).
Propagation by cuttings.

The grape ivy is one of those house plants that can be kept as well in a centrally heated living room as in a cool entrance hall. It will thrive magnificently as long as the temperature does not fall below 8°C (46°F).

Botanists have kept changing their minds about *Rhoicissus capensis*,

Rhoicissus capensis

the only species that we have and which comes originally from South Africa. Consequently we find this evergreen climbing house plant often called by its old botanical name, *Cissus capensis*, and so included not among the vines but among the wild grapes.

The grape ivy has woody shoots covered with brown hairs, and slightly toothed, heart-shaped, bright green leaves growing on long stalks. In mature specimens these grow 15-20 cm (6-9 in) in size, with some brownish hairs on the underside. Flowers appear only on mature specimens, and form red berries.

Cultivation
If you keep the grape ivy in a warm room, you must give it plenty of water; and because it grows so fast it needs a lot of feeding. Plants in cooler rooms can be watered less. You can put the plants out on the balcony in summer, but not in direct sunlight. Repot younger specimens in humus-rich soil every year in the spring—for older specimens this is only necessary every three or four years.

Propagation
You can propagate at any time of the year by taking a green stem cutting as long as your finger and planting it in a very sandy standard compost. It is best to keep the pot under glass at temperatures of 16-20°C (61-68°F).

SAINTPAULIA

African Violet

Evergreen house plant with numerous flowers.

Position shady, in loose lime-free humus-rich soil at temperatures not below 15°C (59°F).
Height 5-10 cm (2-4 in).
Flowering the whole year.
Propagation by leaf cuttings.

In 1890 a German colonial officer, Walter von Saint Paul-Illaire, discovered the blue-flowered plant saintpaulia in the forests of what is now Tanzania. Since then, in its many varieties, it has become one of our favourite house plants under the name of African violet. The short-stemmed leaves of this evergreen perennial form rosettes at ground level. The flowers grow in loose cymes on short stems only just above the leaves.

Species
Saintpaulia ionantha is almost the only species we have as a house plant. It has thick, fleshy, slightly hairy leaves, shiny green on top and with a reddish gleam below. They grow on short, reddish brown stems and form firm rosettes about 25-30 cm (10-12 in) across. This species flowers violet-blue all year round.

Less common is *Saintpaulia confusa,* with violet flowers and thin, green leaves slightly toothed at the edges. Many cultivated forms have been produced by crossing the above two species, some with single, some with double flowers. They bloom in various shades of blue, red and white.

Cultivation
A plant from the tropical rain forest, the African violet cannot tolerate direct sunlight. Keep them in shade, but with plenty of indirect light—a north window is best. Temperatures should be kept at about 18-20°C (64-68°F) all year round and never under 15°C (59°F). Water the roots with lime-free, tepid water, but never sprinkle the leaves and flowers.

Propagation
Even beginners will easily be able to propagate African violets. You can pull off mature leaves complete with stalk at any time of the year and simply insert them at an angle in sandy soil. Young plants will develop in four to six weeks and you can transplant them singly into small pots. Provide sufficient humidity and invert a jam jar or a transparent plastic bag over the leaf cuttings.

Below: *Saintpaulia ionantha*
Bottom: *Saintpaulia confusa*

SANSEVIERIA

Mother-in-law's Tongue, Snake Plant

Very popular evergreen house plant.

Position sunny or half-shady in a warm room, in loamy, nutritious soil.
Height 20-100 cm (9-40 in).
Propagation by leaf cuttings or division.

The snake plant is the undemanding evergreen that you can see on almost every window ledge, waiting room table or hotel reception desk. It is virtually indestructible so long as the room is kept at temperatures about 10°C (50°F). Sansevieria is stemless and has a creeping rootstock. The tough fibres of its long sword-shaped leaves were once used in tropical Africa to make bowstrings.

Species
The species most commonly seen is *Sansevieria trifasciata,* which sometimes develops several leaves on one shoot; the lower leaves are quite small, the upper look like little swords. They can grow up to 100 cm (40 in) long and 7 cm (3 in) broad. They are green with alternate light and dark transverse stripes. The whitish yellow flowers are strongly scented and attractive and grow in spiky panicles on long stems.

There are many forms of this species: 'Laurentii' has broad, golden-yellow borders to the leaves; 'Hahnii' is grown as a dwarf plant, the leaves growing 20 cm (9 in) high and 35 cm (11 in) wide; 'Golden Hahnii' and 'Silver Hahnii' are equally tiny, with broad golden-yellow or white borders to the leaves.

You can tell *Sansevieria metallica*

Sansevieria trifasciata

by its flat leaves, a good deal broader than other varieties and growing obliquely or horizontally. Its leaves are dark green, edged attractively with orange-brown.

Sansevieria cylindrica has three or four leaves to a shoot; they are round in cross section and can grow to 100 cm (40 in). These leaves are also green and have dark green and whitish grey transverse bands.

Cultivation
All species of mother-in-law's tongue should have a light position in the room. They can even stand in the full light of the sun. Do not keep them in the shade or they will grow too tall too quickly.

Sansevieria tolerates dry, centrally heated air very well, but the lower the temperature the less water you should give the plants.

Water regularly in summer, but never water in the hollows of the stems or the rosettes, or the leaves will begin to rot. To prevent rotting the water should also be a little higher than room temperature.

Propagation
The green varieties of sansevieria are propagated by leaf cuttings. Cut the leaves into sections 10 cm (4 in) long and dip them in powdered charcoal before inserting them in a mixture of coarse sand and peat.

Sansevieria cuttings must always be kept warm—20°C (66°F)—or the propagation will not succeed.

Coloured varieties must be divided. If you try to propagate them by leaf cuttings, only green varieties will grow.

SAXIFRAGA

Saxifrage, Mother of Thousands, Roving Sailor

Low-growing perennial with flowers in long-stemmed panicles.

Position half-shady and airy, in humus-rich soil.
Height up to 50 cm (20 in).
Flowering spring through summer.
Propagation by runners and division.

In its mountainous homelands the saxifrage grows very tall. Of the many wild species we have cultivated only a few, mostly as ground-cover plants in rock gardens.

Although they are outdoor plants, some are also kept as pot plants. They differ from one another considerably in leaf shape and in habit, and their flowers, too, are quite different.

Species
Saxifraga cotyledon has fleshy

leaves of oval or kidney shape. They form several rosettes up to 20 cm (9 in) wide. In summer a number of pointed spikes of small white, stellate flowers spread over them like a roof. The flowers of this hardy perennial, also often grown as a house plant, can grow to 50 cm (20 in).

Saxifraga stolonifera, known as mother of thousands or roving sailor, attracts attention by its long, drooping runners, which look like thin, red threads and bear new plantlets at the end. The big, hairy leaves of the mother plant grow flat, forming a thick cushion. The upper side of the leaves is grey-green and interlaced with light veins; the underside is dotted with red. The small white, red-tipped flowers grow in panicles of up to 40 cm (16 in) tall. The smaller and more tender variety 'Tricolor' is especially colourful, with cream, red and green variegated leaves that have bright red undersides.

Cultivation
The saxifrages cannot stand direct sun, but need plenty of light and air if the leaves are not to grow dull. The plants will do well on a balcony in summer; in winter the temperature must be kept at least 8°C (46°F) for the mother of thousands, but *Saxifraga cotyledon,* being originally an outdoor plant, is more robust. Water the species normally, the varieties a bit more freely. Spray from time to time. Always take off dead heads immediately.

Propagation
Mother of thousands produces well-developed young plantlets on its runners. Cut several of them off and insert them together in a pot in humus-rich garden soil. Propagate *Saxifraga cotyledon* by division.

Schefflera actinophylla

SCHEFFLERA

Evergreen, indoor shrub with radially divided leaves.

Position half-shady and warm, in loamy garden soil.
Height up to 150 cm (59 in).
Propagation by seeds.

In the tropics scheffleras are magnificent trees. The genus comprises over 100 different species in which deeply lobed palmate leaves are characteristic.

Only one species has been developed as a house plant, *Schefflera actinophylla,* from Australia. In its homeland the tree will grow to a height of 40 m (131 ft), but if confined to restricting indoor tubs will attain only 150 cm (59 in) and so is suitable as a house plant.

It is common to find 16 separate leaves, as much as 30 cm (12 in) long, growing on a single stalk. The little red flowers appear on their short stems in spring.

Cultivation
If you want the beautiful foliage to last, you must make quite sure that it is growing at the right temperature: in summer between 12-20°C (54-68°F), in winter preferably 15°C (59°F) and certainly not above 18°C (64°F). Give the plants a light and airy spot, but keep them out of direct sunlight and draughts. They can pass the summer in a sheltered place on the balcony. Water freely from spring to autumn, spray frequently and feed once a week. Water less often in winter, but do not let the root ball dry out.

Propagation
Propagation is possible with freshly imported seeds, but they will only germinate with a bottom heat of 21-24°C (70-75°F).

SCILLA

Squill, Wild Hyacinth

Evergreen house plant with delicate racemes of flowers.

Position sunny and airy, in loamy garden soil.
Height up to 50 cm (20 in).
Flowering spring.
Propagation by division.

You will meet most species of the genus growing as pretty spring flowers out of doors. Almost the only species grown as a house plant is the South African *Scilla violacea,* with its beautifully coloured leaves.

Up to 50 cm (20 in) high, *Scilla violacea* grows short-stalked, broadly lanceolate leaves from a bulb growing above ground; their grey-green upper side is spotted with dark green, the shiny underside is deep red. Little yellowish flowers with purple stamens appear in spring, about 20 flowers sometimes growing together on a single delicate, ornamental spike.

Cultivation
This scilla is very little trouble. It just needs a sunny, airy place at temperatures of between 10-20°C (50-68°F). Keep it good and moist throughout the summer.

In autumn the leaves shrink. Set the bulb with its bottom quarter in light, loamy soil to overwinter either cool or warm. Give it only a little water; then, as soon as the first leaves appear, water a little more.

Propagation
Scillas can be easily propagated by division. Carefully separate young offset bulbs from the plant and put them in loamy soil, where they will soon develop.

SCINDAPSUS

Ivy Arum

Evergreen climbing and hanging plant with colourful leaves.

Position warm room, in light garden soil.
Height 2 m (6 ft).
Propagation by cuttings.

Scindapsus climbs like ivy and has borrowed its popular name from it. Its big, heart-shaped leaves are patterned with silver-white spots.

The only common species is *Scindapsus pictus*. This speckled ivy arum does well as a basket plant.

Cultivation
Ivy arum belongs in a warm room, but dislikes too much light. It cannot tolerate sunlight. Even in places where most plants would die for lack of light, the ivy arum still flourishes. The long, oblique stems can either hang down or can be trained up a frame; ideally it should be a moss-covered stake.

It prefers standard compost, or a humus-rich, porous soil mixture. Water with lukewarm water only when the soil feels dry—too much and too cold water can cause brown spots on the leaves. Overwinter the plants at a temperature of 10-13°C (50-55°F).

Pot on every second or third year in the spring if larger plants are wanted. Give a weak liquid feed once a month regularly during the summer.

Propagation
Not only new shoots but any part of the plant bearing a couple of leaves can be used as cuttings. Insert in peat and sand at a temperature of 21-24°C (70-75°F).

Selaginella martensii

SELAGINELLA

Creeping Moss

Evergreen, fern-like indoor plant.

Position shady and airy, in sandy garden soil.
Height 5-30 cm (2-12 in).
Propagation by division or cuttings.

These evergreen, ornamental perennials belong botanically to the sub-group of moss ferns of which there are over 800 species. Most grow along the ground in the tropical rain forests, but they are also to be found in the Canadian tundra. The creeping mosses are valued as house plants for their foliage. The much-branched stems are covered with tiny leaves. Delicate leaf heads grow at the ends of the branches.

Species
Selaginella apoda grows as a mat-like trailer only 5 cm (2 in) high. An undemanding creeping moss of greeny yellow, it is also well suited to cultivation in the cold greenhouse.

The leaves of *Selaginella kraussiana* are bright green. The stems grow to 25 cm (10 in) long, but creep close to the ground. Particularly pretty varieties are the yellow 'Aurea' and 'Variegata', whose leaves have white tips.

Selaginella martensii has erect growing stems of up to 30 cm (12 in) long. The leaves of the species are green, with a shiny surface. A very popular variety is 'Watsonia', with silver tips to the leaves.

Cultivation
All species of creeping moss need a shady, airy place. The species mentioned above can thrive at temperatures of between 5-20°C (41-68°F). *Selaginella apoda* can stand in a fairly cool spot; *Selaginella martensii* prefers more warmth, from about 12°C (54°F). Water with water as free from lime as possible; keep the plants not too moist and not too dry, and spray fairly often to raise humidity. Feed every fortnight in the summer growth period.

Propagation
Propagate *Selaginella apoda* by division. Take cuttings from the other species and put them to root in damp, warm soil. Replant divided parts or new plantlets in sandy soil.

Harry Smith

SENECIO

Cineraria, Dusty Miller

Flowering house plant, generally only annual.

Position in the sunlight, with plenty of water.
Height 40-50 cm (16-20 in).
Flowering spring.
Propagation by seeds.

Cinerarias come originally from the wet, cool hills of the Canary Islands.

Senecio cruentus has large round or heart-shaped leaves with toothed edges and a blue-grey tinge on the underside. The velvety red composite flowers, with red or, less often, yellow centres, grow in clusters.

Its many hybrids flower in every conceivable colour—blue, red and white. They vary tremendously in size, but have the common characteristic that none is worth cultivating after it flowers. Generally the plants die off and have to be thrown away.

Cultivation
Cinerarias prefer a light position but as cool as possible. You can even put them in front of the window as long as there is no frost. In warm, closed rooms they are a positive magnet for aphids and are also susceptible to grey mould and mildew. You will be able to enjoy them longest if you keep them at temperatures of about 15°C (59°F). Keep them even cooler before the flowering period.

Propagation
Cinerarias are only annuals as a rule —even if the experts often write about them as perennials. Seeds, either collected from the plant or simply bought, will give you young plants without any trouble. Sow them in summer, prick them out once and then insert them in pots of 13 cm (5 in) diameter.

SINNINGIA

Gloxinia

Perennial house plant with brilliant, velvety flowers and soft, hairy leaves.

Position light and half-shady, in loose standard compost.
Height 3-30 cm (1-12 in).
Flowering all the year round, depending on species.
Propagation by seeds and cuttings.

Imported from Brazil at the beginning of the last century, the gloxinia commemorates two important botanists: Benjamin Per Gloxin, who lived in the 18th century and wrote a standard contemporary work on botany; and Wilhelm Sinning, a gardener of Bonn University, who studied how to breed this tuberous plant.

It is only through breeding that the original small-flowered plants have developed into the extensive collection of large-flowered, attractively leaved varieties which are now so popular as house plants.

Species
Sinningia barbata, a perennial of upright habit with very attractive foliage, blooms at all seasons. The leaves, dark green and shiny on the upper side and red-brown underneath, grow up to 20 cm (9 in) long. It does not lose its leaves in winter. The white bell-shaped flowers are reddish inside.

Sinningia eumorpha is a decorative house plant with almost round, dark green, shiny leaves. It has creamy bell-shaped flowers with a purple and yellow pattern inside. It flowers in summer and autumn.

Most of the gloxinias we see on window ledges and in nurseries are the so-called garden gloxinias or sinningia hybrids. The common name is deceptive; they are not outdoor plants but house plants. From spring to autumn, they flower white, pink, red, blue and violet, and the blossoms often have patterns of stripes or spots. The plants also have ornamental foliage. The hairy leaves of up to 25 cm (10 in) long are dark green and feel silky to the touch. Florists sell early-flowering, mid-flowering and late-flowering varieties.

Sinningia pusilla is a dwarf gloxinia. These little flowers, just 3 cm (1-2 in) high, have tiny round leaves and equally minute violet bell-like flowers with a white throat. Plant clusters of this species together in bowls to show them off to effect.

With its brilliantly coloured leaves and flowers, *Sinningia regina* is the queen of all gloxinias. The rust red, velvety leaves have striking white veins. The flowers, up to 6 cm (2 in) across and nodding from long stems, are mauve, ornamented with a creamy stripe and dark red spots. Most garden hybrids have been crossed between *Sinningia regina* and *Sinningia speciosa,* the original Brazilian plant.

Cultivation
You can keep gloxinias in the living room all year round, provided that you treat them properly. Put the plants in a light place in the room, with high humidity during summer. There is no harm in opening the window on warm summer days to let the plants get some fresh air.

Give them plenty of water during the growth period, but be careful not to leave any standing water in the pot or the roots will start to rot. Cut down watering from after flowering until the leaves have fallen. Then, until mid-winter, put the pot with the tuber in a light, dry place with temperatures of around 15°C (59°F). Finally, take out the old tuber, remove the root system and the old soil, and insert the trimmed tuber in moist peat at 21°C (70°F). Cover it with a shallow layer of soil and water only for a short time. Do not water it again, and then only sparingly, until the first small leaves appear.

Propagation
Sinningias are propagated by seeds, but only with difficulty. It is much easier to buy plants already in flower and then to cultivate the tuber. Propagation by leaf cuttings is also difficult. Put them with their stalks into moist sand and keep them in the shade at temperatures of about 20°C (68°F). Plantlets will develop after about four weeks.

SKIMMIA

SMITHIANTHA

Species
Most hybrids have been developed from *Smithiantha zebrina,* which bears red-yellow flowers, and from the white-flowering species *Smithiantha multiflora.* The juicy leaves are green, often with a pattern of rusty red. But what has made the hybrids so popular is the luxuriant flowering, which lasts to late summer. The flowers are red, pink or yellow, with darker spots on their light-coloured interiors. The best known hybrids are 'Discolor', 'Golden King', 'Nana' and 'Splendens'.

Hardy evergreen, flowering shrub with brightly coloured ornamental berries.

Position sunny to half-shady, in loamy soil.
Height up to 150 cm (59 in).
Flowering spring.
Propagation by cuttings.

Both growth and leaves are reminiscent of the laurel bush. Of the different species that grow wild, only one, *Skimmia japonica,* is cultivated as a house plant. The leathery, lanceolate or oval leaves of this shrub grow alternately on the much-branched stems. Up to 10 cm (4 in) long, they are light green on top and yellowish green underneath.

Skimmia, up to 150 cm (59 in) high, blooms in spring in long, pale yellow panicles.

If you have both a male and a female plant, round, bright red but inedible berries ripen in the summer, growing in bunches at the end of the branches. They often last until well into the autumn.

Cultivation
Skimmia prefers a light, airy place, but cannot tolerate bright sunlight. You can put it out on a shaded balcony in summer, where you should spray it now and then, and water regularly with lime-free water. In winter keep the plant cool, but away from frosts, and water more sparingly.

Propagation
Take cuttings of half-ripe lateral shoots in autumn, leave them to root in moist, warm sand, then plant in loamy soil.

Skimmia japonica

Tender plant admired as much for its foliage as for its flowers, but which shrivels in autumn.

Position shady, in humus-rich garden soil.
Height up to 70 cm (27 in).
Flowering late summer.
Propagation by division or cuttings.

Like many flowers, smithianthas first attracted attention as house plants when breeders began to crossbreed hybrid forms, distinguished as much by their magnificent foliage as by their flowers. Both species and hybrids have stalked, low-growing, rather downy leaves, growing from tuberous rhizomes. The heart-shaped leaves shrivel in the autumn. The slender blossoms hang down, with an upturned fringe, forming loose clusters above the brownish green stems.

Cultivation
Smithianthas must have a light but shady position, if possible with high humidity. It is important to keep them out of draughts. Keep them at a constant temperature and water moderately with lukewarm water. When the leaves begin to shrivel in the autumn, leave the rhizome to overwinter in dry soil at at least 12°C (54°F). In early spring put the rhizome in new, humus-rich soil and cover it to a depth of at least 2 cm (1 in). Keep in as warm a place as possible—at least 20°C (68°F)—until the plant flowers. During this period feed every fortnight.

Propagation
The rhizomes can be cut into pieces of about 5 cm (2 in) long and left to root—several pieces to one small pot. Later, pot on in a larger pot with humus-rich soil.

Propagation by leaf cuttings is also possible. Let the stalkless leaves root in warm sand, then replant the young plants in soil.

SOLANUM

Winter Cherry, Jerusalem Cherry

Subshrubs and shrubs with bright ornamental berries. A good plant for pot or tub.

Position sunny and airy, in loamy or ordinary garden soil.
Height up to 1 m (3 ft).
Flowering summer.
Propagation by seeds or cuttings.

Many of this numerous and universal genus are cultivated as important food crops. The two best known are the potato and the tomato. The brightly coloured berries are pretty but inedible.

Species

The subshrub *Solanum capsicastrum,* the winter cherry, comes from South America. Its light grey, hairy branches, up to 50 cm (20 in) high, bear elongated leaves with slightly wavy edges. In the variety 'Variegatum' they are marbled with white. Densely growing clusters of flowers precede the ripe, round, orange-red fruits which appear in winter.

Solanum pseudocapsicum, the Jerusalem cherry, grows up to 1 m (3 ft) high. The stalked, lanceolate leaves grow separately on green branches. Small, slightly drooping flowers generally hang in groups of three. The round fruits are orange.

Cultivation

The plants like plenty of sun and air. In summer they will do well on the balcony, and even if they get somewhat unsightly in winter, they will revive by the following summer if you keep them in a light place at about 8°C (46°F) and water them less than in summer. Feed and spray in spring and summer to encourage fruiting.

Propagation

Let the seeds germinate at about 18°C (64°F), in late winter or spring. Or take cuttings of side shoots in spring or summer and insert in a mixture of peat and sand at 13-16°C (55-61°F).

Left: *Solanum capsicastrum*
Below, left and right: *Solanum pseudocapsicum, Sparmannia africana*

SPARMANNIA

African Hemp, Linden Tree

Evergreen, flowering indoor shrub.

Position half-shady and light, in nutritious, porous soil.
Height 60 cm (24 in).
Flowering late winter and spring.
Propagation by cuttings.

African hemp is an extravagant indulgence, not because it is expensive, but because these evergreen shrubs grow quickly, last for years and require a great deal of room.

We cultivate only one species, *Sparmannia africana,* whose hairy, lime-green leaves of up to 60 cm (24 in) long grow on long stalks. Properly looked after, it will flower winter and spring. The white, stalked flowers grow in cymes and are remarkable for their groups of yellow and rusty brown stamens. If you touch the stamens gently, they will automatically open out.

Cultivation

African hemps are strong growers, and so need nutritious soil manured every fortnight. Their large leaves lose a lot of water by transpiration, so during their growth period, from late winter to autumn, water them liberally. Give them less water in the three months of the rest period, but be careful not to allow the root ball to get dry.

In summer African hemps want a warm, half-shady but light position. You can put them out on the balcony, but be careful to shield them from draughts. In winter keep the plants in unheated rooms at temperatures of around 10°C (50°F). Repot after flowering every two or three years. If they are getting too big you can prune the plants after the flowering period.

Ventilate freely during the spring and summer to ensure that the atmosphere is not too humid.

Propagation

Take shrubby cuttings with three or four leaves from flower stems and put them in sandy soil. To stop the cuttings drying out, trim the leaves a little. Put the cuttings in their pot under glass at temperatures of around 20°C (68°F) and stand them in half-shade. The cuttings form roots after about two weeks and can be potted on after two weeks more. Even as young plants, African hemp must always stand in the light or the leaves will turn yellow or actually drop. Revive the plants by restoring proper treatment.

Spathiphyllum floribundum

Stephanotis floribunda

SPATHIPHYLLUM

Peace Lily

Evergreen house plant with brilliant spathes and scented flowers.

Position warm, but not in sunlight.
Height 25-80 cm (10-32 in).
Flowering at any season.
Propagation by division and seeds.

Spathiphyllum has become a popular house plant due to its brilliant spathes. Small, scented, white or green flowers grow on greenish or pale yellow stems. Brilliant white spathes half enclose the spadix. It flowers mostly in spring and summer, but also at other seasons.

Species

Spathiphyllum cannifolium has rounded, evergreen leaves some 20 cm (9 in) long. It grows well in shade, but the temperature must not fall below 18°C (64°F). The spathe is greenish on the outside and white on the inside. The spadix, 10 cm (4 in) long, is green and yellowish.

Spathiphyllum floribundum only grows about 30 cm (12 in) high. Its leaves are a velvety green, and the curved spathe is pale yellow as are the flowers on the green spadix.

Spathiphyllum kochii has thin leaves, growing on long, light-speckled stalks. The spathe, greenish at first, later white, half encloses the 6 cm (2 in) long spadix with its yellow flowers.

Cultivation

Spathiphyllum does best in the greenhouse at temperatures of between 18-20°C (64-68°F), if the humidity is high.

Propagation

You can propagate by division in the spring, or by seeds under glass at temperatures of around 30°C (86°F).

STEPHANOTIS

Madagascar Jasmine, Clustered Wax Flower

Evergreen climbing shrub with highly scented flowers.

Position half-shady and warm, in sandy loam.
Height up to 4 m (13 ft).
Flowering summer and autumn.
Propagation by cuttings.

The supple stems of this long, climbing and twining plant make an attractive decoration for a flower wall or trellis.

Stephanotis comprises only a few species, and only one, *Stephanotis floribunda,* is cultivated. It comes from the Malagasy Republic (formerly Madagascar). Its short-stemmed, opposite-growing leaves are up to 9 cm (3 in) long and 5 cm (2 in) wide. The foliage is leathery, with a shiny green surface, and often comes to a thorny point. Stephanotis produces stellate, highly scented flowers. They may be as much as 5 cm (2 in) across, with white, waxy petals. They are very much like jasmine, both in colour and in scent.

Cultivation

Stephanotis needs a lot of light, but no strong sunlight, and plenty of fresh air. Water freely in spring and summer, feed every two weeks and spray frequently. In winter give it less water, and do be careful about the temperature, which on no account should fall below 14°C (57°F). Always leave the pot in the same place and avoid draughts and fluctuations of temperature.

Propagation

Stem cuttings are best taken in late winter at a heat of at least 25°C (77°F) to make them root. After about a month you can put the plantlets in sandy loam and keep them at about 12°C (54°F).

Stephanotis floribunda

STRELITZIA

Bird of Paradise Flower, Bird's Tongue Flower

Evergreen house plant with attractive flowers.

Position sunny and airy, in sandy loam.
Height up to 2 m (6 ft).
Flowering winter through summer.
Propagation by seeds or division.

In South Africa and the Canary Islands some strelitzias grow into tall splendidly flowering trees. In a cool climate they will only flourish as fine trees in greenhouses. One particu-larly beautiful flowering species makes a very good pot plant for the living room. This is the bird of paradise flower, *Strelitzia reginae,* which can grow to 2 m (6 ft) high. Its large, oval leaves grow on long stems and have a leathery upper surface. Up to eight flowers grow in a greeny reddish spathe that sticks out horizontally like a little boat. The outer bracts are yellow to orange, the narrower, inner bracts bright blue. The flowers will last for weeks.

Cultivation
The bird of paradise flower thrives best in sunny, airy rooms at temperatures of 8°C-14°C (46-57°F). Water it freely all year round and feed frequently until it flowers. If you want the flowers to open early, put the plant somewhere cooler in the autumn and water sparingly.

Propagation
Use only freshly imported seeds for sowing to ensure fertility. If you make sure that the seedbed is always kept at a high bottom heat of 20-25°C (68-77°F), you will get the first flowers after some three years.

Propagation by division is simpler. It is most successful if done in spring or summer.

Strelitzia reginae

STREPTOCARPUS

Cape Primrose

Abundantly flowering evergreen tender perennial.

Position light, but not in direct sunlight, and out of draughts.
Height up to 35 cm (14 in).
Flowering spring and summer.
Propagation by seeds or leaf cuttings.

There are nearly 80 tropical species in the rain forests round the Indian Ocean, but we grow only naturalized hybrids as house plants.

There are many cultivated forms, flowering in all colours from white to violet, but not in yellow; there are

Streptocarpus **hybrid**

also many bicoloured varieties. The flowers are bell-shaped or tubular, and generally with a deckled edge. The leaves form rosettes immediately above the ground, while the flowers grow on long scapes. The pods are twisted like corkscrews.

Cultivation
While it is in flower, the cape primrose prefers warm, half-shady places. It needs high humidity and cannot tolerate draughts. The best potting soil is a mixture of loose humus and peat and sand. Water the plant freely while it is in flower, but in the rest period in late autumn and winter give hardly any at all. During the winter, put it in a cool room with a temperature of 10°-12°C (50-54°F). Repot yearly.

Propagation
Propagation by seeds is difficult because the seeds are very fine and must be pricked out several times. Sow them on top of the soil 18°C (64°F) and do not cover them. Sowing in late winter gives flowers in mid-summer. To get early flowers you must sow in the summer of the previous year. Water seedlings only sparingly. Propagation by leaf cuttings is simpler.

Streptocarpus hybrid

SYNGONIUM

Evergreen climbing shrub with big leaves.

Position half-shady and shady, warm with high humidity, in porous, humus-rich soil.
Height climbing, up to 2 m (6 ft).
Propagation by cuttings.

The leaves and stems of syngoniums contain a harmless, milky sap. It is a long-lived foliage plant, which you can train up a frame or have hanging from baskets. At the nodes of the shoots the plants form aerial roots which you must on no account remove. A remarkable thing about these plants is that the leaves of young plants are lance-shaped, but

Syngonium podophyllum 'Albolineatum'

as they grow older the plants begin to develop complex lobed leaves.

Only established plants flower. As in all members of the arum family, the spadices are framed by spathes, basically of purple-red.

Species
Syngonium podophyllum has a slender stem. The leaves of older plants have long stalks, often enclosed in a sheath. The light green leaves have up to 11 lobes. In contrast, *Syngonium vellozianum* has a much-branched stem and less pale, green leaves; those on the older plants have only five lobes. This species has thick leaves on very long stalks.

Cultivation
Syngonium podophyllum is a foliage plant for warm rooms with high humidity. The best place for it is in a north-facing conservatory, for the plants must not have any direct sunlight. Water freely with lime-free, lukewarm water, and feed once a week to stimulate growth. Reduce the water a little in winter. Repot every year in spring. Use a big pot to accommodate the roots and coarse, porous, humus-rich soil.

Propagation
To propagate syngoniums, take top cuttings in the spring, which will root quickly in sandy compost at temperatures of around 25°C (77°F). Put the young plants in a big pot and keep them at a temperature of 20°C (68°F) under glass. They must be gradually accustomed to the normal tempera-. ture of the room.

THUNBERGIA

Black-eyed Susan

Climbing plant with attractive flowers.

Position sunny, in loamy soil.
Height up to 2 m (6 ft).
Flowering spring and autumn.
Propagation by seeds or cuttings.

Most species can be seen only in botanical gardens. These climbers and shrubs all need the sort of climate that prevails in their African or Asian homeland. However, there are exceptions. They are handsome flowers which are composed of a distinct tube expanding into five rounded, petal-like lobes at the mouth.

Species
Black-eyed Susan, *Thunbergia alata,* is a common plant for the balcony. This annual, which is just as popular as a climbing or hanging plant, comes in a number of varieties, with different-coloured flowers. The colours range from white through bright yellow and orange to brick-red. The stems will climb up to 2 m (6 ft) and bear long-stalked, round or heart-shaped leaves with prominent veins. The black or chocolate brown spot always shining in the middle of the flower gives the plant its name.

Another species, the evergreen climber, *Thunbergia laurifolia,* has recently made its appearance as a house plant. Its flowers are pale violet and cluster in the axils of long, pointed leaves.

Cultivation
Thunbergia alata needs a warm, sunny position. The plants require a well-lit position, but should be lightly shaded during the hottest summer months. It thrives particularly on the balcony, for it likes fresh air. If it has to stay indoors during the summer, ventilate the house when the temperature exceeds 16°C (61°F). It is generally only grown as an annual, but you can get it to overwinter in a light room at about 12°C (54°F), pruning severely in late winter. *Thunbergia laurifolia* can only be grown in light, warm conservatories. Both species must be watered regularly during the growing period and fed once a week. Water *Thunbergia alata* more sparingly in winter keeping the plant just moist. Train these self-clinging climbers against strings or wires

Propagation
Thunbergia alata is sown in late winter at about 20°C (68°F). Prick out seedlings and put them in little pots of loamy soil. If possible, put them on the balcony from spring on. Flowering will begin after three months.

Cuttings taken from *Thunbergia laurifolia* will root in warm, moist sand under glass. Later, put them in little pots, or plant them out in the conservatory.

Thunbergia alata

Tillandsia cyanea

TILLANDSIA

Decorative evergreen house plant.

Position half-shady and warm.
Height up to 30 cm (12 in).
Flowering summer.
Propagation by suckers or division.

Of the tillandsias suitable as house plants, most do best if grown on a branch or stake.

Species
Tillandsia cyanea is valued for its attractive flowers. Pink and mauve bracts grow on a short stem, overlapping one another like scales, and between them, one after another, the great blue flowers appear. Narrow green leaves with red stripes form a rosette around the flowers.

Tillandsia lindenii looks much like *Tillandsia cyanea.* But you can distinguish it by the flower spike standing a long way clear of the leaf rosette, and the light orange bracts.

Another species is Spanish moss or *tillandsia usneoides.* This epiphyte has no roots but twining, thread-like stems with very small, narrow leaves covered with silvery scales and bright yellow-green flowers.

Cultivation
All tillandsias, grown in pots or as epiphytes on a stake, must be kept half-shady and warm, with high humidity. In winter the temperature must not fall below 15°C (59°F), or 12°C (54°F) at night. Give the pot plants plenty of water in summer, less in winter.

Propagation
Some tillandsias form suckers, which you can carefully separate from the mother plant and pot. All species can also be propagated by division.

TOLMIEA

Piggyback Plant, Youth-on-Age

Hardy indoor perennial with tubular flowers.

Position shady and cool in humus-rich soil.
Height up to 30 cm (12 in).
Flowering late spring and early summer.
Propagation by cuttings, air layering, or division.

Every amateur gardener, no matter how inexperienced, can get pleasure from tolmieas. This little North American woodland plant will last for many years by producing young plants of its own accord.
The only species, *Tolmiea menziesii*, more popularly piggyback plant or youth-on-age, continuously produces little buds in the indentations of its long-stemmed, round leaves. When the leaves of the main plant start to wilt, young plants with roots of their own are already forming from the buds. Loose brownish orange flowers cluster between the sappy green leaves.

Cultivation
Tolmiea cannot tolerate sunlight and prefers temperatures of around 10°C (50°F) if it is not to be attacked by lice. The plant needs plenty of water and weekly feeding during the summer. Water less in winter and keep it somewhere cooler but free from frost.

Propagation
The buds on the already developed plantlets can be separated from the mother plant and potted in humus-rich soil. Or stems can be pegged down and cut off when rooted. Older plants can also be propagated by division.

TRACHYCARPUS

Chusan Palm, Fan Palm

Hardy evergreen, slow-growing fan-shaped palm.

Position light and half-shady, in rich, peaty loam.
Height up to 4 m (13 ft).
Propagation by seeds or suckers.

In districts with a mild climate you can take the risk of growing a chusan palm outdoors. It will even tolerate a few degrees of frost.
Of the six species of these fan palms native to central and eastern Asia, we cultivate only one, *Trachycarpus fortunei*. The stems are covered with little, pointed knobs, and a big, almost circular leaf, 80-100 cm (32-40 in) wide, grows at the end of each. These leaves are divided into segments some 50-60 cm (20-24 in) deep, which form fans. The little yellow flowers grow in branching panicles.

Trachycarpus fortunei

Harry Smith

145

Cultivation

Palms, especially in small tubs, must be fed regularly from late winter through summer with organic or chemical fertilizers. They need enough water to ensure that the root ball is always fairly moist and never dries out.

The chusan palm is only seldom attacked by pests and diseases.

Propagation

Soak seeds, which must be as fresh as possible, in warm water at 30-35°C (86-95°F) for two days. Then put them in a mixture of sand and leaf mould and keep them constantly moist and warm. The germination period may differ according to the age of the seeds. Carefully pot the seedlings with the seeds still adhering to them; standard compost is best, but after a week or two you must transfer them to a mixture of old leaf or hotbed soil with loam and some sand and horn meal.

Remove suckers with two or three leaves in spring. Pot up in standard compost and root at a temperature of at least 13°C (56°F).

TRADESCANTIA

Wandering Jew, Spiderwort, Widow's Tears, Creeping Sailor, Little Ship

Evergreen flowering perennial.

Position sunny to shady, in sandy standard compost.
Height up to 40 cm (16 in).
Flowering spring.
Propagation by cuttings.

The hardy species are valued in the garden as spiderwort; the house plants, on the other hand, are known as tradescantia. These indestructible, mostly creeping evergreens are suitable for cultivation in baskets and bowls. Their slender, fragile, sappy stems bear oval pointed leaves which partly clasp the stem at the lower end. The leaves grow alternately on nodes. The flowers, surrounded by little bracts, are not particularly striking in themselves.

Species

Tradescantia albiflora, the wandering jew, creeping sailor or widow's tears, has simple green leaves. They grow without stalks on flat stems or hang down from baskets. The white flowers are infrequent. Prettier than the true species is the variety 'Aureovittata', whose leaves have yellow stripes.

Tradescantia blossfeldiana is notable for its hairy leaves, brown hairs on top and red underneath. This plant, generally growing upright to a height of 20 cm (9 in), bears pink flowers with white interiors.

Among the loveliest tradescantias is *Tradescantia crassula,* an upright plant that reaches a height of 40 cm (16 in), with big, shiny leaves and fine white flowers.

Tradescantia fluminensis, similar to *Tradescantia albiflora,* is of creeping or drooping habit. Its little oval leaves are dark green with a slight blue tinge, and violet on the underside. The variety 'Albovittata' is better known; its narrow leaves have white longitudinal stripes. It does well in hydroponics.

Tradescantia navicularis, the 'little ship', is a pretty climbing plant with mauve folded leaves which look like boats. This succulent variety grows slowly and bears pink flowers.

Cultivation

All these species need a warm, light place, but not in direct sun. The colourful species and varieties like more warmth. All want a lot of lime-free water and a humus-rich standard compost. Feed with liquid fertilizer every fortnight while they are growing quickly.

Propagation

Propagation is child's play. Take cuttings at any time of the year and insert them either in soil containing peat or in a container of water.

Harry Smith

Tradescantia fluminensis 'Variegata'

VALLOTA

Scarborough Lily

Tender, long-lasting, bulbous plant with lovely funnel-shaped flowers.

Position sunny and warm, in sandy loam.
Height up to 40 cm (16 in).
Flowering spring and summer.
Propagation by offsets or seeds.

Vollota speciosa, the Scarborough lily, from South Africa, bears leaves up to 40 cm (16 in) long and 3 cm (1 in) wide, which grow up from a brown, round or oval bulb and spread out like a fan. In late spring and summer a scape some 30 cm (12 in) tall rises from the middle of the leaves, crowned by a magnificent umbel often containing as many as 10 of the great red trumpet-like flowers. Best known of the different var-

**Below: *Vallota speciosa*
Right: *Veltheimia capensis***

ieties is 'Alba', with white flowers.

Cultivation
The plants need a lot of warmth and sun, with regular watering and weekly feeding until the end of the flowering period. After that, keep light and cool at 5-8°C (41-48°F) and water only a little. Unlike other bulbous plants, the leaves must not be allowed to wither.

When you repot the new young plants in the spring, say every four years, be careful to see that the bulb is only two-thirds covered with soil.

Propagation
Small new bulbs form on the bulb, and in the spring you can carefully detach these and plant them in small pots of sandy loam. If you are sowing, use only fresh seeds and let them germinate in warm soil.

VELTHEIMIA

Undemanding, richly flowering bulbous plant.

Position light and cool, in sandy loam.
Height up to 50 cm (20 in).
Flowering late winter to spring.
Propagation by offsets or seeds.

The South African veltheimia is a genus of few species, and only one, *Veltheimia capensis*, is at all common. It is a 'short-day' flower whose blossoms appear in the cold season and last for weeks.

The little tubular flowers are yellow and green with red dots. They grow in a dense cluster on a tall, bare scape some 50 cm (20 in) high rising straight up from the bluish red bulb between the slightly curved leaves, which are wavy at the edges. They grow up to 25 cm (10 in) long and 10 cm (4 in) wide. In the spring the leaves of this bulbous plant die off.

Cultivation
Veltheimia will produce its loveliest flowers in light, cool rooms at about 12°C (54°F). It needs very little watering—hardly any during its resting period from spring to autumn.

In early autumn clean the bulbs and plant them two-thirds down in sandy loam. After that, water fairly frequently and feed from time to time.

Propagation
When you come to replant the bulbs, carefully remove the small new bulbs and plant them in small pots. They will often flower the same year. Fresh seeds are sown in spring, in warm soil. But if you choose this method of propagation, you will have to wait three years for the first flowers to appear.

VINCA

Periwinkle, Band Plant, Cut Finger

Evergreen subshrub with large flowers. Rewarding basket plant.

Position sunny to shady, in humus-rich garden soil.
Height up to 25 cm (10 in).
Flowering spring.
Propagation by cuttings or division.

In the Mediterranean countries and the tropics this evergreen is a widespread ground-cover plant. Of the few existing species, we mostly cultivate two as plants for the hanging basket and for the balcony. Many hybrids have been produced.

The creeping or hanging branches grow densely and bear oval leaves, elongated in some species, rounded in others. They are leathery to the touch and their upper surface is shiny. Large, tubular flowers in various shades of blue grow on stalks at the leaf shoulders in spring.

Species
Vinca major, called the band plant, cut finger, or greater periwinkle, has branches that grow up to 25 cm (10 in) long. Besides the true green-leaved species there are the varieties 'Reticulata' with yellow-veined leaves, and 'Variegata' whose leaves are bordered or spotted with white.

Vinca minor, lesser periwinkle, tolerates sun as well as shade and is not particularly sensitive to temperature. You can put it out on the balcony in summer when it should be watered freely. Keep it away from frost in winter, at temperatures around 10°C (50°F), and water less.

Propagation
Both these species can easily be propagated by division. You can also take cuttings from *Vinca major* at the end of summer for rooting under glass. *Vinca major* and *minor* often form new roots on their stems.

VRIESEA

House plant with decorative leaf rosettes and flowers.

Position half-shady to shady, warm, in garden soil containing peat.
Height up to 50 cm (20 in).
Flowering according to species, the whole year through.
Propagation by offsets.

The numerous species which grow wild on the branches of trees in South America's primeval forests develop leaf rosettes. The leaves, green or brightly patterned and slightly curved, form a big funnel towards the centre, from which the pretty, flat flower heads emerge on a long scape.

Species
The Brazilian species *Vriesea carinata* is one of the green-leaved vrieseas. The little flowers, flaming red and yellow and coming to a point, grow in a loose cluster on a red stalk.

The light green leaves of *Vriesea fenestralis,* up to 40 cm (16 in) long, have a sort of lattice pattern in dark green, and red spots. The underside

Left: *Vinca minor*
Below: *Vriesea splendens*

of the leaves is scaly. The yellow flowers, up to 7 cm (3 in) wide, with greenish bracts dotted with browny red, stand on a scape 50 cm (20 in) high.

Vriesea splendens is another popular species. Its leaves of up to 50 cm (20 in) long and 5 cm (2 in) broad, have rusty red transverse stripes and form pretty rosettes. The long, lance-shaped inflorescence grows on a green scape; slender yellow flowers peep out from crowded, bright red bracts.

There are also a number of hybrids with yellow, orange or greenish-white inflorescences.

Cultivation
Vrieseas can be grown either as pot plants or as epiphytes on a frame. They need plenty of light and warmth, but no full sun. Overwintering temperatures are: for *Vriesea carinata* 15-18°C (59-64°F); for *Vriesea fenestralis* 18-20°C (64-68°F); and for *Vriesea splendens* also 18-20°C (64-68°F), with night temperatures of not below 12°C (54°F). Water the plants only moderately, but always leave some lukewarm water in the leaf funnel.

Propagation
Like most bromeliads, vrieseas form new little rosettes at the foot of the mother plant. Carefully detach these and let them root in conditions of high humidity and at temperatures of at least 25°C (77°F).

Vriesea carinata

YUCCA

Adam's Needle, Spanish Bayonet

Evergreen stem-forming shrub with abundant leaf formation and scented flowers.

Position sunny and airy, in compost.
Height up to 2 m (6 ft).
Flowering summer.
Propagation by suckers or seeds.

Yucca gets its popular names from the spines on its leaf tips. The species we grow in pots or tubs form scaly stems on which a profusion of long, narrow leaves grow, making them look like palm trees. The big, white, bell-shaped flowers grow in long panicles. They have a powerful scent, especially in the evening.

Species
The dark, hard leaves of the slender *Yucca aloifolia* have a bluish colour

and come to a stiff, reddish brown point. The pale borders of the leaves are slightly toothed. This species often produces dark berries after flowering. Best known of the many varieties are the ornamental-leaved 'Tricolor' and 'Quadricolor'.

Yucca gloriosa, or Adam's Needle, has an exceptionally short stem. The grey-green, supple, sword-like leaves are bordered with reddish brown. The flowers have red stripes and in the course of a year their panicles can reach a height of 2 m (6 ft).

The low-growing *Yucca recurvifolia* is an easy plant to grow. Fibrous threads often grow on the drooping leaves.

Cultivation
Since the yuccas thrive and flower best in a sunny, airy position, put them on the balcony or the terrace in summer. Keep them cool in winter at about 6°C (43°F). Give them plenty of water when in flower and feed them every week. After flowering, give them only a little water to prevent rotting. Repot young plants every year in spring, older plants every three or four years at the same time.

Propagation
Suckers grow thickly over the ground at the base of the stem; detach them carefully from the mother plant and plant them in sandy loam. Fresh seeds can be sown in warm, sandy soil, but it will be some time before the seedlings appear.

Yucca aloifolia

ZANTEDESCHIA

Arum Lily

Perennial with magnificent flowers.

Position sunny and airy, in loamy soil.
Height up to 80 cm (32 in).
Flowering winter and spring.
Propagation by division or seeds.

The arum lily is an extremely attractive aquatic plant from tropical Africa. *Zantedeschia aethiopica* has proved particularly successful as a pot plant. It is grown most for its attractive flowers which also do well when cut. A slender yellow spadix grows at the end of a long, straight stem, surrounded by a huge, white spathe, which makes an asymmetrical funnel, opening upwards and turned down at the rim.

The long-stemmed, slightly wavy leaves are generally heart-shaped and deeply grooved. They grow on the ground, in leaf sheaths which spring from fleshy rhizomes.

Cultivation
The arum lily in flower must be frequently watered and sprayed, and fed with liquid fertilizer once a week. At this time the room temperature must be kept at about 15°C (59°F). During the rest period, in late spring and early summer, let the root ball dry out completely, and keep the plant sunny and warm. A place on the balcony suits it very well. Towards the middle of summer plant in loamy soil and slowly begin watering again. In autumn and early winter keep light and cool at a maximum temperature of 10°C (50°F), then move to a warmer place.

Propagation
You can divide well-developed plants with a sharp knife and plant them out again. If you are propagating by seed, let the seeds germinate in warm soil. The first flowers will only appear after about two years.

Zebrina pendula

ZEBRINA

Trailing perennial with prettily patterned leaves. Good basket plant.

Position sunny or half-shady, warm, in ordinary compost.
Height up to 50 cm (20 in).
Propagation by cuttings.

Zebrina is a pretty and versatile foliage plant. In the wild it grows mostly along the ground, but with its creeping, supple stems it can also be kept in a pot or hanging basket. The little violet flowers are not much to look at, but the opposite-growing, symmetrical, oval leaves are extremely attractive.

Species
The most commonly grown species is *Zebrina pendula.* The silver-striped leaves, red underneath, grow closely on red, green-spotted stems. The variety 'Quadricolor' is even more colourful; the alternate leaves bear longitudinal stripes of dark green, white and light pink.

The slightly hairy leaves of *Zebrina purpusii* are reddish blue in colour, often suffused with olive green on the upper side.

Cultivation
Zebrina likes a lot of light and warmth. Keep it in an airy room or on the balcony in summer. Water regularly with lime-free water, spray often and feed every fortnight. In winter zebrina needs a room temperature that does not fall below 14°C (57°F).

Propagation
Propagation by cuttings is possible at any time of the year, but most successful in the spring. Break off stem cuttings 10 cm (4 in) long and plant them in a pot of peaty soil. You can also let the cuttings root in water first and then plant them.

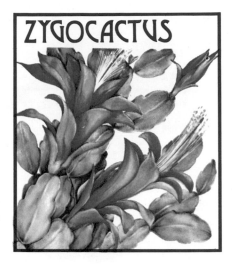

ZYGOCACTUS

Christmas Cactus

Profusely flowering cactus.

Position half-shady, light and warm, in sandy, lime-free humus-rich soil. Do not change the position.

Height up to 40 cm (16 in).
Flowering autumn and winter.
Propagation by cuttings.

Zygocactus used to be called epiphyllum but is better known as the Christmas cactus.

Species
There is only the one species of this leaf-flowering form, *Zygocactus truncatus,* but there are a good many hybrids.

In its home in Brazil the Christmas cactus grows as an epiphyte on trees, but it grows well here in porous, rather sandy soil, which must contain no lime. The plant needs a half-shady position, or else the leaf growths, of up to 5 cm (2 in) long and 2 cm (1 in) wide, will lose their green colour and turn red. New shoots and flowers grow from the ends of these growths. New flowers also grow from areoles in the indentations along the edges of the leaves. They are gener-ally carmine, with drooping tubes and reflexed petals. The Christmas cactus has no thorns or bristles.

Cultivation
The Christmas cactus has its rest period from the end of its flowering period until mid-spring, when its stems (often spoken of as leaves) become a little shrunken. Water generously after this until early autumn, feed once a week and keep in a warm place. Then cut down the water to stimulate the formation of buds, and keep it cooler. From late autumn on, raise the temperature again to 20°C (68°F) and water.

Propagation
You can take cuttings for propaga-tion at any time of year. They root in sandy loam at temperatures of about 22°C (72°F) and must be carefully repotted twice before they shoot.

Zygocactus truncatus

152

Zygocactus truncatus

PLACES FOR PLANTS

If you want to grow house plants well, you must choose the right plants for your house or apartment. Naturally, the first consideration is your personal preference—for flowering plants or foliage plants, climbing plants or hanging plants.

But then you must consider the conditions where the plants will live. Your choice may be limited to those that can survive dry air or a place on the balcony. And remember that if you put a sun-loving flowering plant in a gloomy hall no amount of care will make it flourish.

To help you make the right choice, here is a guide to popular house plants and where they grow best.

FLOWERING PLANTS

Anthurium scherzerianum (flamingo flower), an evergreen from the tropical regions of America. Needs a warm position shaded from direct sunlight, and high humidity in the summer; keep fairly dry in winter. Produces fine spathes, white to dark red, with a straight or curved spadix. Flowers all the year round.

Calceolaria (slipper flower), from South America. Prefers half-shady to cool positions with high humidity. Cannot tolerate draughts. Flowers in spring, with orange-yellow, brown and red, often dappled blooms.

Cyclamen, a perennial tuberous plant from South and Central Europe and Asia Minor. Likes a bright but not sunny position. Must be kept cool when in flower. Long-lived, freely flowering plant in white and all shades of red.

Cyclamen persicum

Hibiscus (rose mallow), a spreading indoor shrub from the tropics. Needs a sunny position in summer and a slightly heated room in winter. Produces large, red flowers amid bright green foliage from spring to autumn. Hybrids also flower white, yellow and orange.

Nertera (bead plant), a perennial creeping plant from the Southern Hemisphere. Needs a cool, half-shady position, not less than 10°C (50°F) in winter. The low cushions of the plant are covered from summer onwards with a profusion of decorative berries.

Rhododendron indicum (indoor azalea), a small evergreen shrub from the Northern Hemisphere. Flourishes only in lime-free soil in half-shady and cool positions. Perennial flowering plant with many different flowers, white and shades of red, according to variety.

Saintpaulia (African violet), a perennial from East Africa. Prefers a light, warm, but not sunny position. Cannot tolerate draughts. Flowers all the year round, violet, pink and white according to variety. Very sensitive to water on the fine hairy leaves, but compost must be kept moist and it needs humidity. Good plant for a bottle garden or terrarium where it will be free from draughts.

BRIGHT FOLIAGE PLANTS

Aucuba, an evergreen house shrub from Asia. In summer needs a light and airy but not sunny position. Overwinters in a cool room. Foliage has gold spots.

Caladium, a tuberous perennial from tropical America. Needs a light, shady and humid position with plenty of warmth. This decorative plant with brilliantly coloured leaves is sensitive to dry air.

Codiaeum (croton), from the Pacific. Needs half-shady, warm position with high humidity. Even in winter the brightly coloured leaves need plenty of light and warmth, or the patterns on them will fade.

Cordyline (sometimes called the flaming dragon tree or scarlet aspidistra), an evergreen from Asia, Africa and Australia. Prefers half-shade, but green-leaved species will also do well in the sun. Spear-shaped leaves. Older specimens flower.

Dieffenbachia, a subshrub from tropical America. Needs plenty of warmth and humidity, brightness but no sun. Leaves are attractively patterned. All parts are poisonous. Wash hands after handling.

Dieffenbachia seguine

Dracaena draco (dragon tree), an indoor shrub from the tropical regions. Needs light, warm position. Leaves have a white pattern. Roots have an aromatic scent.

Gynura, a subshrub from Africa and Asia with bluish red leaves and orange flowers in the autumn. Needs a light, warm but airy position. Keep warm in winter, in artificial light.

Maranta (arrowroot), a perennial evergreen with ornamental foliage, from the primeval forests of Brazil. Needs a light but not sunny position with daytime temperatures about 22°C (72°F), and at nights not cooler than 16°C (61°F). The leaves have coloured veins.

GREEN FOLIAGE PLANTS

Cocos (cocos palm), an indoor shrub from South America. Needs a position with plenty of warmth and high humidity but no direct sunlight. Older specimens of these attractive, feathery palms are less trouble to look after.

Coffea (coffee plant), an evergreen shrub from tropical Asia, Africa and America. Prefers sunny and airy positions. Undemanding. Turn the plant as little as possible.

Fatsia (fig leaf palm, sometimes called castor oil plant), an evergreen indoor shrub from Japan. Needs a light, shady, cool position. May be put out on the balcony, but will not tolerate draughts. Overwinters in cool conditions.

Fatsia japonica

Ficus elastica (rubber tree), an evergreen indoor tree or shrub. Position should be light. Keep in an unheated room in winter, no lower than 10°C (50°F). Drooping leaves are a sign of too much warmth.
Grevillea robusta (silk bark oak), an evergreen tree from South Asia and Australasia. Needs lime-free soil. Likes a light, airy, but not sunny position. Can be put on the balcony. Overwinters in a cool room, 8-10°C (46-50°F).
Howea (often called kentia palm), a tree with narrow fronds, occurring naturally only in the Australian-administered Lord Howe Islands in the Pacific. Needs light in winter but a little shade in summer. Overwinters in slightly heated rooms, 10-12°C (50-54°F). Do not let soil dry out.
Phoenix dactylifera (date palm), from the tropics of Africa and Asia. Needs a sunny position and moist air. Overwinters in the cool. Water sparingly in winter but do not allow soil to dry out.

CLIMBING PLANTS

Cissus antarctica (kangaroo vine), a climbing, trailing plant from Australia. Likes a light, warm position with no direct sun. Can overwinter in a cool room at 8°C (46°F). Some varieties have leaves with coloured patterns.
Ficus pumila (creeping fig), a climbing plant from eastern Asia, considerably less delicate than all the other rubber and fig trees of the same family. Very hardy. Needs a light,

half-shady position. Never let it dry out or it will quickly die.
Hedera (pot ivy), an evergreen climbing plant. Needs brightness and plenty of air, but cannot stand the full glare of the sun. Bright-leaved varieties must be kept over winter in moderately heated rooms. Green species are less delicate and will tolerate shade.

Hedera colchica 'Variegata'

Passiflora (passion flower), a climbing plant from tropical America. Likes direct sunlight and airy positions. Will overwinter in the warm. Can be put on the balcony in summer.
Peperomia (pepper elder), an evergreen plant from the warm regions of America. Needs a light but shady place in a warm room, and in winter needs a warm room with high humidity. There is a fine, grey sheen on its corrugated leaves. If healthy it will produce white flower spikes.
Philodendron scandens (sweetheart vine), an evergreen climber from the warm regions of America. Position should be light, shady and warm, with high humidity. Keep fairly warm during the winter.

Philodendron scandens

Scindapsus (ivy arum), a climbing herbaceous plant. Wants a warm, shady place with moist air. Must overwinter in light, warm conditions. Makes a good hanging plant.
Stephanotis floribunda (Madagascar jasmine), an evergreen climber from the Malagasy Republic. Needs a warm, half-shady position, the air not too dry, and a winter temperature of 12°C (54°F). The white flowers have a powerful scent. Grows quite large. Susceptible to draughts.
Syngonium, an evergreen from Central America. Likes a warm, shady position during the summer, bright and fairly warm in winter. The bracts of the flowers are deep red at the base.
Thunbergia alata (black-eyed Susan), a freely flowering, climbing annual from tropical Africa and Asia. Needs to be in light and warmth, but overwinters in cool conditions.

HANGING PLANTS

Aeschynanthus, an Asian perennial with beautiful flowers. Needs a shady position, high humidity and in summer temperatures around 25°C (77°F). Overwinters in a heated room. Does not tolerate draughts.

Aeschynanthus pulcher

Allamanda, an evergreen plant from Brazil. Often grown as a climber. Needs full sun and damp air. Keep in a light, warm room in winter.
Asparagus setaceus (asparagus fern), not a fern but a perennial evergreen plant from the temperate zones of Europe and Asia. Likes a well-lit, airy position. Can overwinter in a heated room but cannot tolerate dry soil. Bears red berries.
Columnea, an evergreen shrub from tropical America. A very prettily flowering hanging plant which needs high humidity with plenty of warmth and shade. Will overwinter in a mod-

erately heated room and cannot tolerate draughts.

Piper (pepper plant), a perennial tropical plant, occasionally shrubby when grown indoors. Needs shade and warmth. Green species overwinter in unheated rooms, but those with brightly coloured leaves are more delicate. The leaves are prettily patterned.

Piper ornatum

Plectanthrus, from the warm parts of Asia, Africa and Australia. In summer likes a light and shady position. May be put out on the balcony.

Tradescantia, from South America. Does well in any position. Keep bright-leaved species in a good light or they will lose their colour. Attractive as hanging plants in baskets.

Zebrina, related to the tradescantia. Prefers light and sunny positions and can be put out on the balcony in summer with no trouble. After a few years the stems become unsightly and should be cut back.

FERNS

Adiantum capillus-veneris (maidenhair fern), from South America. Should stand in warmth and shade all the year round. Keep damp, but never in standing water.

Asplenium nidus (bird's nest fern), from the rain forests of Africa and Asia. An epiphyte, it prefers a cool, shady position.

Nephrolepis (ladder fern), found in tropical regions all over the world. Likes to be kept in half-shady, warm positions with humid air. Can overwinter in unheated rooms at 10°C (50°F). Very good for cutting.

Phlebodium, from the tropical regions of South America. Grows on the ground and is not an epiphyte. Prefers warm, shady places with high humidity and must overwinter in a warm room. Cannot tolerate lime.

Phyllitis (hart's tongue fern), grows all over the world. Content with cool and shady positions so long as the air is not too dry. Should be kept close to the window in an unheated room during the winter. Water only with lime-free water.

Phyllitis scolopendrium

Platycerium (stag's horn fern), from South Asia but closely related to several species in Central America and Central Africa. Needs a shady place with high humidity. The broad leaves of this fern will die if the roots are allowed to dry out.

Platycerium bifurcatum

Polystichum (often called aspidium or shield fern), an evergreen, completely winter-hardy open-air fern which nevertheless makes a good house fern. Indoor species should have a half-shady position. Keep cool in winter—10-12°C (50-54°F)—and do not water too much.

SHADE-LOVING PLANTS

Aspidistra, a perennial, completely trouble-free member of the lily family. Evergreen foliage plant with inconspicuous flowers.

Aspidistra elatior 'Variegata'

Chlorophytum (spider plant), among the least demanding of house plants. It is content with any position but should have some light or the leaves will turn light and thin.

Chlorophytum elatum 'Variegatum'

Cyperus alternifolius (umbrella grass), a reedy grass found in every continent. Suitable for planting in shallow tanks and pools, but good as a house plant if kept moist or pot stood in shallow water.

Monstera (Swiss cheese plant or shingle plant), an evergreen climber. Likes a shady place so long as it is not too warm. In excessive light the leaves develop brown spots.

Philodendron, similar to monstera in that it prefers shady positions with ample warmth and humidity, and overwinters in a heated room. Does well in hydroponics.

Selaginella (creeping moss), an evergreen plant of the tropical rain forest and the temperate zones. Position should be shady, moist and warm. Cannot tolerate lime. Makes fine hanging basket.

Sparmannia (African hemp), likes some sun but needs light shade in summer. Position must be airy and not too warm. Has light green leaves and little scented white flowers.

PLANTS FOR DRY AIR

Chamaedorea (mountain palm), a decorative little tree from South and Central America. Can tolerate dry air but not dry soil. Needs a warm and shady place. Does well in rooms with central heating.

Chamaedorea elegans

Clivia, with rich clusters of flowers. Suits a place by the window very well. In winter put in a room with only moderate heating and keep almost dry.

Echeveria, a leaf succulent with bright flowers. Needs a light position. Well suited to dry air.

Euphorbia milii (crown of thorns), a thorny shrub. Needs a sunny, airy position. Does not like draughts. You can put it out on the balcony in summer. Can stand dry air as long as the roots do not get dry.

Kalanchoë, a leaf succulent. Wants a light place, which might be on the balcony in summer. In winter needs a room temperature of at least 10°C (50°F). Central heating does not hurt it.

Kalanchoë tomentosa

Sansevieria (mother-in-law's tongue or snake plant), makes no demands at all on its environment as long as it is not too dark. No wonder you see its sword-shaped leaves in every office. Do not overwater or its roots will rot.

PLANTS FOR WARM ROOMS

Acalypha, from the tropics. Needs to stand in a light spot with plenty of warmth and humidity all the year round. Has long spiky flowers.

Paphiopedilum, a tropical orchid from South Asia. Prefers a warm place with plenty of light and high humidity. Water only with previously boiled water.

Rhoeo (boat lily), from Central America with long, lanceolate leaves which form open rosettes. Will do well in a conservatory and can be put in the shade of bigger plants as ground decoration.

Spathiphyllum (peace lily), a low, stemless evergreen topped by a white spathe with yellowish spadix. Hungry for warmth and some humidity. Needs a half-shady position.

Tillandsia usneoides (Spanish moss), from the tropical rain forests

of Central America. Accustomed to a warm position and light but not direct sun. Can be grown as an epiphyte on a special trunk.

Vriesea, mainly from Brazil. Needs a lot of warmth and can be kept best in a half-shady position in a conservatory. Green-leaved and coloured-leaved species.

Vriesea splendens

PLANTS FOR THE BALCONY

Begonia, a very good, hardy plant for the balcony, but should not be placed facing south.

Bougainvillea, a deciduous shrubby climber from the tropics and sub-tropics of America. Blooms freely in summer on a sheltered balcony.

Browallia, an attractive shrub. Mostly kept as a house plant, it does very well in a box on the balcony if kept out of direct sunlight and watered more than usual.

Coleus (flame nettle), a plant that can display the full glory of its brightly coloured leaves only if kept in a light and fairly sunny position. Does well in a box on the balcony if freely watered, but must be sheltered from the wind.

Fuchsia, another popular balcony plant. Should be lightly shaded. Boxes must be kept light and cool during the winter.

Pelargonium (geranium), next to begonia the most common of all balcony plants. Can tolerate sun as well as shady positions and has long flowering season. Put in a light and airy place in a frost-free room during the winter and keep almost dry.

Vinca (periwinkle), a freely flowering subshrub with bright leaves and light blue, long-stemmed flowers. Needs plenty of water.

GLOSSARY

acid—applied to soils with a pH content below 7.0.

acid soil—*see pH value.*

adventitious root—a root that develops from some other part of a plant than a pre-existing root.

aerial root—a root arising on a stem above ground.

aggregate—artificial, chemically inert soil with no organic content. It is often used in hydroponics.

air layering—a method of *vegetative propagation (q.v.)* by separating a part of the stem with the shoots and leaves. Particularly suitable for indoor shrubs. Cut a slit all round the stem and hold the cut open with a sliver of wood or tuft of moss. The *callus (q.v.),* wrapped in damp moss or peat, forms roots. When the roots are fully developed the cut piece of the stem is removed completely.

alkaline—applied to soils with a pH content above 7.0.

alkaline soil—*see pH value.*

anther—the functional part of a stamen which contains the pollen grains. It comprises two pollen sacs or anther lobes joined on a stalk.

apex—the tip of a shoot or root from where growth is extended.

areole—the area occupied by a group of spines or hairs on a cactus.

The sharp spines of the cleisto-cactus spring from areoles.

assimilation—conversion by a plant of inorganic substances into organic, producing carbohydrates, oils and protein. *See photosynthesis.*

axil—the solid angle between a stem and the upper surface of a leaf base growing from it.

bipinnate—a leaf that is divided into several segments which are again subdivided.

biternate—a leaf that is divided and sudivided into units of three.

bract—a modified leaf on stalks developed by plants that have inconspicuous flowers, for the protection of the flowers and sometimes also to attract insects. On many plants, like anthuriums, billbergias and *Euphorbia pulcherrima* (poinsettia), they are wrongly taken to be the flowers.

Billbergias display beautiful bracts instead of flowers.

callus—wound tissue of plants, from which a corky layer grows outwards and a *cambium (q.v.)* later inwards.

calyx—the outer whorl of the flower, consisting of sepals. It is usually green and protects the upended bud.

cambium—layer of actively splitting cells in a plant. Cambium, activated when the plant is cut, makes *vegetative propagation (q.v.)* possible.

chlorophyll—the green colouring matter of leaves, from the Greek words *chloros* ('green') and *phyllon* ('leaf'). Chlorophyll plays an essential part as a catalyst in the process of assimilation, with the aid of sunlight. *See assimilation, photosynthesis.*

chlorosis—the loss or poor production of chlorophyll (the green colouring matter in plants), giving a bleached yellow or white appearance to leaves. In extreme cases, browning and death of tissues may follow. The usual cause of chlorosis is lack of essential minerals, although certain viruses may also be responsible.

cladode—a flattened, leaf-like stalk, performing the functions of a leaf.

cordate—a heart-shaped leaf or one or two lobes at the base.

corm—a rounded, swollen underground stem, with scale leaves, adventitious roots, and buds.

corolla—the general name for the whole of the petals of the flower.

corona—a trumpet-like outgrowth from the perianth.

corymb—a flat-topped cluster of flowers, the stalks of which arise one above the other from a vertical stem or axis.

crenate—with rounded teeth. The term usually applies to a leaf margin.

crocks—broken pieces of clay pots used as drainage material in flowerpots, seed trays, and so on.

cutting—*see vegetative propagation.*

cyme—a domed, flattened or rounded cluster of flowers, usually with several arching branches radiating outwards.

dead-heading—the removal of faded flowers to prevent seeding or to tidy the appearance of a plant.

dentate—applied to a leaf that has tooth-like notches to the margins.

digitate—a term used to describe a leaf that is composed of several radiating leaflets.

distichous—usually applied to leaves that are arranged in two flattened opposite ranks on the stem, creating a fan-like effect.

epiphyte—a plant that grows above the soil, usually clinging to another plant or a rock, especially in the tropical rain forests, where epiphytes climb to the tops of trees in their search for light. Epiphytes are not parasites; they have their own independent feeding system. Well-known epiphytes are orchids and ferns.

Aechmea is an epiphyte from the tropical forests.

etiolation—disturbed growth of plants caused by lack of light. Leaf stalks and stems grow too long, while the leaves remain small. The plants lack chlorophyll and turn a poor yellowish white colour.

filament—the stalk of a stamen (the

pollen producing part of a plant).

friable—referring to a crumbly soil that is easily worked and raked to a tilth.

glochids—bristles or hairs on the surface of a plant that have hooks on them, so that when touched they break off and cling to the skin. These are a troublesome feature of many cacti.

hard water—*see pH value.*

hybrid—a product of accidental or deliberate crossbreeding, generally between two species of a genus, less often between genera. Hybrids are generally indicated by an X in front of the botanical name.

inflorescence—that part of a plant which bears flowers.

lacinate—fringed. Used to describe leaves, bracts, stipules or petals with margins cut into numerous narrow segments.

lanceolate—shaped like the head of a lance. Applied to a base, tapering to a point and at least three times longer than it is broad.

lateral—a side shoot of plants which, when cut off, very quickly forms roots and develops a new plant. It is used in vegetative propagation in many tropical plants.

layer—a horizontally growing shoot of a new plant which is fixed to the ground and so made to form roots. Layering is a method of vegetative propagation. Roots will form only if the shoot has been wounded, possibly where it has been fastened to the ground.

leaf cutting—*see vegetative propagation.*

light mark—a mark made on the containers of house plants, to ensure that the plants can always present the same side to the source of light.

loam—soil consisting of a friable mixture of varying proportions of clay, silt and sand.

mildew—powdery and downy mildew are plant diseases caused by fungi.

mutation—a transmissible, spontaneously developed alteration of the outward appearance of a plant. This is how varieties are bred.

node—a leaf knot or thickened zone on the shoot of a plant from which the leaves develop. Nodes are important in *vegetative propagation (q.v.),* since it is from these points that roots are formed in propagation by cuttings.

offset—a short prostrate lateral shoot arising from the base of the plant.

pH value—the index of acid-alkaline balance of soil. The scale goes from 1 to 14; the neutral point is pH 7, which indicates complete chemical neutrality and in practice is found only in distilled water. Values between 1 and 7 indicate acidity, between 7 and 14 alkalinity. The pH value of the soil is critical to the survival of a plant, though most plants can normally adapt to tolerate a divergence of two points on the scale.

photosynthesis—conversion of atmospheric carbon dioxide and water by means of sunlight into starch and oxygen, using chlorophyll as a catalyst.

phototropism—the tendency of virtually all plants to grow towards the source of light.

pinnule—one of the lobes or segments when a leaflet of a pinnate leaf is itself more or less divided into parts in a pinnate manner.

pistil—the complete female organ of a flower, comprising an ovary, stigma and style. The style may be short or nonexistant.

raceme—a simple inflorescence in which the elongated axis bears flowers on short stems in succession towards the apex.

rhizome—an underground stem or rootstock used as an organ of storage for the winter. Plants grow new, young plants from horizontally growing rhizomes.

runner—a shoot spreading from the plant over or under the ground, which forms new plants.

scape—a stalk, quite or nearly leafless, arising from the middle of a rosette of leaves and bearing flowers.

short-day plant—a plant that begins its growth or flowering in the days when the light does not last long—that is, in winter; thus, a winter-

A short-day plant, *Euphorbia pulcherrima* blooms in winter.

flowering plant.

spadex—a spike with a swollen fleshy axis enclosed in a spathe.

spathe—*see bract.* Spathes are large bracts enclosing one or more flowers.

The brilliant red spathes of the anthurium are very exotic.

sphagnum moss—a leafy moss growing wild and used as a planting medium for epiphytes. It is completely free from lime and is extremely absorbent and water-retentive. Moss peat is based on sphagnum moss.

spores—reproductive organs of ferns, growing in clusters on the underside of the leaves.

succulent—a plant that stores sometimes remarkable amounts of water in its growth above ground. A distinction is made between leaf succulents and stem succulents.

sucker—a strongly growing shoot arising from the base of the stem or from a root.

tubercle—a general term for a small swelling.

umbel—an inflorescence consisting of numerous small flowers in flat-topped groups borne on stalks all arising from about the same point on the main stem.

variety—a deviation in a species of plant in its outward appearance obtained by breeding and given a botanical name. The botanical term for this is a 'cultivar'. Variety names are written in single quotation marks.

vegetative propagation—asexual propagation by division of plants —either of the natural reproductive organs of the plant such as layers, buds, bulbs, or shoots, or of parts of the plant that can produce shoots, which can include roots, leaves, top cuttings or parts of the stem.

159

DICTIONARY OF POPULAR NAMES

Adam's needle— *Yucca gloriosa*
African hemp— *Sparmannia*
African violet— *Saintpaulia*
aluminium plant— *Pilea cadierei*
amaryllis (incorrectly)— *Hippeastrum*
angel's tears— *Billbergia nutans*
arrowroot— *Maranta*
artillery plant— *Pilea*
arum lily— *Zantedeschia*
asparagus fern— *Asparagus setaceus*
azalea indica— *Rhododendron indicum*
band plant— *Vinca major*
Barbados lily— *Hippeastrum*
bay laurel— *Laurus*
bead plant— *Nertera*
begonia— *Begonia*
bellflower— *Campanula*
bird of paradise flower— *Strelitzia reginae*
bird's nest bromeliad— *Nidularium*
bird's nest fern— *Asplenium nidus*
bird's tongue flower— *Strelitzia*
black-eyed Susan— *Thunbergia alata*
black pepper— *Piper nigrum*
boat lily— *Rhoeo*
bottle brush— *Callistemon*
bow string hemp— *Sansevieria*
busy lizzie— *Impatiens walleriana*
cabbage palm— *Cordilyne*
calla lily— *Zantedeschia*
Cape leadwort— *Plumbago*
Cape primrose— *Streptocarpus*
cast iron plant— *Aspidistra*
castor oil plant (incorrectly)— *Fatsia*
chillies— *Capsicum*
Chinese primrose— *Primula praenitens*
Christmas cactus— *Zygocactus*
Chusan palm— *Trachycarpus*
cineraria— *Senecio*
club moss— *Selaginella*
clustered waxflower— *Stephanotis*
coffee plant— *Coffea*
common ivy— *Hedera helix*
common myrtle— *Myrtus communis*
copper leaf— *Acalypha*
creeping fig— *Ficus pumila, Ficus repens, Ficus stipulata*
creeping moss— *Selaginella*
creeping sailor— *Tradescantia albiflora*
croton— *Codiaeum*
crown of thorns— *Euphorbia milii*
curly palm— *Howea forsteriana*
cut finger— *Vinca major*
date palm— *Phoenix dactylifera*
dragon tree— *Dracaena draco*
dumb cane— *Dieffenbachia seguine*
dusty miller— *Senecio cineraria*
dwarf date palm— *Phoenix roebelinii*
dwarf gloxinia— *Sinningia pusilla*
dwarf orange— *Citrus mitis*
dwarf umbrella grass— *Cyperus gracilis*
Easter cactus— *Rhipsalidopsis*
elk horn fern— *Platycerium*

fairy primrose— *Primula malacoides*
fan palm— *Trachycarpus*
fern begonia— *Begonia foliosa*
fiddle back fig— *Ficus lyrata, Ficus pandurata*
fig leaf palm— *Fatsia*
flame nettle— *Coleus*
flaming dragon tree— *Cordyline*
flamingo flower— *Anthurium*
flowering maple— *Abutilon*
fruiting duckweed— *Nertera*
fuchsia begonia— *Begonia fuchsioides*
fuchsia tree— *Fuchsia arborescens*
galingale— *Cyperus*
geranium (incorrectly)— *Pelargonium*
gloxinia— *Sinningia*
gold fern— *Pityrogramma*
grape ivy— *Rhoicissus*
greater periwinkle— *Vinca major*
great flamingo flower— *Anthurium andreanum*
gunpowder plant— *Pilea*
hairy bougainvillea— *Bougainvillea spectabilis*
hard shield fern— *Polystichum aculeatum*
hart's tongue fern— *Phyllitis*
humble plant— *Mimosa pudica*
Indian azalea— *Rhododendron*
Indian mallow— *Abutilon*
Indian rubber plant— *Ficus elastica*
indoor azalea— *Rhododendron*
indoor cyclamen— *Cyclamen latifolium, Cyclamen persicum, Cyclamen puniceum*
ivy— *Hedera*
ivy arum— *Scindapsus*
ivy-leafed begonia— *Pelargonium peltatum*
Jerusalem cherry— *Solanum pseudocapsicum*
kangaroo vine— *Cissus antarctica*
kentia palm— *Howea*
ladder fern— *Nephrolepis*
leaf begonia— *Begonia rex*
lemon— *Citrus limon*
lemon geranium— *Pelargonium odoratissimum*
leopard lily— *Sansevieria*
lesser periwinkle— *Vinca minor*
lilac fuchsia— *Fuchsia arborescens*
linden tree— *Sparmannia*
little flamingo flower— *Anthurium scherzerianum*
little ship— *Tradescantia navicularis*
Madagascar jasmin— *Stephanotis floribunda*
maidenhair fern— *Adiantum capillus —veneris*
mistletoe fig— *Ficus deltoidea*
moth king— *Plectranthus fructicosus*
mother-in-law's tongue— *Sansevieria*
mother of thousands— *Saxifraga stolonifera*
mountain palm— *Chamaedorea*
myrtle— *Myrtus*
Norfolk Island pine— *Araucaria*
old man cactus— *Cephalocereus senilis*
oleander— *Nerium*
orange— *Citrus sinensis*

orchid cactus— *Epiphyllum*
ornamental pepper— *Piper ornatum*
painter's palette— *Anthurium scherzerianum*
passion flower— *Passiflora*
peace lily— *Spathiphyllum*
pepper— *Piper*
pepper elder— *Peperomia*
periwinkle— *Vinca*
Persian ivy— *Hedera colchica*
piggy-back plant— *Tolmiea menziesii*
pistol plant— *Pilea*
poinsettia— *Euphorbia pulcherrima*
pot ivy— *Hedera*
prayer plant— *Maranta*
prickly pear— *Opuntia*
queen's tears— *Billbergia nutans*
red pepper— *Capsicum*
red-hot cat's tail— *Acalypha hispida*
rose bay— *Nerium*
rose geranium— *Pelargonium graveolens, Pelargonium radens*
rose mallow— *Hibiscus*
roving sailor— *Saxifraga*
rubber tree— *Ficus elastica*
saxifrage— *Saxifraga*
Scarborough Lily— *Vallota speciosa*
scarlet aspidistra— *Cordyline*
screw pine— *Pandanus*
sensitive plant— *Mimosa pudica*
shield fern— *Polystichum*
shingle plant— *Monstera*
shrimp plant— *Beloperone*
silk bark oak— *Grevillea*
silver fern— *Pityrogramma argentea*
slipper flower— *Calceolaria*
slipper orchid— *Paphiopedilum*
snake plant— *Sansevieria*
South sea laurel— *Codiaeum*
sowbread— *Cyclamen*
Spanish bayonet— *Yucca*
Spanish moss— *Tillandsia usneoides*
spider plant— *Chlorophytum*
spiderwort— *Tradescantia*
spleenwort— *Asplenium*
squill— *Scilla*
stag's horn fern— *Platycerium*
sweet bay— *Laurus*
sweetheart vine— *Philodendron scandens*
Swiss cheese plant— *Monstera*
sword fern— *Nephrolepis*
tail flower— *Anthurium*
thatch leaf palm— *Howea forsteriana*
touch-me-not— *Impatiens*
tree fuchsia— *Fuchsia arborescens*
Trinity flower— *Tradescantia*
umbrella grass— *Cyperus alternifolius*
urn plant— *Aechmea*
violin case rubber tree— *Ficus lyrata, Ficus pandurata*
wall rue— *Asplenium ruta muraria*
wandering Jew— *Tradescantia albiflora, Tradescantia fluminensis*
weeping fig— *Ficus benjamina*
widow's tears— *Tradescantia albiflora*
wild hyacinth— *Scilla*
winter cherry— *Solanum capsicastrum*
youth-on-age— *Tolmiea menziesii*
Zebra plant— *Aphelandra*

2

Jackson & Perkins® 1978
Seedbook
FLOWERS · VEGETABLES · BERRIES · DWARF FRUIT TREES

INDEX	Page
FLOWERS	
African Daisy	7
Ageratum	4
Alyssum	4
Asters	4
Baby's Breath	10
Bachelor Buttons	7
Begonias, Fibrous	4
Begonias, Floribunda	7
Bells of Ireland	4
Browallia	5
Cactus	5
Calendula	5
Candytuft	5
Carnations	6
Celosia	6
Cleome	5
Coleus	6
Cornflower	7
Cosmos	7
Crownvetch	5
Dahlia	7
Delphinium	6
Dianthus	7
Dimorphotheca	7
Dusty Miller	10
Gazania	10
Geraniums	2, 10
Gladiolus	7
Gloriosa Daisy	14
Gourds	18
Gypsophila	10
Helianthus	10
Hollyhock	11
Houseplants	13
Impatiens	10
Kale, flowering	18
Larkspurs	11
Lobelia	11
Marigolds	8-9
Nasturtiums	11
Pampas Grass	18
Pansies	14
Petunias	12-13
Phlox	14
Portulaca	14
Primula	14
Rudbeckia	14
Salvia	14
Scabiosa	14
Snapdragons	15
Stock	15
Strawflowers	15
Sunflowers	10
Sweet Peas	15
Sweet William	15
Verbena	18
Violas	18
Wildflowers	3
Zinnias	2, 16-17
VEGETABLES AND FRUIT	
Asparagus	20
Beans	21
Beets	21
Berries	20
Broccoli	22
Brussels Sprouts	22
Cabbage	22
Carrots	23
Cauliflower	22
Celery	23
Collards	28
Corn	25
Cucumbers	24
Eggplant	23
Endive	26
Fruit Trees	19
Grapes	19
Herbs	18
Kale	26
Kohlrabi	29
Lettuce	26
Melons	3, 30
Mustard Greens	28
Okra	28
Onions	26-27
Parsley	28
Parsnips	28
Peas	27
Peppers	28-29
Pumpkins	31
Radishes	24
Rhubarb	20
Shallots	see order blank
Spinach	2, 29
Squash	31
Swiss Chard	28
Tomatoes	3, 32
Turnips	29
Walnut Tree	19

See order blank for garden accessories.

2

Geranium — Showgirl

Cantaloupe — Wonder Melon

NEW EXCLUSIVE J&P

Top Crop Hybrids

GERANIUM F₁ HYBRID SHOWGIRL A startlingly beautiful bright pink 1977 All-America winner. An early bloomer that produces many more flowers two weeks earlier than most geraniums. Free flowering, 15-inch high plants bloom with medium-to-large showy, round clusters of lovely, rosy-pink single flowers. Showgirl's semi-dwarf plants . . . thick with foliage and galaxies of blooms . . . grow profusely in window boxes and pots . . . smashing for color impact! And, simply marvelous for creating that "Home Sweet Home" look that's always associated with geraniums blooming in garden bed, patio and porch. *(More geraniums on page 10.)*

Packet	Bonus Pkt.	Jumbo Pkt.
750-P **$1.75**	750-U **$3.35**	750-J **$6.45**

ZINNIA F₁ HYBRID RUFFLES MIX A custom mix, specially selected by J&P! Two 1978 All-America winners (the Cherry and Yellow), a 1974 All-America winner (the Scarlet), and a Fleuroselect winner (the Pink) — all in one incredible collection! And no wonder this Ruffles series has won such recognition. These outstanding cut-and-come-again Zinnias are extremely freeblooming and vigorous . . . give a super abundance of bright 3-inch double blooms on uniform 28-inch plants. Cut all you want . . . more blooms will follow. Colors so brilliant they seem to glow in the sunlight, and fluted petals add depth and texture. *(More zinnias on page 16.)*

Packet	Bonus Pkt.	Jumbo Pkt.
988-P **$1.25**	988-U **$2.35**	988-J **$4.45**

SPINACH F₁ HYBRID MELODY What a boon to spinach lovers! A 1977 All-America winner developed with "bred-in" disease resistance and a hybrid vigor that assures a substantially higher yield than old standard varieties. Plant in spring and fall and you'll have tender, sweet-tasting, nutritious spinach to eat cooked, or as luscious greens in cool summer salads. Large plants grow thick, dark green, round leaves that have greater succulence, provide a fresher, more crisp leaf through the hot summer. A must in any garden! *(More spinach on page 29.)*

Packet	Bonus Pkt.	Jumbo Pkt.
469-P **85c**	469-U **$1.60**	469-J **$3.10**

OUR GUARANTEE IS YOUR PROTECTION!

We promise your satisfaction in every respect. Should any item you purchase from this book disappoint you — notify us any time within one year of purchase. We will refund its cost or replace it prepaid and free of charge — whichever *you* prefer.

DEFINITIONS

Annual — A plant whose life cycle is completed in a single year. Growth is rapid, so gardeners look to annuals for quick, lavish color. Practically all the vegetables except asparagus, rhubarb and parsley are annuals.

Biennial — A plant that takes two years from seed to complete its life-cycle. Some bloom very little or not at all the first year, but come into full bloom the second and then go to seed. Many gardeners treat biennials as annuals, planting new seeds each year to insure steady blooming.

Perennial — A plant that lives on from year to year. Some plants which are true perennials are commonly treated as annuals or biennials by gardeners, because when raised fresh each year from seeds, they produce finer blooms and generally prove more reliable than old plants.

Hybrid — The progeny resulting from crossbreeding between two species, to produce new varieties of flowers and vegetables with greater vigor, uniformity and productivity than the original parent stock. Don't save seed from hybrids — it will revert and not grow true.

All-America Selection or Winner — A distinction awarded to flower and vegetable introductions that have proven themselves superior in a battery of tests under diverse conditions in a nationwide network of 28 test gardens.

A note about our packet sizes — Our regular packets contain more seed by weight than almost any other standard packets we have seen. Our Bonus Packet contains 2-1/2 times as much as the Regular Packet . . . our Jumbo Packet contains 6 times as much as the Regular Packet. And the savings of putting up one larger packet, instead of 3 or 6 standard packets, are passed on to you.

Jackson & Perkins Co.®

World's Largest Rose Growers and Nurserymen • Since 1872 • Medford, Oregon 97501

J&P SUPER EXCLUSIVES

CUCUMBER F₁ HYBRID SUPERCUKE NEW . . . and burpless, too — available only from J&P. Here's the fresh full flavor you want in a cucumber . . . without a bit of bite! Supercuke has crisp, crunchy texture with an extremely high sugar content . . . it's sweet and delicious — and completely edible, the skin is never bitter! It's the result of years of testing, to develop the tastiest, most bitter-free digestible cucumber yet introduced. When compared in taste tests against most of the well known older varieties, as well as the newer hybrids, Supercuke consistently came out way ahead in flavor and quality. And does it ever produce! This is a monoecious F₁ hybrid . . . seed is produced by an expensive hand pollination method. The vines bear fruit over a much longer season than usual — many cucumbers tend to set their fruit all at once, but Supercuke sets slim, straight 12-inch fruits throughout the season. You'll have plenty of glossy, dark green cucumbers all summer long! The vigorous vines are very tolerant to diseases — easily grown on fence or trellis. Try Supercuke this season — we think you'll agree, it's the mildest, tastiest cucumber yet. *(More cucumbers on page 24.)*

Packet	Bonus Pkt.	Jumbo Pkt.
254-P **95c**	254-U **$1.75**	254-J **$3.35**

TOMATO F₁ HYBRID SUPERSTAR Super-delicious! Superstar is one of the most disease-resistant slicing tomatoes in its class — and has an old-fashioned, full-bodied flavor that's impossible to beat! Firm, glossy red fruits grow perfectly round and picture perfect! It's the ideal main crop tomato, with lots of fruit maturing in succession, rather than all at once. These juicy, vine-ripened tomatoes weigh up to one pound, or MORE each! Without a doubt, Superstar is one of the best slicing tomatoes ever created. Get it only from J&P! *(More tomatoes on back cover.)*

Packet	Bonus Pkt.	Jumbo Pkt.
495-P **95c**	495-U **$1.75**	495-J **$3.35**

CANTALOUPE F₁ HYBRID WONDER MELON A short season melon with superior quality and flavor! This new J&P EXCLUSIVE rapidly produces loads of sweet, perfect melons. One of the earliest varieties ever developed! Its vines grow vigorously, flower and set fruit quickly. In only 70 days, you'll harvest plump, 3- to 3½- pound honey sweet melons with firm juicy flesh and a delightful flavor. Ideal for short season areas. In longer season areas, combine with later varieties for a double melon harvest! *(More cantaloupes on page 30.)*

Packet	Bonus Pkt.	Jumbo Pkt.
317-P **95c**	317-U **$1.75**	317-J **$3.35**

NORTH AMERICAN WILD FLOWERS A delightful and carefully selected mix of 21 different wild flower species. This special mix was selected by botanists to include species native to ALL North America, so it will provide a wide variety of blooms in all parts of the country. Includes perennials and self-seeding varieties. Broadcast around an unused area of your property, and then let nature do the gardening! You enjoy the rare beauty of wild flowers in bloom, an ever-changing natural display that few people get to enjoy. Natural beauty . . . completely care free!

Packet	Bonus Pkt.	Jumbo Pkt.
971-P **95c**	971-U **$1.75**	971-J **$3.35**

Cucumber — Supercuke

Tomato — Superstar

Zinnia — Ruffles Mix

North American Wild Flowers

Spinach — Melody

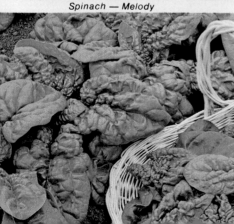

A J&P exclusive
SUPERSTAR TOMATO PLANTS
. . . individually potted!

Not offered in any other catalog! Thriving, hardy SUPERSTAR tomato plants give you a head start on a bumper crop! We have a very limited number of husky, pre-started Superstar plants. These are individually potted, ready to set in the ground — or keep indoors for a couple of weeks until the weather warms up. NOT BAREROOT PLANTS. Elsewhere, tomato plants are often shipped in bunches, with no soil on the roots — not, in our opinion, a satisfactory product for our customers. J&P's EXCLUSIVE POTTED PLANTS GIVE YOU A 2 or 3 MONTH HEAD START! They are already 4 to 5 inches tall when you receive them — fully leafed out and ready to pop into the ground. They are safely shipped in our custom designed shipping tray — they actually keep right on growing on the way to you, and suffer NO TRANSPLANT SHOCK. You eliminate the necessity of starting your own seeds indoors . . . *AND* you'll have the earliest Superstar tomatoes around! Naturally these individually grown plants are costly to produce and ship — but they are surefire work-savers, and a wonderful convenience. And remember! Just *one* healthy plant can give you $5 to $10 worth of tomatoes in a season! Our supply IS limited — please order promptly. Super safe delivery — Superstar plants are grown, and shipped at the right planting time for your area, from points both east *and* west, and sent BY AIR to all but the very closest locations.

Superstar Tomato Plants

3 plants	6 plants	12 plants
4683 **$4.95**	4686 **$8.45**	468-C **$13.95**

Available for delivery to the connecting 48 states and Alaska.

3

Aster—Dwarf Double Gem Mixed

Ageratum—Blue Blazer

Bells of Ireland

Alyssum—Rosie O'Day

Browallia—Blue Bells Improved

AGERATUM
Annual

BLUE BLAZER Large clusters of silvery blue, tassel-like flowers, accented by clear green leaves — this dramatic dwarf F₁ hybrid is ideal for edgings and borders. The earliest of any ageratum! Uniform, very compact 5 to 6 inch plants spread a full foot across. Plant in sun or half-shade for a colorful carpet of bloom from July to frost. Thrives even where ordinary ageratum fails to bloom properly. Stunning combined with petunias or dwarf marigolds.

Packet	Bonus Pkt.	Jumbo Pkt.
600-P **$1.25**	600-U **$2.35**	600-J **$4.45**

ALYSSUM
Annual

Spreads like magic! Carpet your flowerbed with sweet-smelling long-lasting drifts of sunloving alyssum. Thrives in containers — grows about 4 inches high and 12 inches across. Plant seeds in the garden after frost. Thin or transplant to about 6 inches.

ALYSSUM ROSIE O'DAY This All-America winner explodes with deep rose-pink color. Interplant with Carpet of Snow, Royal Carpet and blue lobelia or Blue Blazer ageratum for a striking display.

Packet	Bonus Pkt.	Jumbo Pkt.
606-P **65c**	606-U **$1.25**	606-J **$2.35**

ALYSSUM CARPET OF SNOW The most popular, useful white flower for dense ground covering. Especially effective grouped with clumps of violet-blue Royal Carpet.

Packet	Bonus Pkt.	Jumbo Pkt.
607-P **65c**	607-U **$1.25**	607-J **$2.35**

ALYSSUM ROYAL CARPET All-America winner; the dense purple plant will spread to over 12 inches across. Plant with marigolds or colorful petunias.

Packet	Bonus Pkt.	Jumbo Pkt.
608-P **65c**	608-U **$1.25**	608-J **$2.35**

ASTERS
Annual

Long before Grandma's time, the aster was a beloved, cherished flower. With its great charm and beauty, it is easy to see why it has been planted by generations of gardeners. The softly colored, graceful flowers with dainty petals are borne on tall, stately stems. Grow asters in beds or create matchless border displays with salvia edged with alyssum. Fantastic keeping qualities make asters a favorite flower for arrangements or informal bouquets. Large, festive blooms are yours continuously 'til frost by selecting early and late varieties and sowing them 2 weeks apart. Enjoy Double Powderpuffs early summer to frost — Perfection Mixed in late summer. Plant seeds indoors or in cold frames to be transplanted after frost danger to a sunny spot when 2 or 3 inches tall. Asters are enchanting flowers that will add soft grace and beauty to your garden and home.

ASTER DOUBLE POWDERPUFF MIX Each individual petal tucks itself within the bloom, creating little clusters of "powderpuffs". Stunning bicolor effects of scarlet, crimson, white, rose pink, purple and azure. Pick as large bouquets-in-one — sturdy stems 24 inches long branch freely from the base all season long.

Packet	Bonus Pkt.	Jumbo Pkt.
616-P **65c**	616-U **$1.25**	616-J **$2.35**

ASTER PERFECTION MIXED
A full range of brilliantly coordinated colors including blue, purple, soft pink, crimson, peach and pure white. Four inch blooms on 30 to 36 inch plants.

Packet	Bonus Pkt.	Jumbo Pkt.
614-P **75c**	614-U **$1.45**	614-J **$2.75**

ASTER DWARF DOUBLE GEM MIXED Bright, neat and tidy! True dwarf asters form radiant mounds of double flowers — blue, pink, red and blush cover plants that are only 10 to 12 inches tall. Ideal for containers.

Packet	Bonus Pkt.	Jumbo Pkt.
622-P **85c**	622-U **$1.60**	622-J **$3.10**

ASTER DOUBLE GIANT CREGO MIXED Here's a striking variation of the lovely aster! Called "Giant Ostrich Feathers" because of their long, feathery gracefully curled petals, these huge 5-inch fully double blooms have a delightful "shaggy" appearance. Giant Cregos are long-stemmed and excellent for cutting — mix with your regular asters for an unusual conversation-piece in arrangements! Sturdy 3-foot plants are wilt resistant, blooming in mid-September. These luxuriously-petaled blooms rival the loveliest chrysanthemums for sheer beauty — imagine masses of them in a colorful bed or border! Beautiful range of colors includes blue, crimson, rose pink, white — every color you need for lovely bouquets!

Packet	Bonus Pkt.	Jumbo Pkt.
615-P **65c**	615-U **$1.25**	615-J **$2.35**

BELLS OF IRELAND
Annual

A delightful "old-fashioned" cut flower — superb in dried arrangements. The apple-green, delicately veined bells so prized in the garden are not really the flowers at all. They are the calyxes — outer leaves found at the base of most flowers, only greatly enlarged. Start seeds indoors where summers are short. Elsewhere, seed in sunny warm soil in early summer. To dry for winter bouquets, cut them when they are in their prime, remove the leaves, tie the spikes in clusters and hang them upside down in a cool, well ventilated room to dry.

Packet	Bonus Pkt.	Jumbo Pkt.
642-P **65c**	642-U **$1.25**	642-J **$2.35**

BEGONIA (Fibrous Rooted)
Annual

F₁ HYBRID ORGANDY MIXED Gorgeous shades of red, pink and white flowers will be yours all summer long on neat, uniform plants under a foot tall. Start seed indoors early in the spring and transplant outside after frost, or brighten the winter months by sowing them in pots indoors in September. And begonias are so accommodating — you can even move them in full bloom. Simply scoop up lots of dirt with the roots, relocate and water well. Organdy Mixed begonias feature intriguing foliage; some plants have distinctive bronze leaves, others shiny green.

Packet	Bonus Pkt.	Jumbo Pkt.
636-P **$1.95**	636-U **$3.65**	636-J **$6.95**

4

Begonia—Organdy Mixed

Calendula—Pacific Beauty

Mixed Cactus

Cleome—Pink Queen

Candytuft—Dwarf Fairy Mixed

BROWALLIA
Annual

BLUE BELLS IMPROVED One of the rare true blue flowers! For utter charm, nothing rivals this *improved* strain of lavender-blue Browallia. It cascades gracefully from hanging baskets, flower pots and containers to enhance patios, porches and windows with its neat habit. Decorates rock gardens, window boxes and terraces . . . borders flower beds with its profusion of quaint, bell-shaped flowers that cover with a heavenly shade of lavender-blue. Easy-to-grow in partial shade. Start indoors in spring for outdoor bedding and baskets . . . again in fall for indoor plants.

Packet	Bonus Pkt.	Jumbo Pkt.
644-P **85c**	644-U **$1.60**	644-J **$3.10**

MIXED CACTUS
Perennial

Growing cacti can easily develop into a lifelong hobby when you see the fascinating, fantastic forms take shape. They're interesting even before you get them growing — in the desert, Indians and prospectors courageously climb the large cacti to harvest the seeds for us! You'll note such easily recognized forms as Beavertail, Fish Hook, Barrel, Buckhorn, Prickly Pear plus Giant Saguaro and Cholla.

Plant inside in a shallow container of half sand and half leaf mold. The seeds should be protected and kept warm and moist. You'll notice that some kinds start growing very quickly, while others may take up to two months to sprout. Once the seeds have germinated, they require minimal attention and care. When plants reach the size of a pea, transplant to small pots of sandy soil. Placed on a sunny window sill or in a dry, hot garden spot, your cacti will continue to grow and amaze you for years. A wonderful project for youngsters, too!

Packet	Bonus Pkt.	Jumbo Pkt.
648-P **85c**	648-U **$1.60**	648-J **$3.10**

CALENDULA (Pot Marigold)
Annual

PACIFIC BEAUTY MIXED Few annuals are easier to cultivate or bloom more abundantly. In southerly areas, these bright flowers will bloom nearly the whole year around, and where the climate is less temperate, they will bloom from May until frost. Plants grow 1-1/2 to 2 feet tall — make attractive, free blooming borders, grow rapidly from seed outdoors. Pacific Beauty Mixture has larger flowers (4-1/2 to 5 inches) and is more heat resistant than other varieties. Comes in a beautiful range of colors from a mellow cream to a rich flame orange. Incurving, quill-shaped petals form lovely flowers that have been favorites with florists for years.

Packet	Bonus Pkt.	Jumbo Pkt.
654-P **65c**	654-U **$1.25**	654-J **$2.35**

CANDYTUFT
Annual

DWARF FAIRY MIXED Actually thrives in poor soil, blooms all spring and summer long. The 8-inch mound-like plants form a sculptured carpet of rich colors — white, pink, lavender and crimson. Very good in beds, borders, rock gardens, edgings — lovely in fresh bouquets. Plant after frost in sun or half-shade for profuse blooms in two months. When plants are 2 to 3 inches high, thin to 10 inches apart. Or plant candytuft in late fall in bulb beds for a delightful contrast to your spring blooms.

Packet	Bonus Pkt.	Jumbo Pkt.
660-P **65c**	660-U **$1.25**	660-J **$2.35**

CLEOME (Spider Flower)
Annual

PINK QUEEN Beautiful, carefree tall border plant! Produces bright salmon pink orchid-like blooms on stately 3- to 4-foot plants from July until frost. So easy to grow and care for — cleome is never bothered by insects or disease. Start seeds inside or sow outside after frost. Thin to 18 inches apart when 3 inches high. Plant this All-America Silver Medal winner in striking clusters or masses.

Packet	Bonus Pkt.	Jumbo Pkt.
676-P **75c**	676-U **$1.45**	676-J **$2.75**

PENNGIFT CROWNVETCH (Coronilla varia)
Perennial

The *ideal* ground cover — and that's no exaggeration. Crownvetch is maintenance free, requiring no mowing or irrigation, grows in sun or semi-shade in the poorest soils under some of the worst climate extremes. It stops erosion on the steepest slopes, chokes out weeds, is fire resistant . . . and it's beautiful! The glossy fern-like foliage stays green nearly year around — a neat 12 to 15 inches high. From June until frost the plants are covered with elegant white and pinkish-lavender blooms. Plant any time of the year ground is not frozen or baked hard; allow for two months of growth before freezing weather sets in.

SEEDING KIT You can seed right into weeds or grass cover, then cut down the weeds to serve as mulch. If the area is bare, plan to mulch, or sow seed with rye or fescue as a companion planting. From seed it will take about three years for dense coverage. Kits include seed, Crownvetch inoculant (a must for germination) and instructions.

KIT for small area (1 oz. seed with inoculant)   **$2.95**
Order Cat. No. A-57

KIT for 250 sq. feet (1/4 lb. seed with inoculant)   **$6.95**
Order Cat. No. A-58

KIT for 1,000 sq. feet (1 lb. seed with inoculant)   **$13.95**
Order Cat. No. A-59

FIELD FRESH CROWNS These bareroot crowns or "runners" are healthy, field-harvested systems that are easy to plant. Placed two feet apart, they will establish a lush cover in 2-3 years; for a dense cover in one year, place one foot apart. Can be planted into existing cover or bare soil with no special preparation necessary.

25 crowns for **$9.95**	50 crowns for **$17.45**	100 crowns for **$29.95**
Order Cat. No. 466-L	Order Cat. No. 466-R	Order Cat. No. 466-Y

Penngift Crownvetch

Carnation—Dwarf Fragrance

Coleus — Rainbow Colors Mix

Celosia Cristata—Jewel Box Mixed

Carnation—Chabaud Giant Mix

Celosia Plumosa — Fire Birds Mixed

Delphinium—Giant Pacific Mix

CARNATIONS
Annual

Large, fluffy flowers brimming with spicy fragrance — long, long lasting in arrangements! Plant both these mixtures to have a complete assortment of colorful, plentiful blooms all season. Carnations prefer cool weather and will bloom in 5 to 6 months — they are well worth the wait. For earliest blooms, start seeds indoors 6 to 8 weeks or more before setting out — or sow them outdoors after frost has passed. Although usually treated as an annual, if you take care to mulch and protect them, carnations will bloom for several years.

CARNATION CHABAUD GIANT STRAIN MIX A preferred strain for outdoor bedding, heavily producing magnificent 3-inch blooms topping 18-inch stems. Rich dazzling colors—imagine the beautiful, heady bouquets!

Packet	Bonus Pkt.	Jumbo Pkt.
667-P **65c**	667-U **$1.25**	667-J **$2.35**

CARNATION JULIET 1975 All-America winner. This F1 hybrid bears spicy fragrant, fully-double 2-1/2-inch scarlet flowers of florist quality on strong stems. Silvery green 12-inch plants are tidy and compact.

Packet	Bonus Pkt.	Jumbo Pkt.
671-P **$1.95**	671-U **$3.65**	671-J **$6.95**

CARNATION DWARF FRAGRANCE MIXED Blooms earlier than Chabaud, but dazzling double flowers are of the same size and quality in striking colors of white, red, yellow and rose. Neat and compact — stiff straight stems grow only 12 to 14 inches high.

Packet	Bonus Pkt.	Jumbo Pkt.
666-P **65c**	666-U **$1.25**	666-J **$2.35**

CELOSIA
Annual

Rich, plush flowers of the most unusual shapes — thrive in extreme heat and withstand drought. Two distinct and striking varieties, the bloom of the Crested type (Cristata) is like thick, ruffled velvet and the lavish, graceful Plume type (Plumosa) is accurately named for its feathery bloom. Sparkling colors in vivid reds and yellows. Choice borders — ideal for drying to use in arrangements. Celosias can be started inside about 6 weeks before planting out — or sow directly in the garden when all danger of frost is past and soil is warm.

CELOSIA CRISTATA
JEWEL BOX MIXED Perky rooster comb flowers in a glorious range of gold, scarlet, pink, yellow, copper and crimson are borne on dwarf 6 to 8 inch plants. A gem for containers, low borders and beds.

Packet	Bonus Pkt.	Jumbo Pkt.
688-P **85c**	688-U **$1.60**	688-J **$3.10**

CELOSIA PLUMOSA
FIRE BIRDS MIXED Use this exclusive J&P mixture of brilliant red and gold colored "feathers" to accent your garden; or use in pots — anywhere you want an exotic dash of brilliant color. About 2½ feet tall.

Packet	Bonus Pkt.	Jumbo Pkt.
696-P **75c**	696-U **$1.45**	696-J **$2.75**

NEW EXCLUSIVE J&P

COLEUS
Annual

RAINBOW COLORS MIX These aristocratic house and garden plants are usually found only in exclusive garden shops — and this mix offers a rich assortment of all known coleus colors. Infinite variations of reds, yellows, coppers, pinks, greens, golds — all in beautiful patterns. Technically a perennial; most often used as an annual and quick to grow from seeds, they make superior 15-inch plants for planters, and thrive in shady garden spots. Pot your favorite plants, bring them inside for glorious color during winter days, then set them out again in spring. Cuttings root easily.

Packet	Bonus Pkt.	Jumbo Pkt.
683-P **85c**	683-U **$1.60**	683-J **$3.10**

COLEUS SABER MIX Coleus takes on another leaf form! This one really changes into something novel, new and different . . . bears lance-shaped leaves in a fountain-like habit that gives it an exotic tropical effect. Colored with variations like that of Rainbow Mix . . . more bushy and dwarfed . . . Saber is stunning for indoor plant decor . . . fabulous for pattern interest in outdoor shade beds.

Packet	Bonus Pkt.	Jumbo Pkt.
685-P **$1.50**	685-U **$2.85**	685-J **$5.45**

DELPHINIUM
Perennial

GIANT PACIFIC MIXED Show stoppers at the garden club and traffic stoppers at your home! Giant Pacifics often grow 6 to 8 spikes per plant, each covered with 2½- to 3½-inch flowers, in a magnificent range of colors from white to sky blue to dramatic purple. Plants grow up to 6 feet tall! Create an awe-inspiring hedge with these spectacular perennials.

Packet	Bonus Pkt.	Jumbo Pkt.
724-P **75c**	724-U **$1.45**	724-J **$2.75**

DELPHINIUM BLUE FOUNTAINS MIXED Hardy, compact plants that bloom well under severe conditions. Blue Fountains have the same large size blooms as the Pacific Giants, but are carried on strong, dwarf 3-foot plants. Perfect for windy areas where tall types will be damaged. Mixture contains delightful shades of blue.

Packet	Bonus Pkt.	Jumbo Pkt.
725-P **85c**	725-U **$1.60**	725-J **$3.10**

CORNFLOWER (Bachelor Buttons) — Annual

POLKA DOT MIXED Frilly ruffled flowers in shades of blue, maroon, pink, rose, lavender and white are cool contrasts for bright summer gardens. Double dwarf plants, 15 to 18 inches tall, have beautiful silvery green foliage. Bloom all summer and late into fall. Sow in early spring, again in late June, and even in late fall for the earliest blooms next year!

Packet	Bonus Pkt.	Jumbo Pkt.
703-P **65c**	703-U **$1.25**	703-J **$2.35**

COSMOS — Annual

COSMOS EARLY SENSATION MIXED Largest flowered Cosmos of all! Full range of soft colors, maroon through lavender including white — create a showy array of color in arrangements. Four- to six-inch blossoms atop 4-foot stems truly are sensational in the garden!

Packet	Bonus Pkt.	Jumbo Pkt.
710-P **65c**	710-U **$1.25**	710-J **$2.35**

COSMOS DIABLO 1974 All-America winner! The only *pure* red cosmos. Semi-double two-inch blooms accented by golden centers are borne on 18- to 22-inch plants. Blooms in 60 days, even in the hottest climates. Diablo is luxuriously free flowering — spreads to a full 16 inches for a wealth of color in beds and borders.

Packet	Bonus Pkt.	Jumbo Pkt.
712-P **95c**	712-U **$1.75**	712-J **$3.35**

DAHLIA — Annual

DAHLIA UNWIN DWARF MIXED These lovely 2½- to 3-inch blooms will astound you with their fast growth and beauty. Decorative 15- to 24-inch plants are striking for borders and *en masse*. Their exquisite form and wide range of brilliant clear colors make these dahlias irresistible cutting flowers. Mix includes red, pink, purple, lavender and yellow blooms.

Packet	Bonus Pkt.	Jumbo Pkt.
730-P **75c**	730-U **$1.45**	730-J **$2.75**

DAHLIA UNWIN DWARF TUBERS The same brilliant flowers as described above, but lots quicker because tubers don't require starting indoors. Just plant straight into the ground after frost and enjoy blooms all summer long. Excellent for flower boxes and containers.

10 for **$8.95**	25 for **$17.95**
Order Cat. No. N70	Order Cat. No. N71

DAHLIA REDSKIN A fantastic TRIPLE AWARD WINNER! Holding honors from All-America Selections, All-Britain Trials, and Fleuroselect, Redskin sets double "Unwin" type 3-inch blooms in a dazzling color spectrum — lilac, crimson, yellow, scarlet, orange, white and bright combinations. Tidy plant grows to 15 inches, and has remarkable *bronze foliage!*

Packet	Bonus Pkt.	Jumbo Pkt.
731-P **$1.25**	731-U **$2.35**	731-J **$4.45**

DIANTHUS — Annual

DIANTHUS DOUBLE GAIETY MIXED These are the delightful pinks that grandmother treasured in her garden — and the vibrantly colored fringed flowers with their spicy fragrance still brighten many a bouquet! Bloom profusely on 12-inch plants. The best general purpose mixture of pastel dianthus to be found.

Packet	Bonus Pkt.	Jumbo Pkt.
718-P **65c**	718-U **$1.25**	718-J **$2.35**

DIANTHUS SNOWFIRE 1978 All-America Selection. Hybrid vigor, exceptionally tidy habit and sensational fringed bicolor blooms are the winning features of this unique new dianthus! Blooms are white with cherry centers, and up to 2 inches across. Plant is low growing, and branches from the base to support dense mounds of blooms. Very hardy, blooms for weeks!

Packet	Bonus Pkt.	Jumbo Pkt.
720-P **$1.25**	720-U **$2.35**	720-J **$4.45**

DIMORPHOTHECA (African Daisy or Cape Marigold) — Annual

Daisy-like flowers will add sparkle to your garden — mix includes bright yellow, salmon, rose, apricot-orange and other happy colors. Compact 12-inch plants carry an abundance of 3½- to 4-inch flowers that thrive in full sun. A cheery show all summer!

Packet	Bonus Pkt.	Jumbo Pkt.
735-P **65c**	735-U **$1.25**	735-J **$2.35**

FLORIBUNDA BEGONIAS (Tuberous Rooted)

Marvelous improved new begonia hybrids! Magnificent plants are compact and lush, bear countless iridescent 2-inch blooms for up to FIVE WHOLE MONTHS! Bushy 12-inch well mounded plants take more sun than regular begonias. Six radiant colors — dark red, clear pink, glossy copper, yellow, scarlet and gleaming orange.

6 for **$7.95**	12 for **$13.95**	18 for **$18.95**
Order Cat. No. C42	Order Cat. No. C43	Order Cat. No. C44

GLADIOLUS

PAINT BOX MIXED A custom collection of premium quality, large size bulbs — spectacular new multicolored hybrids with 5-inch blooms, each with two, three, even four colors! Husky stalks soar up to 6 feet. Dazzling in the garden, and what spectacular arrangements! Blooms last and last indoors.

25 for **$5.95**	50 for **$9.95**	100 for **$17.95**
Order Cat. No. 372	Order Cat. No. 373	Order Cat. No. 374

Cornflower — Polka Dot Mixed

Dianthus — Snowfire

Dahlia — Unwins Dwarf Mixed

Cosmos — Early Sensation Mixed

Dianthus — Double Gaiety Mixed

Dimorphotheca

Floribunda Begonia Collection

Gladiolus — Paint Box Mixed

Guys and Dolls

Happy Face

Crackerjack

Marigolds

The cheerful annual flower that asks so little and does so much for sunny borders, hedges, containers, window boxes, mass plantings, rock gardens.

MARIGOLDS HEDGE TYPE F₁ HYBRIDS

Imagine a uniform background or border of tall, gleaming flowers that simply won't stop blooming all summer long! Beautiful new hedge-type marigolds grow 18 to 24 inches high — stand straight and tall with no staking. These tremendous F_1 hybrids vigorously produce gigantic, pom-pom blooms 4 inches across and more!

HAPPY FACE F₁ Hybrid The earliest of early bloomers, this All-America winner branches repeatedly to produce fresh clusters of lemony yellow, 4-inch double blooms, on hedge-size bush, right up until frost.

Packet	Bonus Pkt.	Jumbo Pkt.
823-P **95c**	823-U **$1.75**	823-J **$3.35**

GOLDEN JUBILEE F₁ Hybrid These gorgeous globe-shaped, fully double flowers of the purest shimmering gold are proudly borne well above the fernlike foliage. An All-America winner that resists rain and wind.

Packet	Bonus Pkt.	Jumbo Pkt.
820-P **95c**	820-U **$1.75**	820-J **$3.35**

ORANGE JUBILEE F₁ Hybrid An All-America winner, this early marigold is remarkable for its glowing light-orange color. The stupendous, freely borne flowers are fully double and almost round — always uniform and dense.

Packet	Bonus Pkt.	Jumbo Pkt.
821-P **95c**	821-U **$1.75**	821-J **$3.35**

MARIGOLD CRACKERJACK MIXED (Carnation Flowered)

Our tallest marigold! You'll have huge flowers in all possible marigold colors — primrose, yellow, gold and orange. This "carnation flowered" marigold is not as tightly doubled as the Jubilees, but is, by far, the most popular color mixture available. Tall, 30-inch Crackerjack is extremely hardy and blooms long into the fall when other marigolds have stopped.

Packet	Bonus Pkt.	Jumbo Pkt.
822-P **65c**	822-U **$1.25**	822-J **$2.35**

SPECIAL SAVINGS

A fabulous border of all the new hedge type marigolds! Plant en masse for spectacular effects.
One BONUS Packet each:

Happy Face • Yellow Galore • Golden Jubilee • Orange Jubilee

Order Group No. B-97 . . . **ONLY $4.65**

SUPER SAVINGS! COMPLETE MARIGOLD GARDEN

Graduated Plantings — heights and uses for every spot in the garden.
One packet each: Crackerjack Mix (30″) • Happy Face (24″)
Orange Jubilee (18-24″) • Petite Mix (10″) • Guys and Dolls (6-8″)
Order Group No. T-85 . . . **ONLY $3.25**

GUYS AND DOLLS *(Dwarf Carnation Flowered)* A specially developed mixture of primrose, yellow, gold and orange, perfectly matched for simultaneous blooming and consistent dwarf habit. The compact 6- to 8-inch plants abundantly produce amazingly large 4- to 5-inch blooms that mass effectively for a brilliant carpet of color.

Packet	Bonus Pkt.	Jumbo Pkt.
835-P **75c**	835-U **$1.45**	835-J **$2.75**

Orange Jubilee — All-America Winner

Golden Jubilee — All-America Winner

Petite Spry

Yellow Galore

Bolero — All-America Winner

Primrose Lady

FRENCH MARIGOLDS EXTRA DWARF PETITE STRAIN

Remains dwarfed growing from 6- to 10-inches tall, spreading to 10 inches with multitudes of dainty 1¼-inch blooms.

PETITE MIXED All the Petite varieties below blended to make a dazzling display. A great choice for those who like a little bit of everything!

Packet	Bonus Pkt.	Jumbo Pkt.
829-P **65c**	829-U **$1.25**	829-J **$2.35**

PETITE SPRY Deep mahogany red surrounds the yellow centers of these charming marigolds. They grow 12 inches wide and simply never stop blooming until fall!

Packet	Bonus Pkt.	Jumbo Pkt.
828-P **75c**	828-U **$1.45**	828-J **$2.75**

PETITE YELLOW Brilliantly clear yellow flowers cover the miniature plants all season long. These striking little marigolds are particularly outstanding when planted with blue and red flowers.

Packet	Bonus Pkt.	Jumbo Pkt.
824-P **85c**	824-U **$1.60**	824-J **$3.10**

TWO EXCEPTIONAL ALL-AMERICA HYBRIDS

YELLOW GALORE F₁ HYBRID 1977 ALL-AMERICA WINNER
Bright as the sun, this sensational marigold outshines all others with its *new* shade of pure brilliant yellow. Large double blossoms grow in lively abundance in garden, hedge or pot . . . exceptional hybrid vigor gives you a long, long blooming season.

Packet	Bonus Pkt.	Jumbo Pkt.
838-P **95c**	838-U **$1.75**	838-J **$3.35**

PRIMROSE LADY F₁ HYBRID 1977 ALL-AMERICA WINNER
Rare new carnation-flowered marigold in a primrose yellow color. A full 20 inches tall with multitudes of gorgeous 3- to 4-inch blooms.

Packet	Bonus Pkt.	Jumbo Pkt.
818-P **95c**	818-U **$1.75**	818-J **$3.35**

DWARF FRENCH

Generally the same habit as the Extra Dwarfs but slightly taller, and the bright flowers in this class are 2 inches across.

RED BROCADE A color *rare* in marigolds — 2-inch carnation-like blooms of a solid, deep mahogany red, with edges delicately trimmed in gold for a striking contrast. An early and free-blooming variety.

Packet	Bonus Pkt.	Jumbo Pkt.
836-P **65c**	836-U **$1.25**	836-J **$2.35**

BOLERO The blossoms of this All-America bicolor are a striking bright red variegated with golden markings. These free-blooming plants grow 8 to 12 inches tall and hold their spicy flowers well above the foliage.

Packet	Bonus Pkt.	Jumbo Pkt.
830-P **65c**	830-U **$1.25**	830-J **$2.35**

BROCADE MIXED Aptly named, the varieties included in this selection are all variegated with the exception of a rare pure yellow to add sunny brightness. The bicolor flowers range from gold and crimson to yellow and deep orange-red and are borne on 10 to 14 inch tall plants.

Packet	Bonus Pkt.	Jumbo Pkt.
831-P **75c**	831-U **$1.45**	831-J **$2.75**

CREOLE MIX Festive colors ranging from cinnabar red to brilliant gold! These showy dwarf hybrids range from 10 to 12 inches tall . . . produce a tremendous quantity of spectacular single petalled flowers.

Packet	Bonus Pkt.	Jumbo Pkt.
816-P **65c**	816-U **$1.25**	816-J **$2.35**

LEGAL GOLD AMAZING F₁ HYBRID TRIPLOID Vigorous 12- to 14-inch plant produces an extra wealth of pure, shining gold 2½-inch blooms — offers more flowers per plant than any other marigold only 45 to 50 days after seeding.

Packet	Bonus Pkt.	Jumbo Pkt.
837-P **$1.25**	837-U **$2.35**	837-J **$4.45**

Petite Mixed

Creole Mix

Red Brocade

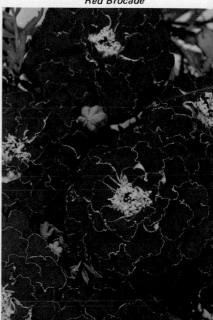

DUSTY MILLER
Perennial

Lacy, small 6 inch plants with delicate silvery white foliage. Plant Dusty Miller for carefree planters or borders — does well even in poor soils. Very showy when combined with Trailing Sapphire lobelia or Blue Blazer ageratum — the perfect contrast as a border for evergreens or bright Sprinter geraniums. A perennial, often grown as an annual — sow directly outside in spring, or in colder climates, start inside in flats in February or March. Does sensationally in pots and window boxes.

Packet	Bonus Pkt.	Jumbo Pkt.
736-P **65c**	736-U **$1.25**	736-J **$2.35**

GAZANIA (South African Daisy)
Annual

SUNSHINE MIXED Dazzling daisy-shaped gazanias originated in Africa. Sunshine mix is an outstanding hybrid strain with glorious and bizarre patterns that few gardeners — even experts — have ever seen. Exotic 2½-inch flowers are borne on 9-inch stems in striking color combinations of red, yellow, brown, salmon, bronze and orange. Foliage is decorative gray green. Drought resistant flowers thrive in full sun and bloom until frost. Plant in April, or when frost danger is past. Fascinating, free blooming and dramatic cut flowers.

Packet	Bonus Pkt.	Jumbo Pkt.
742-P **75c**	742-U **$1.45**	742-J **$2.75**

GERANIUMS
Annual

Continuously blooming through the heat of the summer, geraniums are universally loved for their gorgeous clusters of petite flowers . . . and they are one of the easiest to grow of all annuals. Geraniums are perfect for borders, window boxes, and can even be grown as indoor houseplants. You'll have flowers in July from an April sowing.

SPRINTER *1973 Fleuroselect and All-Britain winner* Gets the jump on every other geranium! In trial after trial, amazing F$_1$ hybrid Sprinter flowered 2 to 3 WEEKS EARLIER than any other seed variety, *on plants three-fourths as tall*. Not only will you have the earliest blooms of all, you'll have the most lavish and you won't have to "pinch" for large flowers. The compact plant presents you with big clusters of brilliant scarlet flowers.

Packet	Bonus Pkt.	Jumbo Pkt.
749-P **$1.65**	749-U **$2.95**	749-J **$5.65**

FLEURISTE MIX A perfectly controlled blend of lavender, pink, red, white and rose colored blooms — all pleasantly offset by handsome ivy green foliage. Standing a neat one- to two-feet tall, these plants will reward you with a vibrant display of lovely flowers during the hottest part of summer.

Packet	Bonus Pkt.	Jumbo Pkt.
748-P **85c**	748-U **$1.60**	748-J **$3.10**

GYPSOPHILA (Baby's Breath)
Annual

COVENT GARDEN WHITE A breathtaking flowered mass of misty-white blossoms. Our Covent Garden White produces the largest flowers 2/3 of an inch across with delicately veined petals on 1½-foot stems. The airy sprays of white "baby's breath" are popular "fillers" for arrangements — especially attractive with asters or sweet peas. Choose an open, sunny location; plant outside in drifts after frost danger has passed. We suggest planting every two weeks so that your display of these sweet flowers never stops. When seedlings are about 3 inches tall, thin to 10 inches apart for fuller plants. Gypsophila can be easily dried by cutting and hanging upside down in a warm dry place.

Packet	Bonus Pkt.	Jumbo Pkt.
761-P **65c**	761-U **$1.25**	761-J **$2.35**

HELIANTHUS (Sunflower)
Annual

Very large flowers in several shades of yellow grow freely in hot dry weather. Sunflowers make useful screens, borders and hedges. Very easy to grow but do require lots of sunshine to develop properly. Sow outdoors in the spring.

MAMMOTH RUSSIAN The biggest flower of all — the gigantic black-centered yellow blooms are borne singly on stems that reach 6 to 10 feet tall! The perfect screen — we suggest staking these huge flowers. Heads bigger than dinner plates fill up with tasty seeds by late summer — they're nutritious and delicious when roasted and salted, if you can beat the song birds to them! Children get a thrill from growing a flower that easily reaches four times their height!

Packet	Bonus Pkt.	Jumbo Pkt.
778-P **75c**	778-U **$1.45**	778-J **$2.75**

IMPATIENS
Annual

F$_1$ HYBRID IMP MIXED Excellent showy flowers to plant in any difficult shady area. The Imp hybrids' large, vividly colored blossoms are prolifically produced on 1 to 2 foot plants. Two-inch rounded flowers are bright crimson, orange, violet, pink, red and pure white. Sow seeds indoors about 6 weeks before the last frost is expected, then transplant to a partially shaded spot in your garden. Cut them back and pot for delightful houseplants during the winter.

Packet	Bonus Pkt.	Jumbo Pkt.
800-P **$1.25**	800-U **$2.35**	800-J **$4.45**

TANGEGLOW Light up a shady spot with the flourescent true orange of Tangeglow, a totally new and different easy-to-grow Impatiens. It'll create a vivid display of brilliant color with large 2½-inch blooms gleaming above dark green foliage, outdoors until frost, then indoors as a bright pot plant.

Packet	Bonus Pkt.	Jumbo Pkt.
801-P **$2.75**	801-U **$5.25**	801-J **$9.95**

Dusty Miller

Gazania—Sunshine Mixed

Gypsophila-Covent Garden

Geranium — Sprinter

Helianthus—Mammoth Russian

Geranium — Fleuriste Mix

10

LARKSPUR
Annual

GIANT IMPERIAL MIXED You won't have to pamper these larkspur! When the ground is still covered with snow, you can sow the seeds and have magnificent spikes of fluffy color in late spring. Buy extra now — save to plant next September — and have early spring bloom. Exquisite florets of lilac, crimson, pink, rose, blue and white are borne on erect spikes 4 to 5 feet tall. Gorgeous flowers retain their color when dried.

Packet	Bonus Pkt.	Jumbo Pkt.
806-P **65c**	806-U **$1.25**	806-J **$2.35**

LOBELIA
Annual

Commonly referred to as "fairy wings" because of the appearance of each clear blue flower. Perfect for a dainty edging by your sidewalk, driveway, or flower bed. Stunning for a hanging basket of luscious cascading color. The seeds are very tiny, so we suggest starting indoors 10 to 12 weeks before planting outside six inches apart. No other annual produces such intense blue flowers all summer long! Lobelia does well in partial shade.

LOBELIA CRYSTAL PALACE Plant for a deep-blue 4 to 6 inch border. Very compact — spreads easily.

Packet	Bonus Pkt.	Jumbo Pkt.
812-P **75c**	812-U **$1.45**	812-J **$2.75**

LOBELIA TRAILING SAPPHIRE Light clear blue flowers with tiny white centers will cascade from hanging baskets, containers or window boxes.

Packet	Bonus Pkt.	Jumbo Pkt.
813-P **75c**	813-U **$1.45**	813-J **$2.75**

A FLOWER ARRANGER'S DREAM
A COMPLETE CUTTING GARDEN — 24 packets in all

One packet each:

Aster — Dwarf Double Gem Mix
Candytuft — Dwarf Fairy Mix
Carnation — Chabaud Giant Mix
Calendula — Pacific Beauty Mix
Celosia — Jewel Box Mix
Cornflower — Polka Dot Mix
Cosmos — Early Sensation Mix
Dahlia — Redskin
Delphinium — Pacific Giant Mix
Dianthus — Double Gaiety Mix
Gypsophila — Covent Garden White
Larkspur — Giant Imperial Mix

Marigold — Crackerjack Mix
    Happy Face
    Petite Mix
Rudbeckia — Rustic Colors
Snapdragon — Spring Giant Mix
Stock — 7 Week Trysomic
Strawflower — Bouquet Mixed
    (Semi Dwarf)
Sweet Pea — Royal Mix
Sweet William — Dbl. Midget Mix
Verbena — Florist Strain Mix
Zinnia — State Fair Mix
    Peter Pan Mix

Order Group No. C-25... **ONLY $14.45**

HOLLYHOCK
Biennial

SUMMER CARNIVAL MIXED Unlike other tall strains, Summer Carnival Hollyhock Mixed blooms the first year it is planted. Gorgeous 1972 All-America winner produces lovely rosette-centered pompom flowers 4-inches across with an outside row of broad, flat petals. Excellent background flower — grows 5 to 6 feet tall, requires staking. Seeds sown 1/2 inch deep in late spring out of doors will grow into plants that bloom in late summer. A rich range of clear, glorious colors — rose, yellow, light pink, white and crimson.

Packet	Bonus Pkt.	Jumbo Pkt.
784-P **95c**	784-U **$1.75**	784-J **$3.35**

MAJORETTE 1976 All-America Award winner — the first truly dwarf Hollyhock mixture, growing just 2 feet tall in a range of vibrant colors — rose, yellow, pink, red, white and crimson. Fluffy, semi-double flowers are closely packed on short plants accented with attractive fig leaf-like foliage — ideal for low borders. And, you never need to stake the plants. Older varieties take 2 years to bloom — Majorette flowers in 4 months!

Packet	Bonus Pkt.	Jumbo Pkt.
785-P **$1.25**	785-U **$2.35**	785-J **$4.45**

NASTURTIUMS
Annual

A popular annual — and just about the most rewarding plant you could grow! They bloom heavily, early, and are excellent ground covers. On the practical side, Nasturtium repels many garden insects — and the leaves, blossoms and even the young seeds are good to eat! Plant Nasturtium in spring bulb beds to quickly cover yellowing bulb foliage. Easy to grow, too — they don't demand rich soil and actually produce more flowers in sandy or gravelly locations. Plant after frost 6 inches apart in a sunny spot. Thin later to 18 inches apart and you'll have loads of flowers until next fall — plenty for cutting too.

NASTURTIUM GLORIOUS GLEAM MIX All-America winner and a glory to behold! Trails or climbs 3 feet and comes in a rich range of colors — salmon, rose, yellow, primrose and red. Long stemmed, large semi-double blooms have a spicy fragrance.

Packet	Bonus Pkt.	Jumbo Pkt.
839-P **75c**	839-U **$1.45**	839-J **$2.75**

NASTURTIUM DWARF JEWEL MIX Twelve inch, compact plants are very free blooming — the large semi-double flowers come in a glorious range of brilliant colors and are held well above the foliage.

Packet	Bonus Pkt.	Jumbo Pkt.
840-P **75c**	840-U **$1.45**	840-J **$2.75**

Impatiens—Hybrid Imp Mixed

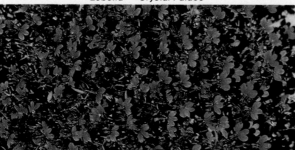

Lobelia — Crystal Palace

Nasturtium—Glorious Gleam Mix

Impatiens — Tangeglow

Larkspur—Giant Imperial Mixed

Nasturtium—Dwarf Jewel Mix

Hollyhock—Summer Carnival Mixed

11

Orchid Cloud

SINGLE GRANDIFLORAS

APOLLO Absolutely stunning white dwarf grandiflora, blooms earlier than any other white petunia in this category. Lightly ruffled blooms of an excellent heavy texture hold up beautifully all summer.

Packet	Bonus Pkt.	Jumbo Pkt.
855-P **85c**	855-U **$1.60**	855-J **$3.10**

HAPPINESS One of the most popular petunias in the country today. Vibrant, bright rose-pink flower — one of the earliest to bloom.

Packet	Bonus Pkt.	Jumbo Pkt.
858-P **85c**	858-U **$1.60**	858-J **$3.10**

ORCHID CLOUD An outstanding extra-large orchid-lavender grandiflora with deep purple striations. Flowers are attractively ruffled and of heavy texture. Weather resistant; an early bloomer and a full season performer.

Packet	Bonus Pkt.	Jumbo Pkt.
859-P **85c**	859-U **$1.60**	859-J **$3.10**

RAZZLE DAZZLE MIXTURE This well-named mixture of variegated grandifloras is truly dazzling. Includes red, deep blue, deep rose, and wine-purple bicolors, selected for matched habit and earliness.

Packet	Bonus Pkt.	Jumbo Pkt.
863-P **85c**	863-U **$1.60**	863-J **$3.10**

Double Delight Mixture

Petunias

FABULOUS F₁ HYBRID PETUNIAS The closest thing there is to an indispensable flower.

Until you've seen *these* annuals, "hybrid vigor" is just a textbook term. These fabulous F₁ hybrid petunias far excel any you may remember from a few years ago. They have been painstakingly developed by controlled hand pollination from selected inbred stock. And each hybrid is more vigorous, bigger, brighter and easier to grow than any of the parent stock from which it came.

There are two main types of petunias — the multifloras, which bear great quantities of blooms 2 to 3 inches across, and the more popular grandifloras, which bear fewer but more spectacular blooms — ranging from 3 to even 5 inches in diameter. Within the two classifications there are both double and single types. Singles are best for show in beds and borders because they resist drooping from collected rain. Doubles are spectacular in hanging baskets, planters, balcony boxes and such, where their cascading beauty is most effective. And the doubles are great cut flowers!

Petunias need a minimum of a half day full sun, but they'll tolerate several hours of light shade. Sow seeds indoors 8 to 10 weeks before the last expected frost. Transplant to the garden 6 to 8 weeks after starting (the seedlings can take light frost). Space young plants 15 to 18 inches apart in the garden.

Plant plenty of petunias — you can't go wrong. Many are fragrant, especially during the evening. Their uses are endless — and with the new hybrids, petunias have never been more breathtaking!

DOUBLE MULTIFLORA

DOUBLE DELIGHT MIXTURE A remarkable color range of solid and bicolor shades — some found in no other blend! Flowers early, excellent dwarf habit. Each variety selected for fullness of the double blooms.

Packet	Bonus Pkt.	Jumbo Pkt.
868-P **85c**	868-U **$1.60**	868-J **$3.10**

PLANTING HINT Petunia seeds are tiny and should be mixed with fine sand before sowing to insure even distribution.

Happiness

Blushing Maid

Razzle Dazzle Mixture

Bridal Bouquet

Indoor Plants

Grow them from seeds! It's easy . . . fun . . . and rewarding!
Sprouting these carefully chosen varieties is almost as easy as growing radishes. Packets contain simple cultural instructions and 100 seeds . . . enough for a jungle of plants for indoor decor and patios. Each of which would cost $10.00 or more full-grown!

Aralia Sieboldi

DOUBLE GRANDIFLORAS
For hanging baskets — the most spectacular flower you can choose!

BRIDAL BOUQUET The finest white double petunia—and the earliest. Extra-large pure white flowers are borne on compact plants. Wonderful for pots as well as beds and borders. Imagine a walkway lined with these lovely full blooms!

Packet	Bonus Pkt.	Jumbo Pkt.
866-P **$1.25**	866-U **$2.35**	866-J **$4.45**

BLUSHING MAID F₁ HYBRID Fresh as spring, this 1977 All-America winner bursts into bloom with a ruffle of *fully double* petals! Its refreshing blossoms are a soft salmon pink. The plants reach 10 inches high and spread to 12 to 14 inches . . . lending themselves to single plantings in pots — or, in a garden border. Blooms early on young plants.

Packet	Bonus Pkt.	Jumbo Pkt.
870-P **$1.25**	870-U **$2.35**	870-J **$4.45**

FANFARE MIXTURE Contains only fully double, early flowering petunias. Full color range includes bicolors of early flowering, uniform double petunias.

Packet	Bonus Pkt.	Jumbo Pkt.
867-P **95c**	867-U **$1.75**	867-J **$3.35**

Aralia Elegantissima

Schefflera Actinophylla

Circus

CIRCUS *1972 All-America Winner* Ideal for hanging baskets — most honored petunia in many years! Lavish blooms are a festive blend of sparkling white and near-flourescent salmon-red. Deeply ruffled flowers are aswirl with the brightest bicolor patterns imaginable. Outstanding habit plus *very early bloom* gives you plenty of color all season long!

Packet	Bonus Pkt.	Jumbo Pkt.
865-P **$1.25**	865-U **$2.35**	865-J **$4.45**

Fanfare Mixture

Christmas Pepper

ARALIA SIEBOLDI *(Fatsia japonica)* Easy-care, lush tropical plants. Leathery, deeply lobed leaves up to 15-inches across are borne on long stems. Natural bushy habit is easily trained upright.
624-P **$1.65**

ARALIA ELEGANTISSIMA (False Aralia) *(Dizygotheca)* Fans of 7 to 10 slender, dark green deeply serrated leaves top striking upright brown and white dappled stems. Decorative leaf form resembles, but is not related to, marijuana (cannabis).
623-P **$3.95**

SCHEFFLERA ACTINOPHYLLA (Umbrella Tree) *(Brassaia actinophylla)* Rapid growing plants with extraordinary shiny foliage. Graceful fronds of radiating "finger" leaves top tall stems in umbrella fashion. Grows as tall or as bushy as you allow.
915-P **$1.65**

CHRISTMAS PEPPER The ideal plant to grow for Christmas gifts! Bright fruit blazes from 10-inch dark green foliage like tiny tree lights, turning green to white, purple and finally scarlet. Start the easy to grow plants in May, one to a 4-inch pot, for holiday decor and gifts. As as attractive outdoor bedding plant, too . . . start in March, transplant in May.
851-P **$2.45**

13

Phlox — Dwarf Beauty Mixed

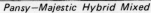

Portulaca—Sunglo	Primrose—Pacific Giants Mixed	Pansy—Majestic Hybrid Mixed	Rudbeckia—Rustic Colors

PANSIES — Annual

Welcome as the robin in spring — pansies are among the best-known and most beloved of all flowers. These hardy varieties bloom early in the spring, continue late into the fall — and the foliage will remain green throughout the winter months. Masses of alluring colors and velvety texture make lush and brilliant borders or edgings. Easily grown in pots and window boxes. They reach 6 to 8 inches in height, and won't object to partial shade. Start indoors then transplant outside as soon as the ground can be worked — or plant early next fall and protect over the winter for really early spring blooms. Pick off faded flowers to encourage continual blooming until frost.

PANSY SWISS GIANT MIXED Vigorous and lush — these extra-large velvety flowers are 3½ to 4 inches across and set atop strong stems. Petals are gently waved and thickly textured. The color range offers dark rich tones of rose, brown, yellow, purple, dark red, blue — accented with white.

Packet	Bonus Pkt.	Jumbo Pkt.
847-P 85c	847-U $1.60	847-J $3.10

PANSY IMPERIAL BLUE 1975 All-America winner remarkable for its dependable ability to bloom, without fading, from early spring through the heat and humidity of summer into fall. Lush spreading 8-inch plants produce 3-inch crystal-blue blooms with navy centers and golden throats for colorful pots and borders.

Packet	Bonus Pkt.	Jumbo Pkt.
850-P $1.95	850-U $3.65	850-J $6.95

PANSY F₁ HYBRID MAJESTIC MIXED An All-America winner — an eye-catcher in any garden. Huge bright blossoms up to 4 inches across that have the bright characteristic pansy "faces." Our formula blend includes shades of yellow, purple, red, rose, scarlet, bronze and white. Majestic Mix blooms several weeks earlier than other pansy varieties.

Packet	Bonus Pkt.	Jumbo Pkt.
849-P $1.95	849-U $3.65	849-J $6.95

PHLOX — Annual

DWARF BEAUTY MIXED One of the showiest, most colorful annuals with large, bright clusters of florets — easy to grow. This vivid mix includes the rare lavender-blue, plus red, pink, white, and deep blue — each dotted with a contrasting "eye." Perfect for sloping areas and rock gardens — compact and heat resistant. Seed in a sunny place after danger of frost — or, since they're slow to germinate, start indoors for earlier blooms. Colorful globed 6 to 8 inch plants bloom 'til fall — spectacular combined with dwarf marigolds and zinnias in borders and flower pots.

Packet	Bonus Pkt.	Jumbo Pkt.
875-P 75c	875-U $1.45	875-J $2.75

PRIMROSE (Primula) — Perennial

PACIFIC GIANTS MIXED This mild sounding perennial will burst out in eye-dazzling shades early in May! Clusters of showy blooms crown slender 10-inch stems, carried above bright green, broad crinkly-textured leaves. Primroses thrive in shady areas — perfect for neglected spots under shady trees or on a sun-filtered patio. Neat, compact habit makes the primrose a favorite flowering houseplant. Seed is slow to germinate — start seedlings indoors, transplant outdoors for a show of color in May and June. Lift plants in fall and bring indoors for winter and spring color.

Packet	Bonus Pkt.	Jumbo Pkt.
887-P 95c	887-U $1.75	887-J $3.35

PORTULACA (Moss Rose) — Annual

SUNGLO New F₁ hybrid Sunglo has *greater vigor* and *uniformity* than any previous variety of this favored and most dependable of hot weather annuals! Thriving in poor soil and hot, dry conditions, Sunglo quickly spreads, forming a brilliant 6-inch tall carpet of white, lavender, scarlet, shades of pink, orange and yellow flowers. Blooming a short 8 weeks after planting, the 2½-inch double blooms are produced in amazing abundance, and look like tiny roses with petals as sheer as tissue paper. Never bothered by insects or disease, amazing new Sunglo is foolproof for sunparched garden areas.

Packet	Bonus Pkt.	Jumbo Pkt.
882-P 65c	882-U $1.25	882-J $2.35

RUDBECKIA (Gloriosa Daisy) — Perennial

RUSTIC COLORS A quaint and charming hybrid that won an All-Britain award before coming to U.S.A. and bringing the old-fashioned "Gloriosa Daisies" in a NEW range of colors. A medley of shades from sunny pure gold through exciting shades and bicolor combinations, to solid rich brown . . . all with velvety brown button centers! Up to THIRTY of these intriguing blooms on *dwarf, uniform* 20- to 24-inch plants. A perennial that's extremely showy in gardens, containers and as cut flowers . . . wintering through most areas to bloom again in profusion for many a summer.

Packet	Bonus Pkt.	Jumbo Pkt.
895-P 75c	895-U $1.45	895-J $2.75

SCABIOSA (Pincushion Flower) — Annual

GIANT DOUBLE MIXED The more of these delightful "pincushion flowers" you pick, the more you will have from mid-summer on. The sphere-shaped flowers 2 inches across and 2 inches deep range from salmon through shades of scarlet, white, pink and popular lavender blue. Broad, frilly flowers crown long stems 2 to 2½ feet tall. Sow seeds outdoors after frost season has passed — for earlier blooms, scabiosa can be started indoors and then transplanted to a sunny location when 3 inches tall. Thin or transplant about 12 inches apart for best results.

Packet	Bonus Pkt.	Jumbo Pkt.
899-P 65c	899-U $1.25	899-J $2.35

SALVIA — Annual

Dazzling spikes of scarlet florets are yours from mid-summer 'til late fall. Stunning in beds or borders, the beautiful warm red is especially striking when combined with low growing annuals such as alyssum, petunias or marigolds. Plant seeds outdoors when danger of frost has passed — or start early indoors. Thin or transplant to about 12 inches.

SALVIA EARLY BONFIRE (18 to 24 inches — use for background)

Packet	Bonus Pkt.	Jumbo Pkt.
911-P 75c	911-U $1.45	911-J $2.75

SALVIA ST. JOHN'S FIRE (10 to 12 inches — border or containers)

Packet	Bonus Pkt.	Jumbo Pkt.
912-P 85c	912-U $1.60	912-J $3.10

SALVIA HOT JAZZ (14 to 20 inches – for border or beds)

Packet	Bonus Pkt.	Jumbo Pkt.
913-P $1.25	913-U $2.35	913-J $4.45

Salvia—Early Bonfire

Scabiosa

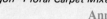

Stock—Dwarf 7 Week Trysomic

Snapdragon—Spring Giant Mixed | Snapdragon—Floral Carpet Mixed | Snapdragon—Little Darling | Sweet Pea—Royal Family Mixed

SNAPDRAGON — Annual

Recent years have shown great improvements in the lovely snapdragons — these showy flowers now come in a range of sizes from 6 inches to 3½ feet and can be used for neat edgings or stately garden backdrops. The exciting new flower form, the dainty "butterfly", is the familiar snapdragon shape without the "snapper" — so more of each petal's color is displayed. We've included the best traditionally flowered snapdragons also — Spring Giant and Floral Carpet. Every one of the gorgeous snapdragons listed below is a vigorous F₁ hybrid and an easily grown mixture of the brightest and clearest colors available. Keep the spikes picked as they mature, and blooms will be continuous.

SNAPDRAGONS SPRING GIANT MIXED Vigorous and extremely tall — 3 to 3½-foot plants make a breathtaking, lavish border. Mix was carefully selected to co-ordinate the colors so that they will bloom at the same time and grow to a uniform height. The florets are the old-fashioned, traditional snap that most of us fondly remember.

Packet	Bonus Pkt.	Jumbo Pkt.
925-P **95c**	925-U **$1.75**	925-J **$3.35**

SNAPDRAGONS BRIGHT BUTTERFLIES Unique flower form — each dainty floret is like a brilliant butterfly. This All-America winner comes in a range of glorious colors — crimson, deep rose, bronze, yellow and white. Vigorous and medium tall, the 2½-foot plants branch freely from the base producing a large number of richly flowered spikes. A wonderful choice for border planting.

Packet	Bonus Pkt.	Jumbo Pkt.
926-P **$1.25**	926-U **$2.35**	926-J **$4.45**

SNAPDRAGONS MADAME BUTTERFLY Many large flowers cover each bright, medium tall 2½-foot stalk. Azalea-type flowers are *double florets* — larger than ordinary snapdragons. A wide range of dazzling colors blooms all summer — pink, red, yellow, bronze, and white. Beautiful in the garden and absolutely lush in arrangements!

Packet	Bonus Pkt.	Jumbo Pkt.
928-P **$1.25**	928-U **$2.35**	928-J **$4.45**

SNAPDRAGONS LITTLE DARLING All-America and All-Britain Selections, this semi-dwarf is a very uniform 12-inches tall. Same butterfly form and bright, clear colors as Bright Butterflies. Removing the vibrant stalks as they pass their peak assures continued mass blooming. Requires no staking — neat for edgings and bedding.

Packet	Bonus Pkt.	Jumbo Pkt.
927-P **95c**	927-U **$1.75**	927-J **$3.35**

SNAPDRAGONS FLORAL CARPET MIXED Extra dwarf strain produces very neat ball-shaped plants that grow 6 to 8 inches high. Early bloomer — produces many short, charming spikes of medium sized florets in a stunning array of colors — bronze, red, pink, rose, orchid, yellow and white. A showy edging plant and wonderful in beds and low borders.

Packet	Bonus Pkt.	Jumbo Pkt.
929-P **$1.25**	929-U **$2.35**	929-J **$4.45**

STOCK — Annual

DWARF 7 WEEK TRYSOMIC The *only* strain that blooms outdoors in the hottest weather. Extra early and hardy, with 85% or more double flowers. Lovely 15-inch-tall, bushy plants are covered with glorious, richly fragrant flower spikes. Colors range from snow white through azure, pink, deep rose, purple and yellow. Sow seeds outside in May — Trysomic begins to bloom when only 6 inches tall — keeps on all summer long!

Packet	Bonus Pkt.	Jumbo Pkt.
919-P **75c**	919-U **$1.45**	919-J **$2.75**

SWEET PEAS — Annual

Fabulously fragrant flowers for sunny garden fences or trellises. The old-time climbers have been remarkably improved and the new bush types are very popular for borders, beds or window boxes. Long favored for cutting flowers — long lasting in cheerful brilliant bouquets. Sweet Peas need rich, deep soil that is fairly moist. Sow seeds outdoors as soon as possible in the spring. Thin plants to 6 inches apart. To have a profusion of colorful sweet peas for as long as possible, pick the flowers before they start to form seed pods.

SWEET PEAS ROYAL FAMILY MIXED The amazing new Royal Family shows improvement in every respect over all other sweet pea varieties. Royals are so easy to train on trellis or fence for old-fashioned garden charm — but never before has a climbing sweet pea offered such outstanding keeping quality as a cut flower too! These beautiful flowers are much larger than common sweet peas, and are borne on unusually long, thick stems — and they really last in arrangements! Royals are a new breed of heat-resistant sweet pea — truly impressive! They have an extremely long blooming period and flower profusely, in spite of hot weather. Enjoy the finest climbing sweet pea you can plant, in the clear brilliant colors that have made sweet peas all-time favorites.

Packet	Bonus Pkt.	Jumbo Pkt.
935-P **75c**	935-U **$1.45**	935-J **$2.75**

SWEET PEAS JET SET MIXED A recently developed bush-type sweet pea! The blossoms are actually 20 per cent larger and come in a rainbow of gorgeous colors from white to crimson. Growing 2 to 3 feet tall and requiring no nets or trellises, Jet Set Sweet Peas are stunning in borders or bright window boxes.

Packet	Bonus Pkt.	Jumbo Pkt.
941-P **85c**	941-U **$1.60**	941-J **$3.10**

STRAWFLOWER — Annual

SEMI-DWARF BOUQUET MIXED Old-fashioned favorite — with many fascinating rich colors . . . white, pink and yellow, through red, crimson, orange, gold and mahogany shades. Uniform 24-inch plants bear dozens of fully-double 2-inch flowers on long straight stems. Plants flower profusely from early August until frost — attractively bright in flower beds and rock gardens. To dry, simply cut when about one-quarter open (they open further as they dry) and hang upside down in a shaded dry place.

Packet	Bonus Pkt.	Jumbo Pkt.
905-P **75c**	905-U **$1.45**	905-J **$2.75**

SWEET WILLIAM — Biennial

DOUBLE MIDGET MIXED Only 6 to 8 inches high, showered with an abundant show of spicy, fragrant blooms in pink, purple, scarlet and white. The stocky little plants are popular for borders, beds and rock gardens. You'll just love their neat compact arrangement of showy blooms. So easy to grow, too — a panorama of garden color the year after planting — protective mulch of straw or leaves should be used where winters are severe.

Packet	Bonus Pkt.	Jumbo Pkt.
949-P **75c**	949-U **$1.45**	949-J **$2.75**

Sweet William—Double Midget Mixed | Strawflower — Semi-Dwarf Bouquet Mixed

15

Peter Pan Cream

Peter Pan Mixed

Sprite Mixed

Thumbelina Mixed

Whirligig Mixed

Zinnias

THE MOST POPULAR ANNUAL OF THEM ALL! And it's very easy to understand why, too — just take a look at these amazing new award winners. They're more beautiful and better than ever! But still just as carefree and rewarding to grow. Zinnias do remarkably well anywhere with almost total neglect — they'll thrive in the hot summer sun and near-drouth conditions, but do well in partial shade, too. In semi-shade they may grow up to six inches taller than the heights listed in the descriptions, to reach for the sun; but they'll still put forth countless blossoms. Wherever you plant them, these zinnias will bloom and bloom all summer long — you'll have plenty in your garden as well as great, gorgeous quantities for cutting.

Out of the multitude of zinnia varieties available, we've come up with this selection. These varieties offer a complete range of size and color — and all of them are tops in their class. We feel that the zinnias on these pages represent the "cream of the crop" — the very best of the new improved zinnias as well as the tried-and-true standbys. As you will see, these super zinnias come in a wide variety of colors, sizes and shapes — from the dazzling giants to the dainty dwarfs. Among these we offer, we're sure you'll come up with just the zinnias you need for your garden, favorite containers, walkways or for indoor beauty in bouquets or arrangements. Zinnias are truly among the biggest bargains in garden beauty available today — they're hardy, colorful, all-purpose busy bloomers!

ZINNIAS **THE AWARD WINNING NEW PETER PAN SERIES**
No other class of flowers has been rated so highly in the 40-year history of All-America Selections as have the Peter Pan Zinnias. As the individual colors of this stunning series have been introduced, they have won All-America awards — and half of them won All-Britain honors as well. These outstanding plants reach a height of 12 to 14 inches and keep a solid, compact appearance. The new growth and blooms have the tidy habit of covering the older ones so the plants are always fresh and full of brilliantly colorful 3 to 4 inch blooms. Grow Peter Pans and you'll discover why they are so widely acclaimed around the world.

ZINNIA F_1 **HYBRID PETER PAN MIXED** A perfectly balanced blend of the five All-America award winning Peter Pan Zinnias, plus two newly introduced colors! Includes Peter Pan plum pink, light pink, yellow, orange, cream, white and scarlet.

Packet	Bonus Pkt.	Jumbo Pkt.
981-P **$1.65**	981-U **$2.95**	981-J **$5.65**

ZINNIA F_1 **HYBRID PETER PAN CREAM** The newest Peter Pan! Included in the mix before its introduction, we now offer Peter Pan Cream individually in honor of its 1978 All-America victory. Like the other Peter Pans, the new cream is a spectacular bloomer, giving more color per plant than any other zinnia. Rich cream color is a true blend of white and yellow, free of green tints! A very useful neutral tone for flower arrangements.

Packet	Bonus Pkt.	Jumbo Pkt.
987-P **$1.25**	987-U **$2.35**	987-J **$4.45**

ZINNIA **CLASSIC** A rare form of the zinnia — unusual *single* golden orange flowers are actually the "true" form of the original wild zinnia. This remarkable flower is one of the very few zinnias that will perform as a perennial in mild climates — elsewhere they are annuals. Bright 1½-inch blooms are profusely borne on hardy 8- to 10-inch plants — excellent as a year around border or ground cover.

Packet	Bonus Pkt.	Jumbo Pkt.
986-P **85c**	986-U **$1.60**	986-J **$3.10**

State Fair Mixed

Giant Cactus Mixed

Classic Zinnia   Chippendale Daisy

Lilliput Mixed

ZINNIA WHIRLIGIG MIX Festive bicolor zinnias to brighten your garden! The 20-inch plants produce many 3- to 4-inch flowers. No two exactly alike . . . and each bright bloom looks almost hand-painted. Their colorful markings and shadings are breathtaking *en masse!*

Packet	Bonus Pkt.	Jumbo Pkt.
980-P **65c**	980-U **$1.25**	980-J **$2.35**

ZINNIA STATE FAIR MIXED Absolutely stunning! Many of these huge, blue ribbon zinnias measure *half a foot in diameter!* At maturity, plants grow 30 to 36 inches tall. Mammoth blooms in bright colors not dreamed possible before this unique strain was developed.

Packet	Bonus Pkt.	Jumbo Pkt.
974-P **65c**	974-U **$1.25**	974-J **$2.35**

ZINNIA SPRITE MIX (Cut-and-come-again) The more of these 2- to 3-inch blooms you cut, the more branches and blossoms appear! Blooms early and continuously all summer. The fully ruffled flowers come in shades of scarlet, pink, yellow, white and lavender . . . on bushy 3-foot plants. Flowers have unique habit of facing outward, an asset in arranging!

Packet	Bonus Pkt.	Jumbo Pkt.
982-P **75c**	982-U **$1.45**	982-J **$2.75**

ZINNIA THUMBELINA MIXED The winner of a coveted All-America Gold Medal, these strong, vigorous miniatures are a great favorite. Wonderfully compact and neat for edgings or for planting in pots, they grow 6 inches tall and 6 inches wide, and are covered with double and semi-double 1¼-inch blooms. Mixture includes pink, red, white, yellow, orange, and scarlet.

Packet	Bonus Pkt.	Jumbo Pkt.
975-P **75c**	975-U **$1.45**	975-J **$2.75**

ZINNIA CHIPPENDALE DAISY Petite, beautifully patterned 2-inch bicolor blooms cover these bushy plants from 65 days after planting 'til frost! Blooms have mahogany red single petals, tipped with intense yellow gold. Dainty and very bright! Twenty-inch plants are self-cleaning, disease and drought resistant.

Packet	Bonus Pkt.	Jumbo Pkt.
989-P **75c**	989-U **$1.45**	989-J **$2.75**

ZINNIA LILLIPUT MIXED Commonly used for borders and edging, not to mention cutting! These dainty flowered Lilliput zinnias are useful in so many ways. They grow quickly and bloom early – simply won't stop producing flowers in a mixture of bright colors until frost. You'll have countless double flowers in a wide range of luscious colors. The mature plants will reach a height of 12 to 18 inches – if planted in partial shade, they, like all zinnias, may grow 6 inches taller.

Packet	Bonus Pkt.	Jumbo Pkt.
983-P **65c**	983-U **$1.25**	983-J **$2.35**

ZINNIA GIANT CACTUS MIXED A distinctive eye-catcher — the flowers of this variety are remarkable because of the spiked and quilled effect of the petals. The 5-inch blooms — some are flat and twisted and some are fluted — come in a range of colors: pink, rose, scarlet, cherry, yellow, orange and cream. The colors of these exotic flowers shade darker toward the center. The 2½- to 3-foot plants are generally planted for background effects — they're particularly striking against shrubbery. And they're unusual and dramatic in arrangements and bouquets for the home.

Packet	Bonus Pkt.	Jumbo Pkt.
976-P **65c**	976-U **$1.25**	976-J **$2.35**

Verbena—Florist Strain Mixed

Flowering Kale

Ornamental Gourds

Violas

Thyme

Pampas Grass

VERBENA
Annual

FLORIST STRAIN MIXED Verbena will provide a low growing carpet of bright clear color all summer. Our variety grows a neat 8 to 10 inches high and spreads to 18 inches – quickly filling window boxes or flower pots. Florist Mix includes white, pink, purple, scarlet – many of which are accented with white in the center. The more of the sweet-smelling branches you cut, the more new shoots the hardy little plants will produce.

Packet	Bonus Pkt.	Jumbo Pkt.
955-P **75c**	955-U **$1.45**	955-J **$2.75**

FLOWERING KALE
Annual

For an unusual and distinctive novelty, grow this cabbage-like, highly ornamental Kale. You sow seeds in May or June, and watch as the foliage turns to either a colorful rose or a pure white in the fall. They add a highly attractive touch to your fall flower garden, providing an easy to care for, low solid bedding of brilliant color. Mix well with other low growing flowers such as alyssum, and make interesting potted plants too! Plants grow from 10 to 12 inches tall — spread 12 inches. Flowering Kale requires cool temperatures to develop color, and is not recommended as a vegetable variety. *(for vegetable garden kale, see page 26)*

Packet	Bonus Pkt.	Jumbo Pkt.
805-P **65c**	805-U **$1.25**	805-J **$2.35**

VIOLAS
Perennial generally treated like an annual

Every garden should include violas. They are truly charming when combined with spring flowering bulbs, and later in the summer, they are stunning with alyssum or other low-growing annuals. The compact 6 to 8-inch plants are covered with dainty little pansy-shaped flowers that brighten every spot they fill. Buy extra to plant next fall — protect over winter and have *early* spring blooms.

Blue Perfection

Packet	Bonus Pkt.	Jumbo Pkt.
967-P **95c**	967-U **$1.75**	967-J **$3.35**

Yellow Perfection

Packet	Bonus Pkt.	Jumbo Pkt.
968-P **95c**	968-U **$1.75**	968-J **$3.35**

GOURDS
Annual

SMALL FRUITED Ornamental gourds quickly cover fences, trellises, porch railings and poles with vines, dense foliage. The brightly colored, hard-shelled, inedible fruit comes in fascinating and unusual shapes and sizes. Our mixture contains vines that can grow as long as 12 feet, and will produce a wide variety of different gourds. By gathering fruit before first frost, you can have unique, long lasting table decorations. Wait until frost danger has passed before seeding – they'll grow just about anywhere but prefer sunshine.

Packet	Bonus Pkt.	Jumbo Pkt.
755-P **75c**	755-U **$1.45**	755-J **$2.75**

PAMPAS GRASS
Perennial

Airy, graceful plumes wave and shimmer with the passing of every breeze. Huge silk-like cream colored feathers are borne on stately spikes up to seven feet tall in late summer and early autumn. Pampas grass is grown as a perennial in areas where the winters are fairly mild – as an annual elsewhere. The showy leaves are narrow and delicately tufted. So easy to grow, too – just plant your seeds in a sunny corner. To dry for arrangements, just cut the plumes as soon as pollen appears and hang upside down in a dry, shady place.

Packet	Bonus Pkt.	Jumbo Pkt.
990-P **95c**	990-U **$1.75**	990-J **$3.35**

HERBS

Herbs are simple to grow and their uses are many. No kitchen is complete without a well-stocked spice rack — and growing your own herbs is a fascinating hobby. Fresh herbs are a delicious gourmet touch to flavor soups, sauces, garnishes, breads, omelets. Ornamental outdoors, they're charming flourishing inside in a windowsill garden. And they can be dried and hung indoors where the rich, pungent fragrance is a delight all winter long.

Order by catalog number . . . 65c each

Sweet Basil 550-P	Coriander 555-P	Rosemary 561-P
Borage 551-P	Dill 556-P	Sage 562-P
Caraway.......552-P	Marjoram 557-P	Savory 563-P
Catnip 553-P	Mint..........558-P	Tarragon 564-P
Chives 554-P	Oregano.......560-P	Thyme........565-P

PRESERVING HERBS

For immediate use, cut herbs and use fresh. Cutting tips encourages bushy growth. Harvest in late summer and dry for winter by using easy instructions that come with seeds. Also, herbs can be frozen. Freezing is a good way to preserve dill, chives, tarragon and basil. Wash herbs as you would for drying . . . tie together and with long end of string, blanch in unsalted boiling water for 50 seconds. Cool in ice water for a few minutes. Remove leaves, wrap in freezer bag and freeze.

GARLIC

What puts zest in stew? Makes spaghetti so good to eat? Garlic — culinary boon to gourmets! Also, serves as a natural pesticide planted in vegetable and ornamental gardens. Grown around rose bushes, it's a deterrent to aphids, blackspot and mildew. Harvest when tops are dry and bent to ground. To plant separate bulbs into cloves — about 1 pound to 20 feet.

1/4 pound	1/2 pound	1 pound
C-21 **$1.95**	C-22 **$3.65**	C-23 **$5.95**

18

J&P's Dwarf Fruit Trees

You can have delicious, full-size, fresh fruit growing right in your own backyard on fruit trees that are half the height of standard trees — or even shorter! Imagine — apple trees — peach trees — pear and apricot trees in the smallest garden plot! Enjoy harvesting bountiful crops every single year. And these amazing miniatures never crowd out your flowers or shrubs. You'll have fruit just as big, colorful and delicious as any grown on large space-taking trees. Early in the season, every branch will be covered with lovely blooms. So profuse and handsome . . . a garden decoration in themselves. And harvesting fruit from these compact little trees is easy! Ideal for the modest garden where you don't have room for larger fruit trees, some may actually be planted as close as 6 feet apart.

J&P's DWARF PEACH
FULL-SIZE PEACHES *AND* ORNAMENTAL BEAUTY!
Garden Gold Dwarf peach trees grow only 4 to 6 feet tall — prized for ornamental beauty, being perfectly formed, compact and dense. These self-pollinating miniatures are true genetic dwarfs . . . not standard varieties grafted on to dwarfing stock. In spring bloom, they're breathtaking! The long lustrous leaves of the dense foliage shade the fruit to the extent that peaches do not always get enough sun to "sugar up" as completely as best standard orchard varieties do. But Garden Gold grows fruit dependably in peach growing areas, planted in sunny garden or container. By the second summer, you'll harvest full size, delicious yellow freestone fruit.

$10.95 each . . . Order Catalog No. 467
3 for $29.95 . . . Order Catalog No. 4673

DWARF PEACH IMPROVED RED HAVEN (HARKEN)
Enjoy an abundant harvest of large, early ripening fruit on this attractive 12 to 14-foot tree. J&P's Improved Red Haven is vigorous, disease-resistant, and even more winterhardy than the old standard Red Haven; bears mature fruit a full 30 days earlier than Elberta! The smooth skin on these freestone beauties has relatively little fuzz and is nearly solid red. Firm, yellow flesh is smoothly textured and extremely sweet — makes for fabulous out-of-hand eating and freezes beautifully, too.

$10.95 each . . . Order Catalog No. 334
3 for $29.95 . . . Order Catalog No. 3343

DWARF BARTLETT PEAR
Most popular pear for cooking, canning *and* enjoying fresh from the tree! Your home-grown Bartletts will be large, golden yellow with a pleasing red blush on the outside — tender, fine-textured and literally dripping with sweet juice inside. You'll have decorative foliage right away . . . and by the third year, you'll be harvesting the most delicious pears imaginable!

$10.95 each . . . Order Catalog No. 330
3 for $29.95 . . . Order Catalog No. 3303

DWARF APRICOT
MOORPARK Big, juicy freestone apricots — and plenty of them! Beautiful red-cheeked yellow fruits are delicious fresh, dried, frozen, and in jams. Vase-shaped ornamental tree grows to 8 to 10 feet. Moorpark is a very hardy variety originally from England. It thrives wherever peaches grow, and is not fussy about soil. For maximum harvest, thin fruits to 3 or 4 inches apart before they are 1 inch wide. When they come free with a gentle twist, get ready for some juicy out-of-hand eating!

$10.95 each . . . Order Catalog No. 333
3 for $29.95 . . . Order Catalog No. 3333

DWARF APPLES
RED DELICIOUS A favorite for eating . . . large, dark red and crisp. *We recommend planting Yellow Delicious trees next to Red Delicious, because the Red Delicious variety is not self-pollinating. This is not necessary, however, if apple varieties other than Red Delicious are already growing in nearby area.*

$10.95 each . . . Order Catalog No. 335

YELLOW DELICIOUS Bright, golden yellow fruit, blushed with rosy pink — really crisp and sweet! Long a popular all-purpose apple — excellent fresh, baked whole, in apple sauce, and homebaked pies of course!

$10.95 each . . . Order Catalog No. 336

BOTH DWARF APPLE TREES Plant these two varieties to assure cross pollination — have a bountiful harvest!
One each: Dwarf Yellow Delicious • Dwarf Red Delicious
for **ONLY $19.95** Order Group No. R36

J&P's Dwarf Peach

CARPATHIAN WALNUT TREE *(Juglans regia)*
You can easily grow *bushels* of fresh, crisp English walnuts for eating, and baking, and have some left for gifting friends! J&P's Carpathian Walnut Trees are famous for their generous yields of high-quality, thin-shelled nuts up to 2-inches long and never bitter! This walnut makes a beautiful shade tree — silvery gray bark is contrasted by dense, dark green foliage. Fast growing, too — up to 3 to 5 feet per year, until it reaches 40 feet. Developed from seedlings found in the Carpathian Mountains in Poland, these long-lived hardwood trees are winter-hardy everywhere in the U.S.A.; bear the 3rd or 4th year after planting. Rarely bothered by pests — the most attention they'll need is in the fall, when you collect your bounty of delicious walnuts right off the ground.

$12.95 each . . . Order Catalog No. 365
2 for $23.45 . . . Order Catalog No. 3652

J&P SELECT DWARF ORCHARD GROUPS

Red Delicious Apple • Yellow Delicious Apple • Bartlett Pear
Improved Red Haven Peach • Moorpark Apricot

One each of the above . . . Order Group No. A50 **ONLY $46.95**
Two each of the above . . . Order Group No. A19 **ONLY $79.95**

Grapes
There's nothing like home-grown grapes vine-ripened until they almost burst with sweetness! CATAWBA GRAPES — these bright red beauties sparkle with flavor, are firm, juicy, keep beautifully. Blue-black CONCORD GRAPES are favorites for juice, jelly, jam, and fresh eating! NIAGARA GRAPES — best known white grapes in the world; firm, tangy and flavorful. Golden-yellow HIMROD GRAPES are very sweet, fine-textured and *completely seedless* — excellent table grapes, make fine raisins, too.

CATAWBA Vines
$1.95 each . . . Order Cat. No. 381
3 vines for **$4.95** . . . Order Cat. No. 3813

CONCORD Vines
$1.95 each . . . Order Cat. No. 383
3 vines for **$4.95** . . . Order Cat. No. 3833

NIAGARA Vines
$1.95 each . . . Order Cat. No. 385
3 vines for **$4.95** . . . Order Cat. No. 3853

HIMROD Vines
$3.45 each . . . Order Cat. No. 337
3 vines for **$8.45** . . . Order Cat. No. 3373

GRAPE VINEYARD SPECIAL

One each:
CATAWBA
CONCORD
NIAGARA
HIMROD

Order Group No. A-20
ONLY $7.45

Asparagus—Mary Washington

Raspberries—September Red

Boysenberries—Thornless Boysen

Rhubarb—Crimson Cherry

Strawberries — Ozark Beauty

Blueberries

RHUBARB PLANTS CRIMSON CHERRY A great old-fashioned touch for pies! Try strawberry-rhubarb pie, or stewed rhubarb for breakfast — it's rich with Vitamin C. You can harvest rhubarb for a few weeks the second season, and a full 8 to 10 weeks the third year. Hardy, vigorous plants produce flat, heavy 2-foot stalks 2 to 3 times larger than other rhubarb. Once established, this permanent addition to your garden will produce for years to come. Handsome plants can even be used as edgings or backgrounds. They need a period of winter dormancy, and don't yield well where temperatures rarely drop below 32°. Plant 30 inches apart in rows 4 feet apart. Six roots will amply supply 2 people with enough rhubarb for fresh eating and freezing. A word of caution — only the stalks are edible. Rhubarb leaves are poisonous and must never be eaten. Warn children against "sampling" the leaves.

| 2 roots for **$2.95** | 4 roots for **$4.95** | 6 roots for **$6.95** |
| Order Cat. No. 5302 | Order Cat. No. 5304 | Order Cat. No. 5306 |

STRAWBERRY PLANTS OZARK BEAUTY So vigorous you can expect one to two quarts of berries from each plant the second year — so disease resistant and hardy they need no pampering to thrive. Iowa State University trials proved Ozark Beauty the most productive home garden variety. These plants quickly multiply by sending out "runners" — new plants. For maximum fruit yield, cut off runners until mid summer. After August 1, let runners propagate new plants. Space new plants 9 inches apart. Or allow them to grow freely for lush foliage in borders and beds.

Strawberries do best in light-textured, well drained soil. Set plants out in early spring 1-1/2 feet apart in rows 3-1/2 feet apart. Fifty plants will thrive in a space the size of a blanket — or try a triple-level "pyramid" planter — grow as many as 75 plants in a 6-foot circle. Allow 25 plants per person for fresh eating, topping ice cream, for jams, pies and freezing.

| 25 plants for **$6.95** | 50 plants for **$12.95** | 100 plants for **$19.95** |
| Order Cat. No. 355-L | Order Cat. No. 355-R | Order Cat. No. 355-Y |

BOYSENBERRY PLANTS THORNLESS BOYSEN These giant berries are rich with the tart, tangy flavor of wild mountain berries — and they're almost seedless! Thornless for easy picking, they should be trained on a trellis for a neat, compact backyard berry garden. The vines are highly productive and the inch-thick berries freeze beautifully. They ripen over a period of 2 months, starting in July of the second year after you plant them. Plant early in spring in fertile well drained soil. Choose a spot that faces south if possible to give the berries continuous summer sun. Plant berries 8 to 10 feet apart in rows also spaced 8 to 10 feet apart. After the canes are well established, train them on trellises or wires 4 to 5 feet high, tying for good support. The first year you'll need to prune shoots to 2-1/2 feet during the summer. The following year, cut side branches to 1-1/2 feet. Three plants yield 6 to 12 quarts per season when fully mature.

| **$2.95** each | 3 for **$7.95** |
| Order Cat. No. 849 | Order Cat. No. 8493 |

RASPBERRY PLANTS SEPTEMBER RED Large 2-year field grown plants give you the largest, bright red berries imaginable — plump and sweet! You'll have a delicious crop this year, and after your plants are established, they'll produce in summer and again in fall.

Plant 2 feet apart in rows 7 to 9 feet apart in deep, sandy, well drained loam, rich in organic matter. Don't set out new plants in the vicinity of wild ones, nor where potatoes, tomatoes, eggplant or melons have grown in the past 3 years. Tie each plant to a pole or if you have a row of them, stretch parallel wires from poles at both ends of the row so the plants are enclosed between them. The vines may also be trained up trellises as they grow. Raspberries are soft when they're ripe — and their sweet fragrance will tell you when they're ready to pick. Harvest daily; they ripen quickly.

| 2 plants for **$2.45** | 4 plants for **$4.45** | 6 plants for **$5.95** |
| Order Cat. No. 8482 | Order Cat. No. 8484 | Order Cat. No. 8486 |

BLUEBERRY PLANTS EARLIBLUE, BLUECROP AND BERKELEY Blueberry heaven — that's the western slope of Oregon's Cascade Mountain range, where these 3 superior varieties are from. And Oregon Blueberry Cobbler has to be *blueberry-eater's* heaven! These heavy bearing plants are extremely winter hardy, disease and insect resistant and require very little care. Space them 6 to 8 feet apart in cool, moist, acidic soil that drains well. The 12- to 18-inch, No. 1 grade plants you receive may yield up to a quart of berries the first season. A single 10-year-old plant can give 12 to 16 quarts — and it may last a lifetime! Two or more varieties must be planted together for cross-pollination. These 3 varieties have been selected for ripening sequence, to give you the greatest number of weekly pickings during the middle and late summer. For maximum flavor, wait a week after the berries turn blue before picking. To harvest, cup your hands around each cluster and gently "roll out" only the ripe berries with your thumbs. Blueberries make beautiful landscape plantings, too, in groups or as hedges. In spring, the white, bell-like flowers are enchanting against the glossy, dark green foliage . . . that then turns a dramatic crimson in the fall. Such beauty and good eating too!

One plant each: Earliblue • Bluecrop • Berkeley
Order Group No. A-21 . . . **$11.95**

ASPARAGUS MARY WASHINGTON A gourmet's delight and one of the simplest vegetables to grow. This delectable perennial produces heavily for 10, 15 or even 25 years. It's at home in the flower garden, too, where the ferns make a lovely foliage background. Mary Washington is the standard of excellence — heavy yielding and rust resistant. From seed, you'll have a light cutting of stalks in 3 years and regular cuttings each year thereafter. Or plant our husky, top grade roots and have tender, delicious spears next spring! Space roots 18 inches apart.

| **Rootstock** | 25 plants for **$4.95** | 50 plants for **$8.95** |
| | Order Cat. No. 533-L | Order Cat. No. 533-R |

| **Seed** | Packet | Bonus Pkt. | Jumbo Pkt. |
| | 100-P **75c** | 100-U **$1.45** | 100-J **$2.75** |

20

Beans—Kentucky Wonder and Kinghorn Yellow Wax

Beans—Thorogreen Baby Lima

BEANS Beans are one of the most rewarding and undemanding of all garden vegetables. They're foolproof — picking will probably be the most attention they'll require all season. Ready in 50 to 60 days, bush beans grow about 2 feet tall and require no staking. Pole beans, ready in 60 to 90 days, can reach 5 to 8 feet tall, and will climb on fences to save space. For non-stop beans, sow a 10 to 15 foot row of bush beans (or 4 or 5 poles of pole beans) every two weeks as soon as danger of frost is past — repeat until two months before the first fall frost. The pole beans and lima beans we offer are also great for shelling and drying. Save money and plant loads — the price of dried beans in stores is up several times what it was last year . . . and there's no end in sight! As a general rule, a 15 foot row of pole beans yields about 18 pounds of beans in 4 weeks. To dry beans, simply let the pods mature on the vine until beige-colored. Then shell and heat in a 130° to 145° oven for an hour, store in a dry place for winter use.

BUSH SNAP BEAN **TENDERCROP** Tendercrop is the finest freezing bean — extra tender and flavorful. Very disease resistant, Tendercrop produces heavy yields of smooth round beans 5½ to 7 inches in length. You'll have plenty of meaty green beans for fresh eating, canning or freezing.

2-1/4 oz. Packet	1/4 lb.	1/2 lb.	1 lb.
114-P **85c**	114-M **$1.45**	114-H **$2.45**	114-K **$4.45**

BUSH SNAP BEAN **TOP CROP** All-America Gold Medal Winner, Top Crop outyields nearly every other variety. Strong, upright disease resistant 2 foot bushes produce plump, 6 inch smooth green pods that grow near the top for easy picking. Several harvests from one planting will give plenty of fine-quality, stringless green beans for eating, canning or freezing.

2-1/4 oz. Packet	1/4 lb.	1/2 lb.	1 lb.
113-P **85c**	113-M **$1.45**	113-H **$2.45**	113-K **$4.45**

POLE SNAP BEAN **KENTUCKY WONDER** The most widely grown pole bean. Long silvery green pods are plump and crisp — and often grow 9 inches long! The buff seeds have a distinctive flavor and are excellent as dried shell beans for baking or soups. Excellent for canning. Vigorous and rust resistant, Kentucky Wonder is foolproof to grow, succeeds everywhere.

2-1/4 oz. Packet	1/4 lb.	1/2 lb.	1 lb.
112-P **95c**	112-M **$1.65**	112-H **$2.75**	112-K **$4.75**

POLE SNAP BEAN **BLUE LAKE** Oregon is famous for this superb pole bean, judged by food scientists throughout the world as the finest flavored bean available. Increasingly scarce — seldom sold in stores because the tender beans are not adaptable to machine harvesting. Climbs 5½ to 6 feet high, covered with slender 6 to 7 inch beans. Suitable for dry shell use.

2-1/4 oz. Packet	1/4 lb.	1/2 lb.	1 lb.
111-P **95c**	111-M **$1.65**	111-H **$2.75**	111-K **$4.75**

BUSH BEAN **NEW BUSH ROMANO 14 ITALIAN GREEN BEAN** True Italian Romano pole-bean flavor now in bush form! Succulent and distinctively flavored green beans are produced on low spreading plants. Take up much less space, and are nearly 2 weeks earlier than the older pole type. Straight, thick 5 to 6 inch pods are ready in 60 to 70 days — full-flavored and great for fresh eating or freezing.

2-1/4 oz. Packet	1/4 lb.	1/2 lb.	1 lb.
115-P **95c**	115-M **$1.65**	115-H **$2.75**	115-K **$4.75**

BUSH BEAN **KINGHORN YELLOW WAX** The earliest of all bush beans — and one of the most delicious! In 50 to 55 days, erect, 15 to 20 inch tall bushes will produce an abundance of tender, stringless yellow pods, 5 to 7 inches long with white seeds. Prolific and all-purpose, Kinghorn is excellent for fresh eating, freezing or canning. One of the longest standing bush beans.

2-1/4 oz. Packet	1/4 lb.	1/2 lb.	1 lb.
117-P **85c**	117-M **$1.45**	117-H **$2.45**	117-K **$4.45**

BUSH BEAN **GOLDCROP WAX** 1974 All-America winner, Goldcrop is especially resistant to hot weather blossom drop. Produces a heavy yield of straight, smooth well-filled pods that are borne high on the plant so they're easy to pick. Mature in 60 to 65 days from planting.

2-1/4 oz. Packet	1/4 lb.	1/2 lb.	1 lb.
120-P **85c**	120-M **$1.45**	120-H **$2.45**	120-K **$4.45**

BUSH LIMA **FORDHOOK NO. 242** An All-America winner and the finest large lima to be found. High yields of 3½ to 4 inch pods even in hot weather. Each pod averages 4 plump tender beans. Fordhook No. 242 keeps buttery rich flavor when canned or frozen. Ready in 75 days!

2-1/4 oz. Packet	1/4 lb.	1/2 lb.	1 lb.
118-P **85c**	118-M **$1.45**	118-H **$2.45**	118-K **$4.45**

BUSH LIMA **THOROGREEN BABY LIMA** Tremendous yields of tender and sweet, buttery-good baby limas are borne on 12 to 15 inch bushy plants. Plump little green pods hold 2 to 4 greenish white baby limas. Vigorous despite hot weather. Keeps fresh flavor even after canning or freezing.

2-1/4 oz. Packet	1/4 lb.	1/2 lb.	1 lb.
119-P **85c**	119-M **$1.45**	119-H **$2.45**	119-K **$4.45**

BEETS Home grown beets are tender as butter! It's a fact — the tender, fibre-free varieties you can grow at home can't be shipped to market without bruising, so commercial growers plant somewhat tougher varieties. And as a home gardener, you can pick beets at the height of perfection — when they're young, small and tender.

Beets are quick and easy to grow, disease-free and fast to produce — insects rarely bother them. Plant 2 crops — just after the ground has thawed in the spring and after mid-summer. Within rows, plants should be 3 inches apart and rows should be 18 inches from each other.

The uses of beets are infinite — tops are delicious fresh in a salad or boiled and topped with lemon butter. Hot buttered beets, shredded raw beets in salad, sauced beets with onions, borscht, pickled or spiced — however you prepare them they'll never be better than when they're fresh from your own garden!

BEET **RUBY QUEEN** Sweet flavor, uniformity and fine texture earned this superior, early beet an All-America Award. Ruby Queen is that rare beet which "slips" in the soil and thereby avoids rocks or clumps in the ground — always growing nicely round and unblemished. Extremely smooth skin, small round size and deep red color throughout make this premium variety the perfect baby beet for canning. Ready in 55 days — best when planted in a crowded condition and harvested while small, young and sweet.

Packet	Bonus Pkt.	Jumbo Pkt.
132-P **65c**	132-U **$1.25**	132-J **$2.35**

BEET **EARLY WONDER** The earliest beet you can plant — in only 53 days you can harvest sweet, tender, deep red beets! Stagger your plantings and you can harvest these smooth, globe-shaped beets through the fall. Lush, tall 16 to 18 inch greens are delicious for boiling. Uniform and fine-grained, Early Wonder is perfect for pickling and canning.

Packet	Bonus Pkt.	Jumbo Pkt.
131-P **65c**	131-U **$1.25**	131-J **$2.35**

BEET **DETROIT DARK RED** Without a doubt the best known beet in the country, Detroit Dark Red is so tender and fibre-free that it cuts like butter! This dark red, medium-sized beet has a small tap root — easy to pull — excellent for canning and freezing. The high sugar content makes it tender and sweet — delicious flavor. Ready in 60 days.

Packet	Bonus Pkt.	Jumbo Pkt.
130-P **65c**	130-U **$1.25**	130-J **$2.35**

Beet—Detroit Dark Red

Cabbage—Ruby Ball

Cabbage—

Brussels Sprouts—Jade Cross Hybrid

Broccoli — Premium Crop

Cauliflower — Snow Crown

Eggplant—

BRUSSELS SPROUTS JADE CROSS HYBRID Unbelievably delicious! Young Brussels Sprouts cooked right from the garden — top them with beurre noir, sour cream sauce or just plain melted butter. Scrumptious! Jade Cross — the first F_1 hybrid — produces *twice as many* tender sprouts as "open pollinated" non-hybrids. This All America winner also matures earlier than any other sprout — does especially well in a moist, cool climate. In only 75 to 85 days you can enjoy tender, bite-sized cabbages with fine, delicate garden fresh flavor. Pick the lowest sprouts first as they mature from the bottom up on the 18 to 24 inch plants. You can harvest them well into fall as they're actually more delicious when touched by an early, light frost. Plant the Bonus Packet for a family of four or Jumbo Packet and freeze some.

Packet	Bonus Pkt.	Jumbo Pkt.
153-P **75c**	153-U **$1.45**	153-J **$2.75**

BROCCOLI Broccoli tops the list of delicious gourmet vegetables you can grow in your own backyard. Garnish with melted butter, creamy cheddar sauce or Hollandaise. Nutritious, too — in fact, broccoli is a prime source of Vitamin C! Cans and freezes beautifully. Start a spring crop in flats and transplant after the last frost. For a fall crop, plant seed outdoors in late May. Plant at least 1½ feet apart in rows spaced 2½ feet apart.

BROCCOLI PREMIUM CROP This 1975 All-America winner produces larger, more solid heads with tighter bud clusters than any other comparable quick-maturing variety. A short 58 days after plants are set out, you will harvest beautiful velvety blue-green broccoli with excellent full flavor!

Packet	Bonus Pkt.	Jumbo Pkt.
144-P **95c**	144-U **$1.75**	144-J **$3.35**

BROCCOLI HYBRID CRUSADER Developed by the famous Japanese firm of Sakata, this outstanding new hybrid broccoli is a smaller, more compact variety than standard broccoli. Grow Crusader where space is limited. Twelve-inch heads are beautifully rounded and uniform, densely covered with tight, firm buds. Extra early — flavorful and tender.

Packet	Bonus Pkt.	Jumbo Pkt.
142-P **85c**	142-U **$1.60**	142-J **$3.10**

CABBAGE Fresh cabbage just can't be beat for making the finest, crispest cole slaw, sauerkraut, or for adding garden-fresh flavor to a boiled beef dinner. One of the most popular garden vegetables, cabbage is not at all fussy about soil conditions and is extremely hardy. When planting cabbage, leave 24 inches between rows and plan on 3 to 5 plants per person for fresh eating and another 3 to 5 plants per person if you plan to make sauerkraut. Sow both early and late varieties in flats and transplant outdoors about 6 weeks later. To insure cabbage through the summer and long into winter, we suggest planting J&P Cabbage Plants for earliest harvest, *and* sowing the seeds of later varieties for fall yield. Beautiful and flavorful purple-red cabbage is often planted in containers for a unique ornamental accent!

CABBAGE F_1 HYBRID SAVOY ACE So outstanding, it's a 1977 All-America GOLD MEDAL WINNER. Superior, uniform heads weigh 4 to

4½ pounds . . . solid with crisp, finely crinkled, very dark green leaves . . . succulent with a sweet mild flavor and tenderness. So good to eat — boiled, stuffed, or for cole slaw or sauerkraut. Not only does Savoy Ace excel in flavor and quality, it matures 5 to 7 days earlier than other hybrids.

Packet	Bonus Pkt.	Jumbo Pkt.
167-P **95c**	167-U **$1.75**	167-J **$3.35**

CABBAGE KING COLE The best sauerkraut cabbage to be found! King Cole is a large, heavier yielding hybrid which matures in early midseason (72 days to maturity). Vigorous, compact plants produce firm, round heads of a uniform size. Fine quality with mild, pleasant flavor, King Cole is disease resistant and an excellent all-around variety for cooking, canning and fresh slaw.

Packet	Bonus Pkt.	Jumbo Pkt.
165-P **85c**	165-U **$1.60**	165-J **$3.10**

CABBAGE RUBY BALL RED This gorgeous, rich red cabbage won the 1972 All-America Gold Medal — a rare distinction reserved for the very best. Red Ruby Ball deserves the honor — hybrid vigor gives greater uniformity and produces small round heads of the finest quality. Neat, compact plants produce very early — 70 days. We highly recommend Ruby Ball, it's the best available — and it's beautiful in salads!

Packet	Bonus Pkt.	Jumbo Pkt.
163-P **95c**	163-U **$1.75**	163-J **$3.35**

CABBAGE PLANTS Full-flavored, garden fresh cabbages in just 4 to 5 weeks! J&P healthy, field-grown Cabbage Plants are already 6 to 8 weeks old and 6 inches tall — shipped direct to you the same day they're harvested. They're extra-hardy and ready for planting as early as the soil can be worked . . . light frost won't hurt them either. By planting Cabbage Plants and seeding other varieties, you'll have delicious cabbage all season long! *(25 plants equal a 50 foot row.)*
Golden Acre *Cabbage Plants*

	25 plants	50 plants
	359-L **$4.95**	359-R **$7.95**

CAULIFLOWER SNOW CROWN Grow this delectable 1975 All-America winning hybrid — and taste the quality of truly fresh, homegrown cauliflower, at a fraction of its supermarket price! Snow Crown produces large 8-inch pure white heads, weighing up to 2 pounds — they're more uniform and vigorous, and mature a week earlier than standard snowball types. Cauliflower is a wonderfully rewarding crop to grow, but it's demanding — more sensitive to heat, frost and lack of water than most cabbage-type crops. Beginning gardeners may prefer to settle for broccoli instead! Where spring weather gets hot, cauliflower is best as a fall crop, planted in late summer. Or in cool spring areas, sow early in spring in cold frames and transplant seedlings after six weeks. Cauliflower requires plenty of growing room — space plants 2½ to 3 feet apart in rows 3 feet apart. When head starts to form, fold the outer leaves over the head to protect from the sun. Interplant lettuce, radishes, or onions between these late maturing plants.

Packet	Bonus Pkt.	Jumbo Pkt.
191-P **85c**	191-U **$1.60**	191-J **$3.10**

22

King Cole

Carrot—Royal Chantenay

Hybrid Midnite

Celery—Tall Utah 52-70

Carrot — Hybrid Spartan Delight

CARROTS Without a doubt, carrots are the home gardener's favorite root crop — and it's easy to understand why if you've ever tasted a young, tender carrot fresh from the garden. The flavor is unbelievably sweeter than <u>any</u> store-bought carrot.

There's a carrot that's just right for every garden in the United States! The main types of carrots are characterized by their shape and length. The long, slim tapered varieties such as Tendersweet and Spartan Delight grow 8 inches and longer and need deep (10 to 12 inches) loose soil to grow in. The shorter, blunter types such as Scarlet Nantes and Royal Chantenay grow 5 to 8 inches long, and so need only a shallowly prepared bed — and their straight shape gives more uniform slices.

Carrots grow in any soil, but do best in sandy deep loam that is well cultivated and free of stones. One packet will plant about 30 feet — enough for 3 people. Plant plenty; thin by pulling some to serve as tiny gourmet size carrots. Sow seeds outdoors 2 to 3 weeks before the last frost is expected. To keep your crop of tender young carrots coming all season, plant seeds every two weeks until mid summer. For winter storage, leave your carrots in the ground until just after the first frost, then pull them and store in a moist, cool place. They'll keep for several months.

CARROT DANVERS HALF-LONG Fine grained, bright orange carrots will be ready to pull in 75 days. Danvers is a popular favorite that is all-around excellent for fresh eating, storing or freezing. Tender, rich and sweet, 6 to 8 inch carrots taper to a blunt end and are nearly coreless. An excellent choice to plant for a fall crop.

Packet	Bonus Pkt.	Jumbo Pkt.
180-P **65c**	180-U **$1.25**	180-J **$2.35**

CARROT ROYAL CHANTENAY Fine flavor, interior color and smooth skin make Chantenay a favorite for cooking or canning and freezing. Neat, cylindrical, blunt-ended, 5 to 7 inch roots are 2½ inches at the shoulder. Plant at intervals and enjoy spring, summer and fall crops of these bright reddish-orange tender carrots — ready in 69 days.

Packet	Bonus Pkt.	Jumbo Pkt.
177-P **65c**	177-U **$1.25**	177-J **$2.35**

CARROT SCARLET NANTES Unsurpassed in quality and flavor, Scarlet Nantes grows 6 to 8 inches long and has scarcely any core. Excellent for freezing. Blunt ended, attractive carrots are crisp, tender and fine grained . . . ready to eat in only 68 days.

Packet	Bonus Pkt.	Jumbo Pkt.
176-P **75c**	176-U **$1.45**	176-J **$2.75**

CARROT SPARTAN DELIGHT Exceptionally long — averaging 10 to 14 inches of the crunchiest, sweetest carrots you've ever tasted! Ready in only 68 days, this outstanding F_1 hybrid with slender, tapering bright orange roots will quickly become your family's favorite carrot for fresh eating!

Packet	Bonus Pkt.	Jumbo Pkt.
181-P **75c**	181-U **$1.45**	181-J **$2.75**

CARROTS TENDERSWEET (IMPERATOR 58) Wonderful all-purpose carrot — delicious for fresh eating, canning, freezing or cooking. Fine grained, deep orange carrot is truly coreless — attractive, smooth roots are 2 inches at the top, 7 to 10 inches long, tapering to a point. This fine

quality All-America winner is the sweetest carrot on the market — ready in 73 days.

Packet	Bonus Pkt.	Jumbo Pkt.
179-P **65c**	179-U **$1.25**	179-J **$2.35**

CELERY TALL UTAH 52-70 Celery takes patience and lots of water — but the reward is flavor never found in stores. Tall Utah is a popular, widely adaptable variety that is unexcelled for crisp, extra long stalks. Celery is generally started in the house and later transplanted outdoors. Tall Utah's 23-inch plants with 11-inch stalks will be ready in 90-100 days from the time of transplanting. Rich soil, plenty of water and a rather cool climate are requirements for growing good, fresh celery. Use the delectable tender hearts and center stalks for salads or festive relish trays. Braise celery with green pepper, oregano and onion for a scrumptious vegetable casserole — or try serving au gratin for a real gourmet delight.

Packet	Bonus Pkt.	Jumbo Pkt.
200-P **75c**	200-U **$1.45**	200-J **$2.75**

EGGPLANT One of the most delicious delicacies a gardener can grow! The two varieties that we offer produce strong, compact plants about 24 to 32 inches tall, with large, jet-black fruits. The fruits are tasty at all stages of growth — best picked when they're 3 to 6 inches in diameter. Four to six plants will feed a family of four the entire season. Try eggplant baked, fried, broiled, stuffed or scalloped in a casserole. Absolutely delicious as a main course or a vegetable side dish.

EGGPLANT BLACK BEAUTY Ready to eat 80 days after the plants are set in your garden. The compact, sturdy 24 to 30 inch plants produce good quantities of smooth, glossy fruits with firm, golden flesh. Tender and tasty at all stages of growth, the ever-popular Black Beauty retains its brilliant and uniform color — weighs 2 or more pounds at maturity.

Packet	Bonus Pkt.	Jumbo Pkt.
262-P **75c**	262-U **$1.45**	262-J **$2.75**

EGGPLANT HYBRID MIDNITE Husky, vigorous plants bear even *earlier than Black Beauty*. This F_1 hybrid also bears a *larger* crop of its outstandingly glossy, dark pear-shaped fruits. The tall 28- to 30-inch plants are strong and upright — keep the fruit from touching the ground. This has our highest recommendation for home garden use — and top quality and flavor make Midnite unbeatable for cooking!

Packet	Bonus Pkt.	Jumbo Pkt.
261-P **65c**	261-U **$1.25**	261-J **$2.35**

Cucumber—Hybrid Patio Pik

Cucumber—Hybrid Burpless

Cucumber — Pot Luck

CUCUMBERS Cool, crisp cucumbers on ice in August! A fast, refreshing taste-treat right from your garden! There are many varieties of cucumbers available today — but the two things they all have in common is that they are rapid growers and they don't need much pampering. Every cucumber that we feature here is a vigorous, heavy producing hybrid. Plant 10 to 12 seeds in hills about 48 inches apart then thin to 4 or 5 plants. You can train them on stakes or trellises, or they can be grown on a fence too — to save space. *(See Supercuke on page 3.)*

CUCUMBER HYBRID POT LUCK We highly recommend this sensational new hybrid — a vigorous, very dwarf plant that grows regular sized cucumbers! Pot Luck's vines grow to no more than 18 inches in length, yet they produce plenty of excellent quality, 6¹/₂- to 7-inch slicing cukes. Great eating, and a practical choice for small gardens or container gardening.

Packet	Bonus Pkt.	Jumbo Pkt.
256-P **75c**	256-U **$1.45**	256-J **$2.75**

CUCUMBER HYBRID PATIO PIK A very unique hybrid because of its dwarf, bush-like plant habit. You can neatly grow Patio Pik in a tub on your patio or even in a small city garden! Produces extra early, high yields of multi-purpose cucumbers. When small, use for pickling as tiny whole gherkins. As it grows a little larger Patio Pik makes an excellent pickler for chips and spears. At maturity, fruits develop into beautiful slicing cucumbers which complement the best salads!

Packet	Bonus Pkt.	Jumbo Pkt.
251-P **85c**	251-U **$1.60**	251-J **$3.10**

CUCUMBER F1 HYBRID VICTORY 1972 All-America winner. Outstandingly resistant to disease, this award winner is one of the best hybrid slicing varieties available. The vigorous vines are busy all summer long producing loads of remarkably uniform, smooth glossy dark green cucumbers that are always crunchy and flavorful. A real treat in summer salads!

Packet	Bonus Pkt.	Jumbo Pkt.
250-P **75c**	250-U **$1.45**	250-J **$2.75**

CUCUMBER HYBRID BURPLESS *Completely digestible!* Narrow, deep green cukes are best harvested when they are 9 to 10 inches long, when the tender fruits can be enjoyed by everyone. It is not even necessary to peel the smooth skin for eating. Vigorous, heavy yielding plants are staked or grown on a trellis for best results — fruits are ready in 62 days. Burpless makes delicious full-flavored pickles — or serve fresh on an attractive relish tray.

Packet	Bonus Pkt.	Jumbo Pkt.
248-P **85c**	248-U **$1.60**	248-J **$3.10**

CUCUMBER SALTY A pickler par excellence! This vigorous F1 hybrid produces quantities of superior pickling cucumbers in only 50 days. Handsome cylindrical fruits are perfect pickling size and shape — and they retain their rich dark green color even as they grow larger. The hardy vine is highly disease resistant. Get your pickle recipes ready!

Packet	Bonus Pkt.	Jumbo Pkt.
255-P **75c**	255-U **$1.45**	255-J **$2.75**

RADISHES The fastest, crunchiest, easiest vegetable you can grow! Just 10 feet will give you an ample supply of radishes for one person. The Bonus Packet will generously feed a family of four — plant plenty! Plant radishes ½ inch deep in rows 6 inches apart. In a few short days, when radishes develop smooth, firm crisp roots, pull and eat fresh or serve braised slices with slivers of celery and green pepper.

It is a good idea to plant seeds every two weeks to keep the crop coming all season long. Radishes are often planted in among other larger, slower growing crops like corn to make maximum use of garden space. Many people mix in a few radish seeds with the seeds of other root crops like carrots, beets and parsnips when planting. This helps to mark the rows of the slower growing vegetables and as you pull the early radishes, you automatically thin out the other crops and give them room to grow.

RADISH CHERRY BELLE This All-America selection was developed in Holland — its bright red color and small round shape give it a remarkable resemblance to a cherry! A very early radish, Cherry Belle is ready to pull in 22 days. Tops are 2½ to 3 inches and quite short. Cherry red, solid, smooth, crisp and globular shaped roots encompass a white flesh which is mild in flavor, sweet, crisp, and firm. These ideally shaped radishes reach ¾-inch in diameter and retain their good eating qualities for an exceptionally long time.

Packet	Bonus Pkt.	Jumbo Pkt.
453-P **65c**	453-U **$1.25**	453-J **$2.35**

RADISH CHAMPION Imagine a beautifully rounded, bright crimson radish — larger than any you've ever seen before. That's Champion — a larger edition of Cherry Belle. This ALL-AMERICA WINNER with picture-perfect form is ideal for fancy hors d' oeuvres — just split lengthwise and top with cottage cheese, deviled ham, or rich Gorgonzola cheese. Harvest tremendous yields in just 28 days — even in blazing hot weather!

Packet	Bonus Pkt.	Jumbo Pkt.
456-P **65c**	456-U **$1.25**	456-J **$2.35**

RADISH FRENCH BREAKFAST Oblong in shape, 1½ to 2 inches long — a bright scarlet-rose color with a pure white lower tip. Its white flesh is crisp, juicy and delightfully sweet. Very quick — only 23 days from sowing seed. Radishes show above the ground for easy harvest.

Packet	Bonus Pkt.	Jumbo Pkt.
457-P **75c**	457-U **$1.45**	457-J **$2.75**

RADISH WHITE ICICLE Cool, crisp, with a frosty, fresh flavor — this unique white radish *tastes* as delightfully different as it *looks!* The flavor is sweet, mild, delicate — not like any red variety we've tried before. This gracefully tapered variety stays firmer and crunchier longer in hot weather than other early radishes. Unusual tapered shape reaches a full 6 inches — excellent for slicing or serve on picks to dip into a savory herbed cheese dip.

Packet	Bonus Pkt.	Jumbo Pkt.
454-P **65c**	454-U **$1.25**	454-J **$2.35**

Radish—Cherry Belle

Radish—White Icicle

CORN SUGARDADDY A medium early (76 days), heavy yielding hybrid, plants produce good-sized, hearty ears of sweet, tender corn! Each 8 to 8½ inch ear contains 16 rows of delectable, golden-sweet, milky kernels protected by light silks and strong husks. A great variety for the home canner and freezer.

2-1/4 oz. Packet	1/4 lb.	1/2 lb.	1 lb.
232-P **$1.25**	232-M **$2.15**	232-H **$3.65**	232-K **$5.95**

CORN YUKON An excellent mid-season selection. Yukon produces fine quality 8- to 9-inch golden yellow ears in 75 days. Outstanding F_1 hybrid vigor makes this one a heavy yielder — plan an August barbecue and put on a huge feast of sweet and tender, garden-fresh corn!

2-1/4 oz. Packet	1/4 lb.	1/2 lb.	1 lb.
241-P **$1.25**	241-M **$2.15**	241-H **$3.65**	241-K **$5.95**

CORN GOLDEN CROSS BANTAM The most famous corn grown — the standard by which all hybrid sweet corn is judged. Six foot stalks — noted for their uniformity — carry large, 8 to 9 inch ears packed with rows of juicy, deep golden kernels of sugary sweetness. Ears are slightly tapered and are compactly filled with 10 to 14 straight rows; ready in 85 days.

2-1/4 oz. Packet	1/4 lb.	1/2 lb.	1 lb.
233-P **95c**	233-M **$1.65**	233-H **$2.75**	233-K **$4.75**

CORN IOCHIEF A well-deserving All-America gold medal winner, hybrid Iochief produces extra BIG 8½ to 9 inch ears with 14 to 16 rows of sugary-sweet kernels in 86 to 90 days. A good husk protects the extra tender, milky kernels even during the hottest weather. Strong, wind-resistant stalks receive top ratings for their high yields, fine flavor, and drought resistance. Ears stay in prime eating stage longer than Golden Cross. Definitely one of the most outstanding sweet corn introductions ever!

2-1/4 oz. Packet	1/4 lb.	1/2 lb.	1 lb.
237-P **95c**	237-M **$1.65**	237-H **$2.75**	237-K **$4.75**

CORN COUNTRY GENTLEMAN All the merits of the old favorite white Shoe Peg variety, plus "hybrid vigor." The yield has nearly been doubled, the fine, deliciously sweet flavor has actually been increased — and a strong disease-resistance added. The 7-foot stalks produce an abundance of 8 to 10 inch ears tightly packed with SNOW WHITE, tender, sweet kernels irregularly arranged on the ear. Ready to eat in 95 days, when most other corns are overripe. This outstanding hybrid is the finest corn you can grow for cream-style corn or corn chowders — as well as canning or freezing.

2-1/4 oz. Packet	1/4 lb.	1/2 lb.	1 lb.
235-P **$1.15**	235-M **$1.95**	235-H **$3.35**	235-K **$5.65**

HYBRID SWEET CORN Did you know that the sugar content in a fresh ear of sweet corn begins to turn to starch the very minute it is picked? It's a fact, and that's why the only sweet corn worthy of the name is that picked fresh from your own garden, shucked then and there and dunked into a ready pot of boiling water. If you've never experienced it, take our word for it — there's nothing to compare with the flavor of garden-fresh corn-on-the-cob, the milky, tender, sugary-sweet kernels bursting with natural flavor and slathered with butter!

Any good garden soil which is well drained and receives 6 full hours of sun a day is suitable for corn. Run the rows north to south for maximum sun.

Each stalk produces one or two ears, so make several sowings of early-maturing corn 2 weeks apart, or plant early, midseason and late varieties at one time, then repeat the same varieties about 3 weeks later. They'll mature in succession, and you'll enjoy corn all season.

Hybridization has created phenomenal corn yield increases in the past few decades. Hybrids have greater vigor, are more tender and flavorful, and produce larger quantities of beautiful, more uniform ears — they are more disease resistant than standard "open pollinated" varieties, too. However, you cannot save the seeds from a hybrid for future planting. The seeds will "revert" and will not grow true.

A ¼ pound packet plants 100 feet. Plant plenty for fresh eating, canning and freezing.

CORN EARLY SUNGLOW The earliest sweet corn to be found — ripens three weeks to a month earlier than most sweet corn varieties — ready to harvest in about 60 days! A hardy, early hybrid that is particulary resistant to cold and frost. Early Sunglow with its high sugar content and slim 7-inch cobs was primarily developed for on-the-cob freezing. So plant plenty for fresh eating and pop extras in the freezer for wonderful summertime treats in January!

2-1/4 oz. Packet	1/4 lb.	1/2 lb.	1 lb.
236-P **$1.15**	236-M **$1.95**	236-H **$3.35**	236-K **$5.65**

CORN ROYAL CREST This excellent F_1 hybrid bears cylindrical 6½- to 7½-inch ears well-filled out to the tapered ends, in only 64 days. Plant plenty for freezing — simply husk, wrap in freezer paper and pop in the freezer without any cooking. Later in winter, heat for 15 to 20 minutes in a 350° oven and enjoy garden fresh sweet corn all over again!

2-1/4 oz. Packet	1/4 lb.	1/2 lb.	1 lb.
240-P **$1.25**	240-M **$2.15**	240-H **$3.65**	240-K **$5.95**

CORN EARLIKING Largest of the early (66 days) sweet corn we offer. Excellent for all areas, and is especially popular with home gardeners in northern states with shorter growing seasons. Hybrid Earliking produces ears 7 to 8 inches long, packed with 12 well-filled rows of *extra* sweet and flavorful plump kernels. Delicious fresh or in chowder or fritters.

2-1/4 oz. Packet	1/4 lb.	1/2 lb.	1 lb.
238-P **95c**	238-M **$1.65**	238-H **$2.75**	238-K **$4.75**

LETTUCE Lettuce is exceptionally easy to grow — thrives in so many locations in the garden — even tucked away in empty nooks and crannies as space fillers. Will grow in partial shade.

There are three main types of lettuce — the best known is the HEAD type with crisp texture and mild, sweet flavor. The heads are quite compact and heavy. Often included in this category are the Bibb lettuce varieties, including Buttercrunch which has a smaller head with rich green outer leaves that are much looser than standard head lettuce and are very tender. ROMAINE or COS type lettuce is tall, cylindrical with stiff, crisp leaves. The flavor of Romaine is tart and distinctive. LEAF LETTUCE is spreading and very quick to grow. The crisp, usually frilled leaves are refreshingly mild-tasting. Make successive plantings and you'll have beautiful, crisp summer salads all season long. Find a spot to plant in a flower border — lettuce is decorative, too!

HEAD LETTUCE ITHACA ("Improved Iceberg") These rich, green heads have all the crispness and fine texture that you expect from good Iceberg lettuce! Well-wrapped, firm, disease-resistant heads grow to 5½ inches in diameter and 4¾ inches deep! Plants mature at a slow rate — 85 days.

Packet	Bonus Pkt.	Jumbo Pkt.
305-P **95c**	305-U **$1.75**	305-J **$3.35**

HEAD LETTUCE GREAT LAKES Won an All-America Award because of its ability to succeed under the most adverse conditions! Large, thick leaves fold over the fresh green heads to preserve their crackling crisp quality. Disease resistant, fine-flavored and exceptionally choice.

Packet	Bonus Pkt.	Jumbo Pkt.
306-P **65c**	306-U **$1.25**	306-J **$2.35**

LEAF LETTUCE BLACK SEEDED SIMPSON Will produce a mass of extra-large, crinkled leaves anywhere in only 45 days! Termed the "ever-bearing lettuce" because of its amazing dependability — it will grow crisp, good quality lettuce of the most delicate flavor all through the season. Harvest the light green leaves and new ones will grow from the center.

Packet	Bonus Pkt.	Jumbo Pkt.
302-P **65c**	302-U **$1.25**	302-J **$2.35**

LEAF LETTUCE PRIZE HEAD A super quick grower — only 45 days until you can enjoy surprisingly sweet, crackling crisp lettuce right from your own backyard! Leaves are reddish-brown, edged in delicate pink, and are quite frilly. They branch out from very compact centers which are tender and unusually mild. The perfect variety to grow in areas where hot weather presents a problem.

Packet	Bonus Pkt.	Jumbo Pkt.
303-P **75c**	303-U **$1.45**	303-J **$2.75**

LEAF LETTUCE SALAD BOWL An All-America winner selected for superb quality and the ability to retain its delicate tenderness indefinitely! Rich in Vitamins A and C — healthful and appetizing. In 47 days you can pick decorative rosettes of sweet, wavy notched leaves which will fill a salad bowl. Different from other leaf varieties because leaves are deeply lobed which gives them the attractive appearance of endive.

Packet	Bonus Pkt.	Jumbo Pkt.
304-P **65c**	304-U **$1.25**	304-J **$2.35**

BIBB LETTUCE BUTTERCRUNCH An All-America winner — and for good reason! Buttercrunch forms loose "butterheads" brimming with high quality characteristic of Bibb types, but plants are much larger and have a good tolerance to heat. Anyone can grow Buttercrunch; vigorous and dependable, leaves are thick and crisp. The heart of the loosely folded, deep green leaves is the most delicious part of the plant. The delicate flavor and gourmet quality will delight you — enjoy it all season! The Jumbo packet will enable you to make successive plantings April through August, about every 65 days you'll enjoy a fresh crop.

Packet	Bonus Pkt.	Jumbo Pkt.
307-P **65c**	307-U **$1.25**	307-J **$2.35**

ROMAINE LETTUCE VALMAINE (Cos Type - "Paris White") A variety much prized for its fresh crispness and disease resistance. Tightly-folded green leaves form a compact head ready to eat in 68 days. Plants have an endive-like flavor — they're tender and sweet! An attractive and dependable type producing greens of 10 to 11 inches in length and 3 to 4 inches wide.

Packet	Bonus Pkt.	Jumbo Pkt.
308-P **85c**	308-U **$1.60**	308-J **$3.10**

ENDIVE GREEN CURLED RUFFEC Large, finely cut and curled leaves with pure white midribs are high in vitamin content and have a distinctive tart flavor. Intriguing and attractive in salads and garnishes — or bake or braise, and top with a creamy roquefort sauce. Ready in 95 days — plant anytime from early spring until mid July in northern states. Seeds sown in July will grow fresh salad greens for fall and winter use. Endive is sown in rows 18 inches apart, and the plants are later thinned to 8 to 12 inches apart. Easy to grow, endive is best when heads are white to pale yellow. Blanch by tying the low-spreading plants when they are nearly full grown (15 to 18 inches across). Ruffec will produce tender, sweet hearts — a delicacy in salads!

Packet	Bonus Pkt.	Jumbo Pkt.
272-P **85c**	272-U **$1.60**	272-J **$3.10**

KALE DWARF BLUE CURLED This hardy, low-growing vegetable produces leafy curled greens straight through the fall and into winter! It's at its best when there's a nip in the air — and the flavor of the ruffled leaves is never better than when they're touched by a light frost! Young, tender kale shoots make delicious greens, or use as a garnish just like parsley. Use in salads or sandwiches in place of lettuce — or boil and top with sauce Béarnaise or vinaigrette. Kale is not only delicious but also packed with vitamins and high in calcium, too. Blue Kale is so attractive it is often planted as a border or in containers. The hardy productive plants will grow 15 inches tall and spread to 30 inches wide in about 65 days — sow in early spring and again in July for a maximum harvest.

Packet	Bonus Pkt.	Jumbo Pkt.
282-P **85c**	282-U **$1.60**	282-J **$3.10**

Endive

Kale

Head Lettuce—Great Lakes

Bibb Lettuce—Buttercrunch

Evergreen Bunching Onions

ONIONS Onions comprise a large, vigorous family with an infinite variety of uses — eating, garnishing, flavoring, cooking, slicing and pickling! And so easy to grow that every home garden should include them. Once you get them started, you'll have onions for every use you can think of. Pull them while young and enjoy fresh green onions — boil the small bulbs and serve creamed. Wait until the bulbs mature and use them full-flavored and fresh in salads, sliced on hamburgers, for flavoring a variety of different dishes. Plant plenty and store the mature onions in a dry place for use all winter long. Plan on a 50 foot row for each person and you'll have a year's supply at hand.

A hardy vegetable, onions like a loose, well-drained soil in a sunny location.

Shallowly plant seeds 2 to 3 inches apart in rows 18 inches apart. If you want fully-matured onions, thin the seedlings when they are 3 to 4 inches tall so that they will have sufficient room to develop without crowding each other. When bulbs are mature, bend down the tops to speed-up ripening before harvesting. When pulling bulbs leave on top of ground to dry in the sun for two days. Clip tops to a 1/2-inch stem. Store in net bags and hang in cool dry location.

ONION EVERGREEN BUNCHING
Whether you live in the North or South, you can grow fresh, sweet green onions in just 60 days! Clumps of 4 to 6 tender green shoots sprout from each seed! No bulbs are formed on Evergreen Bunching. Stagger plantings and have mild, sweet onions all summer and longer — they winter well; enjoy scallions next spring, too.

Packet	Bonus Pkt.	Jumbo Pkt.
364-P 75c	364-U $1.45	364-J $2.75

ONION RINGMASTER (WHITE SWEET SPANISH) (For Northern Latitudes)
The perfect onion for crisp golden onion rings! Large, sweet Spanish type grows only one center — makes perfect rings, slice after slice. Delicious in salads, too. Ready in 110 days — excellent keeper.

Packet	Bonus Pkt.	Jumbo Pkt.
365-P 85c	365-U $1.60	365-J $3.10

ONION YELLOW SWEET SPANISH (For Northern Latitudes)
The ideal large onion! Pick early — tiny onions are delightful glazed or creamed. Mature onions often weigh a pound or more. Heavy, golden-brown skin protects sweet onion inside — firm, crisp and exceptionally mild. Excellent slicer; good for storing. Ready in 115 days.

Packet	Bonus Pkt.	Jumbo Pkt.
366-P 75c	366-U $1.45	366-J $2.75

ONION BURGUNDY (For Northern Latitudes)
These deep red skinned onions are sweet and mild — tops for hamburgers, sandwiches and beautiful in salads. Medium size, flat-globe shaped onions slice perfectly. Crisp flesh is white and always mild — ready to enjoy in 95 days.

Packet	Bonus Pkt.	Jumbo Pkt.
367-P 85c	367-U $1.60	367-J $3.10

ONION WHITE BERMUDA (For Southern Latitudes)
An excellent onion for the South, although it can be grown in the North for tiny pearl and pickling onions. The mild, crisp white flesh of these onions is so sweet that some people eat them like apples! Plant White Bermudas close together and harvest delicious small pickling onions. For larger, flat-shaped slicing onions, plant 3 to 4 inches apart — they'll be ready in 90 days.

Packet	Bonus Pkt.	Jumbo Pkt.
371-P 75c	371-U $1.45	371-J $2.75

ONION SETS
An onion "set" is simply a tiny onion, which you plant and allow to continue growing. You then have the choice of pulling them as "green" onions — or allowing them to grow on and go to seed, at which time they're pulled to dry in the sun, for winter storage. The advantage of planting sets rather than seeds is that they mature in 1/3 or less the time. You can harvest green onions from sets in 25 to 50 days. Just like onions from seeds, they may be crowded to produce small onions particularly suited for pickling or boiling, or set them far enough apart to produce full-sized mature onions.

Australian Brown *Onion Sets*

1/2 pound	1 pound	2 pounds
C-18 $1.65	C-19 $2.95	C-20 $5.25

ONION PLANTS
You'll have bigger, milder, sweeter onions than any grown from seed! Imagine — 2 weeks after planting, you'll pull green onions for a tossed salad . . . shortly after, there'll be larger onions to serve glazed or creamed . . . or let them mature to husky slicing size — they're ready fast! Your fully mature onions are ready about two weeks earlier than onions from sets. These hardy, field grown onion plants are shipped the same day they are dug. Because they are field grown, they are not susceptible to "transplant shock" . . . so you can put them out extra early to take full advantage of the growing season. Once you've seen the extra-big yield you get with onion plants, you'll always want to plant them! Plant 4 inches apart, or thicker if you plan to thin for early green onions. Shipped at the right planting time for your area.
One bunch equals approximately 75-85 plants; allow 150 plants for a 50-foot row.

White Sweet Spanish Ringmaster *Onion Plants*

2 bunches	3 bunches	5 bunches
4742 $4.95	4743 $6.75	4745 $10.45

Yellow Sweet Spanish *Onion Plants*

2 bunches	3 bunches	5 bunches
4862 $4.95	4863 $6.75	4865 $10.45

Red Burgundy *Onion Plants*

2 bunches	3 bunches	5 bunches
4882 $5.95	4883 $7.95	4885 $11.45

White Bermuda *Onion Plants*

2 bunches	3 bunches	5 bunches
4902 $4.95	4903 $6.75	4905 $10.45

Easy-to-grow Onions!

PEAS
Planting peas is one of your best gardening bets! You'll have the incomparable enjoyment of fresh, sweet and plump garden peas — and when you see the price of market peas next spring, you will know you really saved money! So now's the time to stock up, and plan to plant plenty. Peas are super easy to grow — a packet will plant about 15 feet, enough for one person to have loads of fresh, delicious tender peas. For economical, great tasting frozen peas, plant another 25 to 30 feet per person. Our quarter-pound packet plants 25 feet. While the cost of seed peas has gone up dramatically, the quality of the seed we offer is the very best obtainable. We still feel that planting peas now is a better investment than ever before.

PEA MELTING SUGAR (Snow Peas)
Here are the tender sweet edible pods used in Chinese dishes — the kind you can usually enjoy only in restaurants. "Snow Peas" are eaten whole — no need for shelling. They cook in seconds — or enjoy their crisp, sweet flavor in salads. Vigorous 4-foot bushes should be supported on stake or trellis or grown on a fence; pods are picked just as peas begin to form inside but are still tiny. Ready in 72 days.

2-1/4 oz. Packet	1/4 lb.	1/2 lb.	1 lb.
413-P 95c	413-M $1.65	413-H $2.75	413-K $4.75

PEA LITTLE MARVEL IMPROVED
Biggest selling EARLY bush pea! This improved version of America's most popular dwarf pea needs no trellis or poles for support. The low, compact plants produce tremendous quantities of tender, sweet dark green peas. Ready to eat in about 63 days. A long-time favorite and *still* a superior garden variety.

2-1/4 oz. Packet	1/4 lb.	1/2 lb.	1 lb.
414-P 85c	414-M $1.45	414-H $2.45	414-K $4.45

PEA WANDO
Specially bred to stand up to hot weather — excellent mid-season producer even under drought conditions. Dwarf bush plant grows just 2½ feet tall — needs no support. Excellent for fresh canning and an outstanding freezing variety; harvest choice, tender peas in 70 days.

2-1/4 oz. Packet	1/4 lb.	1/2 lb.	1 lb.
415-P 85c	415-M $1.45	415-H $2.45	415-K $4.45

PEA MORSE'S NO. 60
Known as the "best in the west" this outstanding pea is an all-time favorite. Sturdy, erect bush plants grow just 28 inches high, producing long slender pods up to 5 inches in length, filled with 8 to 10 plump peas. Delicious fresh, canned or frozen. Harvest in 75 days.

2-1/4 oz. Packet	1/4 lb.	1/2 lb.	1 lb.
416-P 95c	416-M $1.65	416-H $2.75	416-K $4.75

PEA SOUTHERN BLACKEYE
Here's the perfect choice for a small planting area. This excellent bush variety is easy to contain without staking. And talk about flavor — it's considered most delicious of all by Blackeye "connoisseurs." The vigorous, upright disease-resistant plants reward you with quarts and quarts of large easy-to-shell peas. If you can grow Bermuda grass, your area is warm enough for this traditionally southern-grown pea.

2-1/4 oz. Packet	1/4 lb.	1/2 lb.	1 lb.
417-P 95c	417-M $1.65	417-H $2.75	417-K $4.75

Edible Pod Peas—Melting Sugar

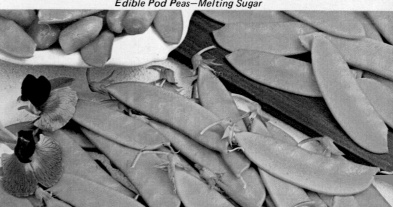

Pea—Morse's No. 60

Collards—Georgia Southern

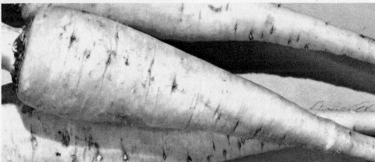

Mustard Greens—Southern Giant Curled

Okra—Clemson Spineless

Parsnips—All American

Chard—Fordhook Large Ribbed Dark Green

Parsley—Extra Triple Curled

SWISS CHARD FORDHOOK LARGE RIBBED DARK GREEN The
best available! Chard is one of the most rewarding and useful vegetables to grow — because it is so easy *and* it just keeps on producing for months! Unlike most other greens, chard doesn't bolt to seed in hot weather, and it is also extremely hardy to cold — so if you plant in the spring, you'll have fresh chard available FROM EARLY SUMMER CLEAR INTO NEXT WINTER! Both the leaves and stems are good eating. The broad leaves are delicious fresh, used like lettuce in salads and sandwiches, or cooked as you would spinach, topped with sour cream or flavored with bacon. The thick stems, stripped of the leaves, are cooked and eaten like asparagus. Fordhook Large Ribbed is an early producer — in only 55 days you'll have large yields of broad, dark green leaves packed with vitamins and iron. A packet plants a 25 foot row — plenty for a family of four.

Packet	Bonus Pkt.	Jumbo Pkt.
210-P **65c**	210-U **$1.25**	210-J **$2.35**

COLLARDS GEORGIA SOUTHERN Best known in the South, but easy
to grow anywhere! Ready to harvest in 75 days, Georgia Southern provides you with fresh greens all summer long — delicious new leaves grow back each time you pick. Add the tender, slightly crumbled leaves to a salad with toasted sesame seeds, small bacon bits, dill and basil, and top with vinaigrette dressing. Plant grows 2 to 3 feet high — fall frosts sweeten flavor.

Packet	Bonus Pkt.	Jumbo Pkt.
220-P **65c**	220-U **$1.25**	220-J **$2.35**

MUSTARD GREENS SOUTHERN GIANT CURLED A fine all-time
favorite and All America winner that produces choice, tender greens in only 40 to 50 days. One of the fastest crops you can plant and harvest in your garden — the young leaves add sharp, tangy flavor to fresh green salads. The mature, wide leaves are bright green and frilled at the edges, and served fresh or cooked like spinach, have a mild, pleasing flavor. Very rich in iron and vitamins A, C and B$_2$. The plant is large, upright and slightly spreading in growth. Plant the seeds 5 to 6 inches apart in rows spaced 12 to 18 inches apart. Make successive sowings up to the time weather gets hot. For late fall use, plant in August and plan to freeze some for the winter!

Packet	Bonus Pkt.	Jumbo Pkt.
344-P **65c**	344-U **$1.25**	344-J **$2.35**

OKRA CLEMSON SPINELESS Traditionally used to flavor famous New
Orleans seafood gumbos — just as delicious french fried, baked, or hot with butter sauce. Pick the crisp, emerald green pods when they're about 2 to 2½ inches long — when they're young, tender, at the peak of their unique flavor even though they're still tasty when twice that size. Cook for 8 to 12 minutes in a small amount of boiling water — great with stewed tomatoes. This ALL-AMERICA WINNER is grown extensively in the south — but the 4 to 4½ foot plants will produce anywhere in the U.S. where the summer months are warm. (A good rule of thumb is that if your garden will grow good sweet corn, it will grow good okra.) Seedlings should be thinned 12 to 18 inches apart in rows — in 55 days they will yield pounds of straight, smooth, tapered pods up to 6 inches in length.

Packet	Bonus Pkt.	Jumbo Pkt.
354-P **65c**	354-U **$1.25**	354-J **$2.35**

PARSLEY EXTRA TRIPLE CURLED The indispensable garnish! Start
it indoors early in spring . . . snip fresh parsley as soon as plants are a few inches high. The favorite garnish for soup, omelets, roasts, salads — easy to grow; thrives in sun or shade. Transplant outdoors when warm weather comes — enjoy a dooryard garden with these vigorous bushy plants displayed in containers on porch or patio. So attractive you'll plant it as a compact edging in flower beds — it's winter hardy, comes back year after year. Grows 8 to 9 inches tall. Nutritious as well as flavorful — rich natural source of Vitamins A, C and B!

Packet	Bonus Pkt.	Jumbo Pkt.
393-P **65c**	393-U **$1.25**	393-J **$2.35**

PARSNIP ALL AMERICAN This tender, fine-grained parsnip fairly melts
in your mouth! Firm, slender roots are a full 12 inches long, and 3 inches in diameter at the crown, tapering to a smooth point. Superb flavor is sweet and sugary — delicious sautéed or baked au gratin. Sow seed ¼ inch deep; thin to 4 inches in rows 24 inches apart. Tender and delicious late in the fall — especially after a frost which adds sweetness to the flavor. May be stored for winter use or, as they are improved by freezing, just leave some in the ground all winter to harvest as needed or for use in early spring.

Packet	Bonus Pkt.	Jumbo Pkt.
403-P **65c**	403-U **$1.25**	403-J **$2.35**

PEPPERS Ask anyone who has grown their own green peppers
how they like the store-bought kind, *now!* There's just no comparison. And all the peppers we offer here are tops in flavor and very easy to grow — produce decorative, lush green plants and delicious crisp peppers for eating, cooking, pickling and canning. Sow seeds in flats and transplant seedlings when they are 3 or 4 inches high and set out in the garden when all danger of frost is past. Plan rows 30 inches apart, spacing the plants 18 inches apart in the rows. Three plants per person is plenty for fresh eating, another 3 to 5 for canning and processing. Pepper plants are one of the most decorative in the garden — these lush, erect dark green plants are actually prized as shrubs in tropical climates!

PEPPER CALIFORNIA WONDER 300 One of the best stuffing peppers
— an unusually firm, extra-thick walled sweet bell. Specially bred for resistance to tobacco mosaic, bane of many green peppers. Taller than most, it produces over a long season — bears dozens of 4-inch emerald green peppers that mature to rich crimson.

Packet	Bonus Pkt.	Jumbo Pkt.
428-P **65c**	428-U **$1.25**	428-J **$2.35**

PEPPER **HYBRID BELL BOY** An All-America winner and great all-purpose pepper. Bell Boy has excellent "setting" ability — producing abundant yields of large, thick-walled fruits with a distinctive sweet flavor. The peppers form high on the large plants — under ample foliage to prevent sunburn — and reach full size in 70 days from setting out plants. Resistant to tobacco mosaic virus; glossy green fruits mature to deep red. Excellent pepper for cooking — adds color and zest to dozens of dishes.

Packet	Bonus Pkt.	Jumbo Pkt.
432-P 95c	432-U $1.75	432-J $3.35

PEPPER **HUNGARIAN YELLOW WAX** The earliest of the hot peppers — ready in 60 to 65 days. Compact plants produce large amounts of 6-8 inch long, smooth tapered fruits. Waxy canary yellow fruits turn brilliant red when ripe. An excellent variety for home canning and hot pickles — used fresh or dried, Yellow Wax is a must for hot spicy flavoring in stews and homemade soups.

Packet	Bonus Pkt.	Jumbo Pkt.
430-P 75c	430-U $1.45	430-J $2.75

PEPPER **LONG RED CAYENNE** An early maturing variety (70 to 75 days), this hot bright red pepper can be used the year round — it's best to pickle, can or dry. Five-inch long, slim peppers grow on bushy plants 20 to 24 inches high. Fruits turn from waxy green to rich crimson and have a hot pungent flavor.

Packet	Bonus Pkt.	Jumbo Pkt.
431-P 65c	431-U $1.25	431-J $2.35

PEPPER **LONG SWEET BANANA** This All-America winner appears to be a hot pepper, but is actually a sweet pickling variety! Bright banana yellow, gradually turning brilliant red. Either color, they make delicious eating. Plants produce heavy yields of 6 to 7 inch fruits. No. 1 pepper for pickling — also great fresh in a crisp, colorful salad.

Packet	Bonus Pkt.	Jumbo Pkt.
429-P 75c	429-U $1.45	429-J $2.75

SPINACH Leafy, tender green spinach is a delightful treat from your spring garden — and it's rich in Vitamins A, C and B_2. Spinach adds unique flavor to green salads — or steam and garnish with butter and nutmeg, slivered almonds or crumbled bacon. Plant every two weeks until summer and again in early fall. Allow 5 to 10 feet per person for fresh eating — add another 15 feet for freezing. A packet will sow 25 feet of row; thin plants to 4 inches apart in rows 2 feet apart. Just harvest the outer leaves as they're ready — let the center continue to produce new leaves until it grows a flower stalk and bolts to seed. Spinach may be mulched with straw or grass and survive winter — plants pop up again next spring. *(See Melody Spinach on page 3.)*

SPINACH **BLOOMSDALE SAVOY** Long standing Bloomsdale Savoy will produce heavy yields in only 48 days. Uniform plants supply luscious greens until the hottest days of summer — produces about 2 weeks longer than other varieties before going to seed.

Packet	Bonus Pkt.	Jumbo Pkt.
466-P 65c	466-U $1.25	466-J $2.35

SPINACH **NEW ZEALAND** There should be room in every garden for New Zealand, the "summer spinach", because there's nothing like having fresh, home-grown, fine flavored greens during the summer months when regular spinach gives up! Hardy, spreading bushlike plants produce large quantities of rich green leaves. This is the "mock spinach" to plant if your summers are hot and ordinary spinach bolts to seed. Easy to grow — ready to eat in an average of 70 days.

Packet	Bonus Pkt.	Jumbo Pkt.
467-P 75c	467-U $1.45	467-J $2.75

TURNIP **TOKYO TOP** This outstanding F_1 hybrid is *perfect* for fresh eating, pickling and garnishes. Sweet, pure white turnips are ready to eat in only 50 days, when 2 to 3 inches in diameter — wonderful boiled and buttered, or steam the tender greens. Sparkling crisp white turnips are exceptionally disease resistant and not affected by late autumn frost — your crop will be virtually flawless!

Packet	Bonus Pkt.	Jumbo Pkt.
511-P 75c	511-U $1.45	511-J $2.75

TURNIP **PURPLE TOP WHITE GLOBE** Largest and best all-around turnip to be found! Precedes other vegetables in the spring and bears longer into the fall. Purple Top White Globe produces turnips 5 to 6 inches in diameter in an average of 55 days. Tender roots are deep lavender on top and creamy white on the lower portion — but the delectable interior flesh is white, sweet and fine-grained.

Packet	Bonus Pkt.	Jumbo Pkt.
509-P 65c	509-U $1.25	509-J $2.35

KOHLRABI **EARLY PURPLE VIENNA** A little-known, excellent vegetable whose succulent, delicious bulb-like stems form above the ground. The enlarged stem base is similar to a turnip in appearance and taste — but many people consider its subtle flavor superior. A rapid grower (mature in 60 days) that is harvested when the bulbous stem is 2 or 3 inches in diameter — that's when the creamy white flesh is young, crisp and tender. Kohlrabi can be prepared like turnips — or eaten raw, it is a tasty and different addition to fresh salads. Stagger the planting of seeds — they may be sown from late April up to August in rows that are 18-24 inches apart — you'll have a continuous crop.

Packet	Bonus Pkt.	Jumbo Pkt.
293-P 65c	293-U $1.25	293-J $2.35

Pepper—Long Red Cayenne

Pepper—California Wonder 300

Turnip — Hybrid Tokyo Top

Pepper—Hungarian Yellow Wax

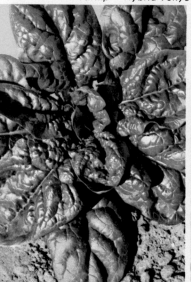

Spinach—Bloomsdale Savoy

Kohlrabi— Early Purple Vienna

Pumpkin — Hybrid Spirit

Summer Squash—Goldneck

MELONS It's a fact — store-bought melons simply can't compare with home grown melons. Here's why. The home gardener can grow the tender, melt-in-your-mouth varieties that commercial growers find too delicate or too large to ship. Also, home gardeners can pick their melons vine-ripe, after they've developed full sweetness and flavor. Cantaloupe, for instance, don't continue to ripen off the vine — rather they drop in sugar content right after picking.

For the price of one or two store-bought melons, you can plant 2 or 3 packets of seeds and have bushels of sweet, vine-ripened fruit! You must give them room, sun and plenty of water, but other than these simple requirements, melons are carefree to grow. And we're sure you'll find your home grown are superior in every way.

When planting cantaloupe, allow 60 inches between hills (one packet plants 12 hills). For watermelon, leave 96 inches between hills (one packet plants 6 hills). Plant 6 seeds per hill and later thin to 2 plants. Harvest when melon twists easily off the stem.

CANTALOUPE (Muskmelon) **JUMBO HALE'S BEST** One of the finest! Jumbo Hale's Best isn't usually grown for commercial purposes and the best way for you to enjoy the excellent, uniquely sweet flavor of this cantaloupe, is to grow it yourself! An early (86 days) large version of the famous Hale's Best, with small seed cavities and a strong rind. Produces beautiful 4-pound melons even in hot weather.

Packet	Bonus Pkt.	Jumbo Pkt.
319-P **65c**	319-U **$1.25**	319-J **$2.35**

CANTALOUPE (Muskmelon) **HYBRID CLASSIC** This wonderful new hybrid produces excellent yields of large, 4 to 5 pound fruits of a sweet refreshing flavor. Classic is an early variety with firm, delicious, deep-orange flesh. Highly improved disease resistance assures you of a good crop. Ready to pick in 80 to 90 days.

Packet	Bonus Pkt.	Jumbo Pkt.
318-P **95c**	318-U **$1.75**	318-J **$3.35**

MELON HONEY DEW Best known of all, this melon boasts fine textured, thick emerald green flesh with a sweet, delicate flavor. Fruits average 7 to 8 inches in length and 6 inches across, with a smooth, creamy white rind. Honey Dew needs a long growing season (110 days) — and produces best in warmer areas. If harvested fruits are stored where they won't freeze, they'll keep for a long period.

Packet	Bonus Pkt.	Jumbo Pkt.
320-P **75c**	320-U **$1.45**	320-J **$2.75**

WATERMELON HYBRID DIXIE QUEEN Huge 35 to 50 pound watermelons! Ready to eat in only 80 to 85 days! Vigorous, productive vines bear large, top-quality melons — with crisp, firm flesh that is sparkling red and deliciously sugar-sweet. Fewer seeds and fine texture make this hybrid a superb home garden variety. You'll have extras for friends — or to set up your own fresh melon booth.

Packet	Bonus Pkt.	Jumbo Pkt.
331-P **95c**	331-U **$1.75**	331-J **$3.35**

WATERMELON HYBRID YOU SWEET THING An extra early watermelon for short season areas — 70 days from planting 'til sweet eating! This round, dark-skinned family-sized melon has thick black stripes and reaches 13 lbs. when mature. Thin rind allows for more of the extra sweet 'n juicy flesh — the finest taste of any melon we've ever eaten! Highly disease resistant vines produce in abundance.

Packet	Bonus Pkt.	Jumbo Pkt.
330-P **95c**	330-U **$1.75**	330-J **$3.35**

WATERMELON HYBRID SWEET FAVORITE This All-America winner for 1978 produces large, striped melons averaging 20 pounds apiece! Excellent quality, thin-skinned home garden type fruit are full flavored, extra-sweet, *and* they mature quickly for fruit this size — only 85 days from planting. A vigorous, highly productive hybrid, Sweet Favorite is an unbeatable choice for average growing season areas.

Packet	Bonus Pkt.	Jumbo Pkt.
336-P **75c**	336-U **$1.45**	336-J **$2.75**

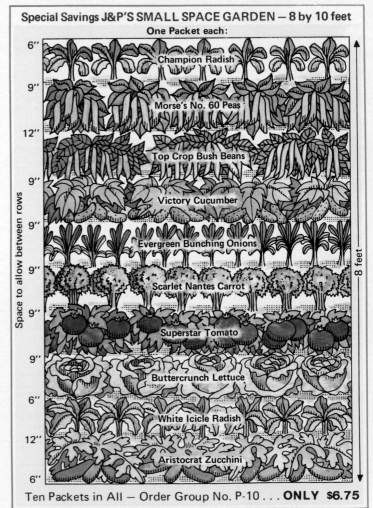

Special Savings J&P'S SMALL SPACE GARDEN — 8 by 10 feet

One Packet each:

6" — Champion Radish
9" — Morse's No. 60 Peas
12" — Top Crop Bush Beans
9" — Victory Cucumber
9" — Evergreen Bunching Onions
9" — Scarlet Nantes Carrot
9" — Superstar Tomato
9" — Buttercrunch Lettuce
6" — White Icicle Radish
12" — Aristocrat Zucchini
6"

Space to allow between rows

8 feet

Ten Packets in All — Order Group No. P-10 . . . ONLY $6.75

MORE SPACE SAVING HINTS FOR A SMALL GARDEN

Grow squash, cucumbers, pole beans, peas, tomatoes, on a 6-foot fence of wire mesh. Cantaloupe can even be grown this way — simply put the ripening melons in a mesh sack and wire to the fence. Plant 3 corn plants so the leaves will be touching. Quite a few of these "triangles" can be tucked into even a small garden.

Summer Squash—Aristocrat Zucchini

Winter Squash—Table Ace

Summer Squash – Greyzini Zucchini

Summer Squash—Patty Pan

Winter Squash—Waltham Butternut

PUMPKINS Plant easy-to-grow pumpkins! Deep rooted American tradition makes them an essential and delicious part of Halloween and Thanksgiving. They take partial shade and may be planted among corn to save space, or in hills 6-8 feet apart. Store whole in cool dry place for winter . . . freeze or can the flesh.

PUMPKIN F₁ HYBRID SPIRIT You'll have room for Spirit — semi-bush habit takes only a 5-foot space to grow and produces big yields of 12-inch, 15-pound pumpkins! Smooth, uniform in shape, bright in color, this 1977 All-America winner inspires you to carve a face. Matures early to the joy of pumpkin-eaters who love its thick, rich succulent meat.

Packet	Bonus Pkt.	Jumbo Pkt.
445-P **$1.25**	445-U **$2.35**	445-J **$4.45**

PUMPKIN FUNNY FACE This excellent new F₁ hybrid provides a heavy yield of nearly perfectly round, bright orange pumpkins. The 10- to 15-pound fruit is uniform in size and shape, and matures in *less than 80 days*! Unusual semi-bush plant habit with only a 5-foot vine makes Funny Face ideal for small gardens. Terrific for carving and pies!

Packet	Bonus Pkt.	Jumbo Pkt.
444-P **95c**	444-U **$1.75**	444-J **$3.35**

PUMPKIN BIG MAX A real State Fair Special — Big Max is *BIG!* Grows up to 70 inches around and averages 100 POUNDS or MORE if given fertilizer and plenty of water. Grown mainly for novelty and for HUGE Jack O' Lanterns, the 3/4 inch thick flesh is also good for pies and canning. Flattened round fruits are attractive apricot-orange.

Packet	Bonus Pkt.	Jumbo Pkt.
443-P **95c**	443-U **$1.75**	443-J **$3.35**

SQUASH There is a thrill in growing squashes that experienced gardeners or even beginners shouldn't miss! With almost no care at all, the plants grow like magic and produce large quantities of delicious, choice garden fresh eating.

Squash is truly one of the least demanding and most rewarding of all vegetables to cultivate — and growing squash is a great way to introduce children to the thrill and excitement of gardening.

SUMMER SQUASH There are many scrumptious ways to serve the tender summer squashes — slice and boil in salted water, sauté in butter, bake in a casserole with parmesan cheese, or stuff a zucchini with herbs, onions, peppers and bread crumbs. Summer squash can be par-cooked and frozen for winter use. Summer squash is best when picked very young — the thumb nail should easily pierce the skin with little pressure. Plant in "hills" spaced 60 inches apart — thin to the 2 or 3 strongest plants when the seedlings have 3 or 4 leaves. Then . . . 50 to 60 days later, put the water on to boil and harvest your first crop! One packet will plant about 8 to 10 hills.

SUMMER SQUASH HYBRID GOLDNECK Hybrid vigor is shown in the tremendous yields and superior flavor of this yellow summer crookneck type. Goldneck is a very early maturing hybrid (45 to 50 days) and is especially delicious when picked early as 4 to 5 inch fruits but remains tasty when full grown at 10 to 12 inches long. Bushy plants remain very compact and can be spaced close together — excellent for small gardens.

Packet	Bonus Pkt.	Jumbo Pkt.
478-P **95c**	478-U **$1.75**	478-J **$3.35**

SUMMER SQUASH HYBRID PATTY PAN (Early Bush Scallop) Shaped like a beret with scalloped edges! This is the green tinted type which stays delicious and tender just a little longer than the old pure white variety. Plants are rather small and bushy — quite productive. Delicate pale green fruits average 3 to 4 inches in diameter at picking time. Delicious when served topped with a well-seasoned, buttery, lemon sauce — a real canning and freezing favorite.

Packet	Bonus Pkt.	Jumbo Pkt.
479-P **95c**	479-U **$1.75**	479-J **$3.35**

SUMMER SQUASH F₁ HYBRID ARISTOCRAT ZUCCHINI Outstanding 1973 *All-America winner* with a vigor that produces one of the earliest crops . . . bears dozens of firm, smooth, deep green squash month after month. Aristocrat Zucchini is particularly prized for its tender and delicately flavored fruit — delicious baked, stuffed, fried or boiled!

Packet	Bonus Pkt.	Jumbo Pkt.
477-P **95c**	477-U **$1.75**	477-J **$3.35**

SUMMER SQUASH GREYZINI ZUCCHINI You just won't believe that a plant can produce *so* much *so* rapidly as this All-America hybrid — bears dozens of medium green squash with distinctive silver-grey markings month after month. *And* your harvest begins only 50 days from planting! Widely adapted — an excellent producer in every area of the United States. The fruits (best picked when 5 to 6 inches long) are tender and delicately flavored — delicious steamed and topped with melted butter, salt, pepper and parmesan.

Packet	Bonus Pkt.	Jumbo Pkt.
483-P **85c**	483-U **$1.60**	483-J **$3.10**

WINTER SQUASH Winter squash may be enjoyed fresh from your garden in the fall, or harvested and stored. To keep for winter use just store in a cool (45° to 55°F.), dry place. Popular favorites, the rich Butternuts and Acorns are luscious halved and baked with butter, or mashed and topped with brown sugar, cream, spices and chopped walnuts. And the fruits of your vines can be cooked and frozen or canned for convenient use all year. The "winter" squashes are harvested in the fall — 85 to 110 days after planting, after they have matured fully and developed a hard rind. Always pick your squashes with part of the stem attached. When planting, allow 6 feet between hills. One packet of seeds will plant 6 to 8 hills.

WINTER SQUASH TABLE ACE A *new hybrid* acorn squash. Shiny, near-black and uniform in size and shape, it's beautiful to serve . . . just bake with savory spices . . . or cooked and mashed with butter. The rich, smooth-and-sweet flesh fairly melts in the mouth. Grows with a semi-bush habit, taking up much less space, yet yielding an abundance of 4½- x 5½-inch, thick and meaty, quality fruits. Matures with a hybrid vigor 5 to 10 days earlier than common acorn strains — to harvest and eat in the fall . . . or store for winter use.

Packet	Bonus Pkt.	Jumbo Pkt.
487-P **85c**	487-U **$1.60**	487-J **$3.10**

WINTER SQUASH WALTHAM BUTTERNUT A 1970 All-America award winner, Waltham Butternut produces larger, high quality yields of 7 to 9 inch fruits in 91 days. Almost 90% solid meat and heavy for their size, the thick, straight-necked, blocky fruits have sweet, rich pumpkin-colored flesh with small seed cavities. The hard rind protects the tender, rich-flavored meat — months after the snows set in, you can be serving the squashes you harvested and stored in the fall. Enjoy hot Butternut squash with melted butter on a cold day in January!

Packet	Bonus Pkt.	Jumbo Pkt.
481-P **75c**	481-U **$1.45**	481-J **$2.75**

SUMMER SQUASH F₁ HYBRID SCALLOPINI Something really different! This 1977 All-America winner is dark green, like zucchini . . . round as an apple with slightly scalloped edges, very meaty. It has a distinct flavor all its own! Delicious boiled or fried . . . especially good in raw salads. Easy to grow plants reach 2- to 2-½ feet and bear heavily. An exciting new vegetable for your garden!

Packet	Bonus Pkt.	Jumbo Pkt.
485-P **$1.25**	485-U **$2.35**	485-J **$4.45**

WINTER SQUASH TABLE KING ACORN 1974 All-America winner, Table King produces 4 to 7 large 1½-pound squashes on each compact, bush-type plant — requires much less garden space than ordinary acorn squash. You can plant about 3½ feet apart. The thick golden yellow flesh has excellent flavor. Ready in 75 days from seed planting.

Packet	Bonus Pkt.	Jumbo Pkt.
484-P **85c**	484-U **$1.60**	484-J **$3.10**

31

Beefmaster

Floramerica

Small Fry

Wonder Boy

Springset

Heinz 1350

TOMATOES

Nothing beats walking into your own garden, picking a fresh, ripe tomato, washing it off with the garden hose and eating it. You can't get vine-ripened tomatoes in stores, because they're picked when still green before the flavor has developed. The alternative is to grow your own — it's easy and fun! We recommend that you plant a combination of small early tomatoes with the later, whopper hamburger size for the longest season possible — once you've tasted garden fresh tomatoes, you won't want to stop until the frost forces you! Many gardeners plant crops of 20% early . . . 60% main and 20% late varieties.

We've carefully selected only the most improved, DISEASE RESISTANT hybrid varieties, bred for resistance to fusarium wilt, nematodes and other tomato-attacking diseases. This is J&P's way of assuring you outstanding crops on healthy, vigorous, disease-free plants. *"Days" shown means approximate time from setting out plants started inside, until first ripe tomatoes.*

F_1 HYBRID SMALL FRY (Earliest Cherry Tomato) Ready to eat in 53 days, this All-America hybrid bears clusters of 7 or 8 one-inch tomatoes on a strong, bush-type plant. Has the juiciness and flavor of larger tomatoes. Great for canning!

Packet	Bonus Pkt.	Jumbo Pkt.
498-P **65c**	498-U **$1.25**	498-J **$2.35**

F_1 HYBRID TOY BOY (Early) Grow this *novelty* to trail gracefully from baskets . . . to hang tantalizingly overhead. Or, set in a window box or pot to look decorative and delicious. Grows fast . . . produces small, very tasty tomatoes.

Packet	Bonus Pkt.	Jumbo Pkt.
502-P **75c**	502-U **$1.45**	502-J **$2.75**

F_1 HYBRID PATIO (Early) Ornamental 24- to 30-inch plant grows regular sized 2-inch tomatoes! Developed for growing in pots, but makes an excellent garden plant too. The sweet, firm, scarlet red fruit is ready in only 70 days. Plant is bushy, compact, and very productive.

Packet	Bonus Pkt.	Jumbo Pkt.
499-P **75c**	499-U **$1.45**	499-J **$2.75**

HYBRID FLORAMERICA 1978 All-America Selection. A great new hybrid that produces in all parts of the country! Tolerant to *seventeen* plant diseases and able to set fruit under cool, hot or humid conditions, this dependable performer gives outstanding yields of big 3½- to 4-inch tomatoes. And larger! Fruits are slightly flattened, firm, deep red — excellent flavor fresh, canned or juiced! The long vines produce in just 81 days, a week earlier than most main-crop tomatoes.

Packet	Bonus Pkt.	Jumbo Pkt.
503-P **65c**	503-U **$1.25**	503-J **$2.35**

Don't miss J&P's exclusive F_1 hybrid tomato SUPERSTAR on page 3. You'll want this big, new slicing tomato in your garden this year!

Toy Boy

Patio

F_1 HYBRID SPRINGSET (Extra Early) The first tomatoes of summer! Sets blossoms while weather is cool . . . producing juicy, medium-sized, globe shaped tomatoes in 60 to 65 days. Double, disease-resistant, compact plants quickly yield large quantities of delicious, all-red tomatoes.

Packet	Bonus Pkt.	Jumbo Pkt.
497-P **65c**	497-U **$1.25**	497-J **$2.35**

HEINZ 1350 (Main Crop) Extremely productive, particularly disease and crack resistant. Developed by the tomato experts for good flavor and firmness in home canning. Carried on short vines, gorgeous fruit is ready in 75 days, ripe-red inside and out.

Packet	Bonus Pkt.	Jumbo Pkt.
493-P **65c**	493-U **$1.25**	493-J **$2.35**

F_1 HYBRID BEEFMASTER (Late) Improved and the largest of the Beefsteak-type. Some weigh 2 pounds and MORE! Deep scarlet red color and lack of seeds makes this firm, meaty tomato perfect for slicing and canning. In 88 days, the vigorous, long vines produce fruits which are mild, juicy and extra fine quality.

Packet	Bonus Pkt.	Jumbo Pkt.
494-P **75c**	494-U **$1.45**	494-J **$2.75**

F_1 HYBRID WONDER BOY (Main Crop) One of the largest and most delicious . . . weighs up to a pound, and MORE! Eighty days produces great quantities of scarlet tomatoes. Vigorous vines with dense foliage protect globe-shaped fruit. Can be staked or allowed to spread.

Packet	Bonus Pkt.	Jumbo Pkt.
496-P **75c**	496-U **$1.45**	496-J **$2.75**

Jackson & Perkins Co.®
World's Largest Rose Growers and Nurserymen • Since 1872 • Medford, Oregon 97501

Z